The Religious Heritage of Japan

The Religious Heritage
of
Japan:

foundations for cross-cultural understanding
in a religiously plural world

Edited by

John Ross Carter

BOOK EAST

Acknowledgements:

Picture of "Image of the Buddha": printed by courtesy of Rissho Koseikai, Tokyo, Japan.
"Ten Oxherding Pictures" from *Manual of Zen Buddhism* by Daisetz T. Suzuki: printed by courtesy of GROVE/ATLANTIC, INC., New York, NY.

Printed in the United States of America

ISBN: 0-9647040-4-8

BOOK EAST
P.O. Box 13352, Portland, OR 97213

In Memory Of

Sumiko Kudo
and
Minor Lee Rogers

PREFACE

This volume is the result of the activity of a sterling group of scholars in Japan who agreed that a program of lectures introducing American undergraduates to dimension of the religiousness of Japanese men and women would provide a significant learning experience. These scholars were diligent in arranging for a program to be set up almost entirely by correspondence months in advance, and they were faithful in discharging their assignments in spite of their very tight schedules. The lectures, given in Kyoto and Tokyo, indicate the religiously plural context in which life is lived in Japan. Comments on American and Japanese intellectual and cultural contacts introduce the sequence of lectures which contain reflections on the city of Kyoto, in which much of the program took place, some themes of the Protestant Christian experience in Japan, aspects of the Buddhist testimony, particularly Jodo-Shinshu, which, when combined with Jodo-shu, represents by far the most popular form of Buddhist piety in Japan, and Zen, and also the witness of Shinto

We wish to express our gratitude to Minoru Tada, of Otani University, for his assistance in making some of the arrangements for the program in Kyoto, and to the President of Otani University for a warm reception. We express our appreciation to Mr. Masuo Nezu, who began organizing for the program at Rissho Kosei-kai in Tokyo, and to Dr. Michio T. Shinozaki, Dean of Rissho Kosei-kai Seminary, who provided the American students with wonderful facilities in Tokyo. We enjoyed a brief presentation about Rissho Kosei-kai given by Mr. Keichi Akagawa, too brief to be included here. We warmly acknowledge the hospitality provided by Rev. and Mrs. Okano, of Kodo Kyodan in Yokohama, and their conversations about the significance of lay Buddhist witness. We are indebted, further, to Professor Hajime Nakamura (1912-1999) for leading a discussion on key issues in Buddhist thought and for introducing Gudo Nishijima Roshi. We are deeply appreciative of Professor Gaijin Nagao, whose profound understanding of Buddhist thought appears only briefly, regrettably, in this volume, but whose presence for informal discussions greatly enhanced the learning experience of all the undergraduates. Professor Ryusei Takeda, of Ryukoku University, arranged for a context of exchange and deepening understanding between American and Japanese students in a university classroom. We also express our thanks to Alex Vesey, a disciple of Keido Fukushima Roshi, for a memorable tour of Tofukuji, one of Japan's most beautiful Zen temples. And the staff of the Urasenke Foundation graciously contributed to cross-cultural understanding by means of the way of tea.

Professor Naofusa Hirai and colleagues at the Institute for Japanese Classics and Culture, of Kokugakuin University in Tokyo, contributed significantly to the program and to this volume. To Professor Hirai and the Institute we also express our deep gratitude for making it possible for special offerings and ritual dances to be performed at the Meiji Shrine in Tokyo, at Nikko, and at the grand Shrine of Ise on behalf of the program. Professor Hirai's contribution to this volume is adapted with permission from "Shinto" in *Encyclopaedia Britannica*, 15th edition, © 1974 by Encyclopaedia Britannica, Inc. Mr. Norman Havens, of the Institute of Japanese Classics and Culture, provided subtle insights while accompanying the undergraduates to Nikko. Rev. Toyotaka Ogaki, as arranged by Professor Hirai, met the students at Ise and led in a discussion after giving them an extended tour of the Shrine complexes.

Although numerous were the ways these distinguished scholars and representatives of religious groups in Japan contributed to the program, the modes of their participation could not readily be structured in a format designed for publication. They, nevertheless, made a stellar contribution to greater international understanding and deeper humane sensitivity to religiousness in Japan.

To each of the contributors to this volume, the editor expresses his deep appreciation for their willingness to prepare their lectures, to journey to the different locations and to present them, to engage the students in discussions, and to follow through, now several years later, to provide revisions of their lectures in preparing them for publication. For the ones participating in the program that lies behind this volume, the sincerity with which the lectures were given and the authenticity of the discussions contributed on each occasion to a qualitative sense of "one lifetime, one meeting" (*ichigo ichie*).

Marie A. Nardi, who also followed the course of lectures in Japan, patiently completed a transcription of the lectures which became the first rough draft of the volume. It was the editor's task to revise that draft, to send copies to all contributors for their revisions, and, receiving those revisions, to prepare the final copy of this book for publication. Garda Parker assisted in maintaining timely correspondence with the publisher and in providing oversight in copying and mailing the final copy for publication. Financial support for this publication project was provided by the Fund for the Study of the Great Religions of the World, Colgate University.

To Christopher John, my son and fellow student in the program, I express my thanks for his timely questions related to issues of the course and his outright help in keeping a word processor on track. Thanks, too, to Mary Elizabeth, my daughter, for her enthusiasm in this and all ventures in understanding between Japanese and Americans. A special word of gratitude I express again, and anew, to Sandra, whose husband I am, for demonstrating in speech and act that quality of human understanding to which the printed words in this volume testify.

This volume is dedicated to two persons whose lives have exemplified the rewards of seeking understanding of humankind's religiousness, particularly in the conversation fully developing among Americans and Japanese.

Sumiko Kudo was for several years a much admired secretary at the Institute for Japanese Culture and Classics at Kokugakuin University, held in great affection by her Shinto colleagues. At the same time she was a devoted Zen disciple of the late Zenkei

Shibayama Roshi, former abbot of Nanzenji in Kyoto. Sumiko Kudo was the translator of two important works by Shibayama Roshi that have made their way from Japan to the bookshelves of undergraduates and others in America: *A Flower Does Not Talk* (Rutland, Vermont: Charles E. Tuttle Co., first edition, 1970, fifteenth printing, 1993) and *Zen Comments on the Mumonkan* (New York: Harper & Row Publishers, 1974; New York: New American Library, 1975). Her life was characterized by being ever cheerful, alive to the moment, compassionately aware of others.

Professor Minor Lee Rogers, former DuPont Professor of Religion at Washington and Lee University, and co-author with Ann T. Rogers of *Rennyo: The Second Founder of Shin Buddhism - with a translation of his letters* (Berkeley, California: Asian Humanities press, 1991), was a teacher of teachers, having a remarkable ability to listen intently, to ask the creative and probing question to enable one to find one's way. Through his scholarship and a profoundly authentic rapport with the delicate dialectic at the depths of Jodo-Shinshu, it would seem that he heard the request to follow, the supportive urging to go, and the calming invitation to come of which Christians and Jodo-Shinshu Buddhists have spoken.

John Ross Carter
Hamilton, New York

TABLE OF CONTENTS

LIST OF CONTRIBUTORS

ASOYA, Masahiko B.A., M.A., Kokugakuin University; M.A., Claremont Graduate School; D. Litt., Kokugakuin University; Professor of Shinto Studies, Kokugakuin University.

BANDO, Shojun B.A., M.A., University of Tokyo, British Council Scholar, Oxford; Lecturer, University of Kyoto; Visiting Professor, Oberlin College, University of Hawaii; Professor, Otani University; Professor, Ueno Gakuen College; Head-priest, Bando Hoonji.

CARTER, John Ross B. A., Baylor University; B. D., The Southern Baptist Theological Seminary; M.Th., King's College and the School of Oriental and African Studies, University of London; Ph.D., Harvard University; D.Litt., Kelaniya University; Professor of Philosophy and Religion, Chair of the Department; Robert Hung-Ngai Ho Professor of Asian Studies, Director of Chapel House, Director of the Fund for the Study of the Great Religions of the World, Colgate University.

EILERT, Håkan Th.D., Uppsala; Visiting Fellow, Center for the Study of World Religions, Harvard University; Associate Director NCC Center, Kyoto, 1983-1991; Vicar in V. Karaby Parish, Diocese of Lund, Sweden.

HIRAI, Naofusa B.A., *Gakushi*, Kokugakuin University; M.A., Divinity School, University of Chicago; D. Litt., Kokugakuin University; Professor emeritus, Kokugakuin University, Director, Institute for Japanese Culture and Classics, Kokugakuin University 1990-1993; Past President, Society for Shinto Studies, Tokyo; former Standing Committee Member, Japanese Association for Religious Studies, Tokyo, 1981-1992.

HIROTA, Dennis B.A., University of California, Berkeley; M.A., San Francisco State University; Ph. D., Nagoya University; Visiting Fellow, Center for the Study of World Religions, Harvard University; Visiting Professor, Colgate University; Head Translator, "Shin Buddhism Translation Series," Hongwanji International Center, Kyoto, Japan; Visiting Fellow, Center for the Study of World Religions, Harvard University; Numata Professorship at Harvard Divinity School; Professor of Asian Cultural Studies, Chikushi Jogakuen College.

HLAWATSCH, George Oliver B.A., Pomona College; Research Associate Kyoto University; M. A., Ph.D., University of Hawaii, Honolulu; Associate Professor, Kansai University of Foreign Studies, Center for International Education.

INAGAKI, Hisao   Ph.D., School of Oriental and African Studies, University of London; Professor at Ryukoku University; Numata Professorship at the University of California, Berkeley, and the University of Hawaii at Manoa.

NAGAO, Gadjin   *Bungakushi* (M.A.), Kyoto Imperial University, *Bungaku-hakase* (D. Litt.), Kyoto University; Professor emeritus, Kyoto University; Member of the Japan Academy; Visiting Professor, the universities of Wisconsin, British Columbia, Calgary, and Michigan, Ann Arbor.   Former Director and President of numerous academic associations.

NAKAMURA, Kyoko Motomochi   M.A., the University of Chicago; M.A., the University of Tokyo; Ph.D. candidate, the University of Tokyo, Professor of the History of Religions, Kawamura Gakuen Woman's University; Director, International Institute for the Study of Religions.

NISHIJIMA, Gudo Wafu   Graduate of Tokyo University, Law; Recipient of the Transmission of Dharma from Master Renpo Niwa; Advisor of Ida Ryogokudo Company; Soto Zen Master.

NOMURA, Nobuo   B.A., M.A., Ryukoku University; M.T.S., Harvard Divinity School; Professor of Buddhist Studies, Ryukoku University; Professor of Buddhist Studies, Kyoto Women's University.

SHINOZAKI, Michio   T.B.S, Saitama University; Rissho Kosei-kai Seminary; M. A., University of Chicago; Ph.D., Vanderbilt University; Dean, Rissho Kosei-kai Seminary.

TADA, Minoru   *Bungakushi* (M. A.), Kyoto University; Visiting Fellow, University of California at Los Angeles; former Dean of Post-Graduate Studies, Otani University; Professor of English emeritus, Otani University.

TOKUNAGA, Michio   B.A., Osaka University of Foreign Studies; M.A., Ryukoku University; Visiting Fellow, Center for the Study of World Religions, Harvard University; Numata Professorship at Harvard Divinity School; Professor of Buddhist Studies, Kyoto Women's University.

UEDA, Kenji   Professor of Shinto Theology emeritus; D. Litt., Kokugakuin University; Past President, Society for Shinto Studies; Former Director, Institute for Japanese Culture and Classics, Kokugakuin University.

INTRODUCTION

Japanese men and women have been religious for a very long time and they have manifested this quality of life in a variety of ways. Upon thinking about Japan an American might recall images of Buddhist temples or Shinto shrines and conclude that Japanese have a kind of unusual "mixed religion," yet with exotic charm. Some Americans, dependent on the media for information about Japan, might be led to conclude that the religion of Japan is Zen Buddhism.

The more closely one looks, however, the more variegated the manifestations of faith become. What would the remarkable practice of calm seated meditation, known as *zazen*, have in common with an exuberant festival of the Gion Shrine in Kyoto (*gion matsuri*) in mid-July, or a carefully choreographed dance of shrine maidens with a spontaneous and private recitation of praise for Amida Buddha (*nembutsu*), or wherein would commonality be found in the word *kami*, used both to designate the God of Abraham, Isaac and Jacob, the father of Jesus the Christ and also the fox-*kami* as at the Fushimi-inari shrine (*jinja*) just south of Kyoto, or various mountain deities with ultimate reality known as the Great Buddha? One could go on and on, of course, peeling back, as it were, layers and layers of ritual practices, pilgrimage sites, texts and institutions, and doctrinal formulations, to find that the variety is immense, the alternative perspectives are numerous, and the intellectual structures are complex.

No, Japan is certainly not synonymous with Buddhism, nor Shinto, nor Christianity, nor Folk Religion, nor Confucian ethics. Hardly.

Further, Japan is in transition, and radically so. The demographic shifts from rural to urban settings have been rather thoroughly studied. Within the urban settings, however, there are secondary demographic shifts; elderly persons who had done rather well in holding a community sense within their urban sub-districts are beginning to sell their urban property to corporations in some cases planning to construct condominiums in that space. Younger families are entering recently reconstructed residential areas devoid of traditional structures and are finding primary loyalties developed no longer on the basis of residence but focused solely on one's employer-company and particularly grounded, as it were, *at* the site of employment. One reason for the intensity of company loyalty in recent years is due, in part, to the concomitant breakdown in primary identification based on residence and also on family trade. With the demographic mobility has come a democratization of trade skills: one can learn at the factory or store what was, to a considerable extent, passed down in the family or through hereditary teachers to students.

Further, more and more Japanese are well-informed in international matters and the old question, arising from deep within Japanese cultural patterns, of discerning one's proper place arises afresh and in very complicated ways on the global scene. There is a tendency to wait several years, even a decade perhaps, to learn what people in other countries expect of them before the slowly moving gears of Japanese political action are gradually set into motion. An American, say, might often tend to lose patience with Japanese on political matters, arguing that the movement of political action is too slow, the process is too indecisive. In reality, though, Japanese leaders are giving expression to the degree of respect they have for their foreign counterparts and the extent to which they are striving to maintain a favorable evaluation from those foreign counterparts.

Finding one's proper place, therefore, is a complex matter for Japanese men and women, one made much more complicated and involved by the currents of social, economic, and political change in Japan today. Much more consequential than this, however, is finding one's proper place in the grand scheme of things: in one's life, but also in the dimension of human awareness into which one's life is placed.

The fragmentation of our corporate intellectual life resulting from the sharply drawn demarcations of academic disciplines, so often seen in our universities, is not the result of pure intelligence reflecting upon itself. There are political ideologies at work in the rise of the disciplines, seeking both power and prestige in the name of freedom from a particular world view or, uncritically, ironically, on the basis of an assumed ideology. The irony involved in this is, of course, that in the name of freedom from, let us say, religion--and meet the challenge head on--a new ideology has been put in place, one hardly giving evidence of either maintaining what is most noble in us or constructing alternative altruistic loyalties that will sustain our human ventures into our common future.

Japanese men and women are involved in this process also, because the cross-currents of the Western academic tradition run through much of Japanese society today. The point that one would want to note, therefore, is that more and more Japanese young men and women are finding themselves to have become more or less cut adrift from the infrastructures that enabled them to discern religious meaning in the dynamics of human relationships based on their place of residence, on their family temple, on their relationship with their teachers, or from their involvement in the academic tradition.

Things are changing in Japan.

It is becoming increasingly difficult for young men and women in Japan to determine what is fitting, how they fit in and what the fundamental rationale undergirding their own understanding of their place in human relationships might be. Of course there is little difficulty in finding what is fitting in one's work place, in the place of one's employment. If there be clear indications of older Japanese normative behavior still around, one would see them most readily in the infrastructures of corporations. In such context, hierarchy tends to be clear, the benefits of longevity are spelled out, face-to-face loyalty in sub-groups is maintained. Forming abiding and mutually supportive relationships, bonding, occurs through corporate goal oriented achievements and through routinized parties and end of day informal camaraderie at long patronized bars.

Japanese men who are successful in receiving employment and who work hard will not long search for a sense of brotherhood among their peers. It is not the same for Japanese women, and surely there is a price to be paid by young families for this particular sense of brotherhood.

There have been movements of late to introduce clearly articulated religious themes in the Japanese work place. Meditation sessions and meetings for congregational singing have become a part of the daily or weekly routine of some businesses. Ethical formulations are becoming more pronounced in some companies, whether discernibly Confucian or patently Rotarian. There are signs of self-conscious attempts to provide some deep grounding for motivation, for maintaining obligations, without an irreversibly debilitating sense of being driven.

One concludes that Japanese men and women are living in a period of transition -- once again.

We are well aware that analyses of human life are very complex, that one can hardly freeze-frame, as it were, an entire cultural heritage in any country, in any century, in any decade, or year, or in any province or village. Human life is too dynamic for that, assuredly. Nor for that matter can any analysis of any one country from any one point of view be considered definitive, really. In our quest for human understanding we are left, happily, with a pragmatic procedure for acquiring greater knowledge; a kind of cumulative participation in which gradually more information is gathered and shared and made the basis for further reflection and tentative conclusions so that in time the horizons of intelligibility are extended and we discover, simultaneously, that our understanding of others, of ourselves, and of what it means to be genuinely human has been gradually significantly enhanced.

Certainly Japanese culture is not Zen. In fact, today one would have to look very hard indeed to find much of Zen in Japanese culture. And "the Way of the *Kami*" is not synonymous with the way of the Japanese. We have known this for long. Further, no one would mistake the status of the environment in Japan, the increasing pollution, the pressure of the pace, with either the Pure Land, the Land of Ease discerned as being closer than one's own pulse by Japanese Buddhist saints, or the quietude of calmly enunciating the *nembutsu*. Christians learned long ago that they would have to refocus their interpretive lenses to enable them no longer to conceptualize their enterprise as the Christianization of Japan but to understand their endeavor as an engaged mutuality of sharing whereby they give to others precisely what matters most to them with the assurance that such a gift and such an attitude of giving will lay the foundations for a friendly future, one mutually supportive.

The study that awaits us in these pages contributes to that pragmatic procedure, represents the collective activity of scholars offering their observations about deeply significant things to students eager to learn in an effort to add to our cumulative knowledge of the religiousness of men and women in Japan.

THE RELIGIOUS HERITAGE OF JAPAN

I
The Meeting of Two Cultures
Minoru Tada

We begin our study by noting that our study had already begun over a century ago when persons of adventuresome spirit and inquiring minds sought to understand others on this globe. Professor Minoru Tada, who has studied the reciprocal involvement of Americans and Japanese learning of each other, launches our series of reflections by providing a context for our grasping the significance of our own participation in cross-cultural understanding that this study represents.

A popular nineteenth century novelist, Rudyard Kipling, on a passage to India, wrote "East is east, West is west, Never shall the twain meet again!"[1] lamenting that Westerners will not understand, or cannot understand, men and women in India. We are worlds apart.

Earnest Francisco Fenollosa (1853-1908), an American, whose father was Spanish and whose mother was from Salem Massachusetts, composed a poem, "East and West," that complements, but affirmatively, what Kipling had to say. We *can* understand mutually, and we *should* understand, mutually.

Our first example of this attempt to understand in the meeting of cultures is Sir William Jones (1736-1794). He was a British solicitor sent to India to learn about and to explore Indian culture. He was a very good linguist and studied Arabic, Sanskrit, Pali, and other Indian languages. So, he made an exploratory study of the Indian classics. In those days Indian documents, whether classic, ancient or recent, were not immediately translated into English. The English, though they occupied the country, did not know and were not particularly interested in learning Indian languages, so they did not know very much about the people of India.

Jones started research on the Indian *Code of Manu*. He met an Indian princess and came across the *Bhagavadgītā*. He started to translate these works into English. In a sense, this was the origin of what came to be called Oriental Studies. The first volume of his work, *Asiatick Researches*, appeared in 1788. The *Bhagavadgītā*, Kalidasa's *Śakuntala, Hymn to Narayana, Institutes of Hindu Law: or the Ordinances of Manu* appeared in 1794. These contributed greatly to the understanding of and interest in India. For the first time, people understood something about the ways of people in India.

These findings made a very strong influence on the age of Romanticism, which took place in Germany in the late eighteenth century. Writers who were much influenced included Goethe, Schiller, and Kant. German romantics borrowed many themes from the Indian stories. From these English translations, subsequently translated into German and French, the transposition through Europe was rather easy. William Jones belonged to a club in London, Dr. Johnson's Club, whose members included Edmund Burke (a political philosopher), Joshua Reynolds (a famous painter), and David Garrick (a famous Shakespearean actor). Benjamin Franklin was also a member of the club. In those days, Franklin was a representative of the colonies in England, under George III, and traveled a great deal between London and Boston. It did not take much time for the English books on India to travel to Boston, and thus spread interest in India to North America. This greatly interested the "transcendentalists" like Emerson, Thoreau, and others.

Also in those days, there was a lively trade between Boston and China. Merchant sailors brought back many things from China--things like silk and paintings. They also imported books, both Confucian, and Buddhist.

Centuries ago, Indian Buddhism traveled along the Silk Road to China and then to Tibet. It traveled as far as Japan through Korea, around 552 A.D. Thus with the spread from Europe to North America, we have Buddhism spreading around the world in two directions, 1,300 years apart.

Japan was ruled by *shogun*s for a long time, during the Edo period. After long years of isolation, the "black ships," commanded by Commodore Perry, arrived in Japan in 1853, in Tokyo. Perry surprised the Japanese, with his ships and their black smoke. Japanese of the time had never seen such huge ships. In 1868, with the Meiji Restoration, the Imperial rule was restored. The capitol was transferred to Edo (Tokyo) and the motto of "Rich Nation, Strong Arms," began. This occurred at almost the same time as the Civil War in the United States. It marked the beginning of the modernization of Japan. The Japanese wanted to take in Western culture. In the United States, after the Civil War was over, a great surge in industrialization began. We began, similarly, at the same time.

About ten to fifteen years following the Meiji Restoration, the government hired a considerable number of people from abroad, from many countries, German, American, English, French, and others, mostly technicians and scholars. In those days, the government paid about 300 yen a month, plus accommodations, etc. In comparison, Japanese "novices" or recent graduates from schools, were paid only 10 yen a month. The new government was not rich, yet they paid these foreign advisors so much to bring them to Japan, so earnest was their desire to modernize. They hired about 500 people a year.

Earnest Fenollosa was just a Harvard graduate, twenty-five years old, when he came to Japan. He was recommended by Edward Morse, an oceanographer and modernist, who wanted to conduct research on Japanese shells. Morse came here and was asked to give advice on many things, including establishing departments in the newly founded Tokyo University, and other matters such as mining, shipping, and sewage systems and so forth.

Around 1879, just ten years after the beginning of the Restoration, Fenollosa came to Japan, invited by the University of Tokyo, and became a professor of philosophy, sociology, and economics. The students were very clever and eager to learn about Western ways. Fenollosa had an eye for aesthetics--paintings, sculpture. He had been to an art institute in Philadelphia as well as to Harvard. He came to Japan with what in those days were very modern tastes, including Darwinism and Hegelian philosophy, and he incorporated these theories into many of his classes.

The usual policy was for foreign advisors and teachers to leave Japan after one year. However, in Fenollosa's case, his visit was extended for as long as eight years, because he was so popular. During this time, he had a very strong influence on many people, including, of course, his students. After the Meiji Restoration, all of the people wanted to take in Western culture, and were almost throwing away their indigenous culture. They wanted something new, something Western. When Fenollosa came to Japan, many extraordinarily valuable antiquities, curiosities, were being offered cheaply for sale.

Fenollosa was very impressed with Japanese art and culture. Because most of the people who came to Japan did not speak Japanese, the only way they could take in the culture was through art and other cultural expressions. Fenollosa started to study the crafts and arts, to learn about Buddhist scrolls and sculptures. He became absorbed in Japanese studies. He urged the Japanese to re-examine their heritage and to discover the wealth there.

After eight years, Fenollosa returned to Boston with many curios, paintings, and wares. After his death, all of these things were put into an oriental department in a museum. Many other people brought back precious things from Japan. These became very fashionable to have.

In 1893, in Chicago, an exposition was held in honor of the four hundredth anniversary of Columbus landing in America. Chicago was the edge of the "new west" in those days, and that is one of the reasons the exposition was held there. Just to have an exposition was not enough for many Americans, after the chaotic years following the Civil War; they also wanted something spiritual. So, they decided to have the first world conference on religion.

In those days, Catholics and Protestants disagreed to a great extent, and Buddhism was regarded by some as being evil. It was difficult to think that people holding so strongly such widely different views would come to such a conference. Buddhists and Catholics alike were hesitant. They were afraid that if they went they would be subjected to criticism. In 1893, it took many days to get from Japan to Chicago. Steamships crossed only once a month. In spite of their hesitance, contingents of Buddhist, Confucian and Taoist priests decided to participate. Four courageous Japanese Buddhist priests attended. One of them was named Soyen Shaku, a Zen Buddhist. From India, Sri Ramakrishna, Swami Vivekananda, Anagarika Dharmapala and other famous religious figures came. The presentations took several days.

Soyen Shaku was a Zen master from Kamakura, near Tokyo, who had many disciples. One of them was Natsume Soseki, a Japanese novelist of the Meiji period. He had studied eighteenth century English literature in England for three years. Soseki was originally a professor at Tokyo University, but later resigned his position and devoted himself to writing. He died in his early fifties. Many of his novels are considered classics of modern Japanese literature.

Also among Soyen Shaku's disciples was D. T. Suzuki. Shaku read a paper at this conference. In the audience was Paul Carus, a German American scholar, who was editor of a religious and philosophical journal called *The Monist,* among whose contributors was John Dewey. Carus was very impressed with Soyen's presentation, and asked his help in finding someone to help him translate Chinese writings into English. Soyen recommended Suzuki, then only twenty-eight years old. Suzuki, upon arrival in the United States, stayed with Paul Carus for eleven years. As there were virtually no Japanese in the Mid-West area of the United States, Suzuki had no contact with other Japanese during this period. He studied English and American culture while continuing his Zen practice. He wrote very many letters to his friends in Japan and to his master, Soyen Shaku.

Suzuki went on to become world famous as a man of Zen. But in those days he was just a sincere young man. He wrote in his letters about how hard it was to eat American food. The difficulty he experienced in being so far from his home showed in his letters. When he returned to Japan, he began teaching English. He later taught at Gakushu-in Academy, the Peer's School and then at Otani University for thirty-five years. He died a quarter century ago, in 1967, at the age of ninety-six. He left more than thirty books in English and more than one hundred in Japanese. The English volumes were widely read throughout the world.

D. T. Suzuki's wife, Beatrice Lane Suzuki, was a disciple of Madame Blavatsky, a Russian and a theosophist who studied Buddhism in Tibet for many years. In those days, Madame Blavatsky was hesitant to say she was a Buddhist because of possible criticism, particularly from the Roman Catholics. So, she went to London. She wanted to set up a field for theosophy in the universities. In 1875, she started teaching in New York City together with others, including an American, Colonel Olcott.

Madame Blavatsky and Col. Olcott started the Theosophical Society in New York City. This was during a great flourishing of spiritualism in the United States. New religions were a source of novel and exotic ideas. The number of devotees of Eastern religions increased along the east coast of the United States. Just as exploration in America moved ever westward, so did Buddhism in one form or another.

Fenollosa wanted to have American and Oriental cultures merge. He wanted a culture in the United States more subtle than what he saw as the "Westward ho!" culture. The United States, influenced by industrialization and Darwinism, was an expanding country. Fenollosa wanted a more "feminine" culture, one more gentle, in the image of the Bodhisattva. This is why he composed the poem "East and West" mentioned earlier.

Fenollosa's master was a Buddhist priest at the Miidera temple in Otsu. Fenollosa devoted himself to Buddhist teachings. In his will, he asked that his ashes be buried at Miidera. When he died in London, some of his ashes were taken to Miidera. He is sometimes spoken of as the first American Buddhist as well as the first Japanologist.

Other Americans followed Fenollosa's example, and many Japanese followed in the footsteps of Suzuki and went to the U.S. These two personalities, therefore, were important in the history of the meeting of the U.S. and Japan.

Suzuki returned to Japan and started the Eastern Buddhist Society at Otani University in 1921. With his wife, Beatrice, he edited *The Eastern Buddhist* and wrote many articles for this important journal, still being published. Among his major writings were *Essays in Zen Buddhism*, which Christmas Humphreys, then an English barrister, arranged to have published in London in 1927. This work had a strong influence on the spread of a type of Zen thought in the English-reading world. Another person influenced by this was the Irish poet W. B. Yeats, in his later years, around 1930-1939. Many American writers were also drawn to Suzuki's writings. Examples are J. D. Salinger and Gary Snyder.

One of D. T. Suzuki's close friends and followers was a British poet, Reginald Horace Blyth. He was teaching English in Japan before World War II. During the time that he was detained in a detention camp, he wrote books on Zen and, later, books on *haiku*. Many American poets and teachers read his books on *haiku*. He was also a tutor to the present emperor after the war was over.

Soyen Shaku had many disciples also. One was Sokatsu Shaku, who went to the United States in the early 1920's. In those days, a utopian mode of thinking was very popular in Japan. Encouraged by this way of thinking, Sokatsu Shaku and his disciples wanted to set up a new village on the west coast of the United States. One of his disciples, Sokei-an Sasaki, settled in New York City and started the first Zen Institute in New York, in 1931. It is still in existence. Sokei-an Sasaki was confined in a concentration camp in the United States because he was Japanese and died before the war ended. Ruth Sasaki, his wife, was a devotee of Zen. After the war was over, she came to Japan and wanted to practice *zazen* and to continue his work. Her daughter's husband was Alan Watts. Watts also wrote many interesting books.

In a conversation with Mary Farkas, a long-time member of the Zen Institute in New York, I learned that J. D. Salinger came to the Institute in New York in 1950.

On the west coast, Zen influence was seen through the works of the "Beat Generation" of poets. It produced poems, the City Lights Books Store in San Francisco, and *Howl* with Alan Ginsberg, Gary Snyder, Jack Kerouac, and Philip Whalen. Later a Zen Center was opened in San Francisco by Shunryu Suzuki, a Soto Zen monk from Japan. Suzuki wrote a best-selling book, *Zen Mind, Beginner's Mind*.

Another disciple of Shoyen Shaku was Nyogen Senzaki. He also had some connection with D. T. Suzuki. Paul Reps, a well-known artist, studied under Nyogen Senzaki. He also wrote with Senzaki a number of books on Zen, notably *Zen Flesh, Zen Bones*. Soen Nakagawa was also a disciple to Nyogen Senzaki, as is Tai Shimano, who is now the abbot at the New York Zen Center. This is an illustration of an American "lineage" of Zen.

There is another lineage, so to speak, an artistic line that follows from Fenollosa. Fenollosa bequeathed his papers to Ezra Pound. Although Pound left his writings to William Carlos Williams, Pound influenced and was a friend of W. B. Yeats, whose "Vision" is based on theosophy. J. Krishnamurti from India was also a theosophist for a number of years. He declared independence from the theosophical movement near the end of his life and started teaching in Los Angeles, travelling frequently to Kent, England. He was in contact with many American students.

Robert Aiken, a student and friend of R. H. Blyth, is still very active as a Zen Roshi in Hawaii. Aiken worked in construction projects in Guam before the war. He was arrested after hostilities began and was sent to Japan to be placed in a detention camp. There he met and was influenced by R. H. Blyth. (Blyth wrote a large number of influential books on Zen and Japanese culture. His four books on *haiku* are now classics. I found in the New York City Library that J. D. Salinger recorded his name on the borrower's card for these volumes.)

Christmas Humphreys, whom we have briefly mentioned, became the head of a Buddhist Society in London. Being an English barrister and later a judge, coincidentally, he worked as a prosecutor at the international war crimes court following World War II. He had first met D. T. Suzuki in 1927. After the war he asked Suzuki to publish his writings in London, and also persuaded him to return to England to give lectures on Zen Buddhism. Another member of the court at the war crimes trial after World War II was Philip Kapleau. He studied under Zen Roshi Harada and remained in Japan under another Zen Roshi, Hakuun Yasutani, for thirteen years, until he returned to Rochester, New York, where he started a Zen Institute.

Zen was the first form of Buddhism to come to the United States. Now Jodo Shinshu is also becoming popular, especially on the west coast and particularly among Japanese Americans. In fact, since the Meiji Restoration (1868) many Japanese have immigrated to California. Through them, Shin Buddhism has been propagated. Zen seems to have been popular because many Americans were reacting against what they saw as fundamentalism and were attracted to Zen's simplicity.

This then is a glimpse of the coming of Zen Buddhism to the United States, and a simple outline of a cross-cultural network over the world. Many coincidences took place, like Ben Franklin being a member of a club to which Jones belonged, and Jones passing along to him some writings, which were then brought to the United States. The inter-connected lineage continues. For example, Keido Fukushima Roshi, who has visited several American Universities, was a disciple and personal attendant of Zenkei Shibayama Roshi, who was a close friend of D. T. Suzuki. The lineage is worth studying. Many Japanese Buddhists as well as American Buddhist scholars are not aware of this historical background of the meeting of two cultures.

II
Kyoto: The City that Represents Japan
George Hlawatsch

In the study of a religious heritage and the rest of a culture other than one's own one is fortunate to be able to visit a city that has been a magnetic center for centuries, drawing to it the interests and contributions of persons because, to a large extent, they themselves had noticed that others preceding them already discovered a particular setting both attractive and immensely informative. So it has been for long with Kyoto, the anchor in space and time of much in Japanese history. Persons continue to come to this fascinating city to discover what others who have passed this way have known. Professor George Hlawatsch introduces us to a city of countless charms, enabling us to discern the place of Kyoto in Japan and thereby to understand more fully its place in our global human history.

Last night I had an interesting experience regarding the place of Kyoto in Japan. I was at an East-West Center alumni meeting near the Kyoto train station. After the meeting, a friend in the group, a high school principal, said he had to go to his school just a few blocks away. I asked why he had to go to his school at 9:30 p.m. on a Saturday night, and he replied that he had to check the school because the Emperor was coming. I offered to help, and we carefully checked the roof, saw that the doors were securely locked, and so on. Indeed, the Emperor is now in Kyoto. You have probably seen a lot of police moving around the city. All of the palace area, though not exactly off limits, is undergoing a thorough safety check. I just saw a policeman knocking on the garbage cans around a Mr. Donut. All around Kyoto it is the same.

I mention this because Kyoto does enjoy a special place in the history of Japan with regard to the emperor, though that place has changed significantly over the years. As a matter of fact, today's visit by the emperor is just a visit. The emperor no longer lives in Kyoto, and that is a very significant change for this city. The emperor is a visitor. Of course, he is not the only visitor. Something like 33 million visitors come each year to Kyoto, a city of only about one million people. Many of them come on Sundays, especially when the weather is very nice. They come, of course, because of the antiquity of the city, because of the artifacts, the remains of that antiquity, the temples and gardens. Kyoto's twelve hundred years of history is its chief drawing point today. And one aspect of that antiquity is the artifacts related to the emperor.

Kyoto figures quite prominently in the foreign descriptions of Japan. There is an advertisement in a 1927 issue of the *National Geographic*, which promotes a romantic approach to the city:

Sip tea in a satiny house. Look out through windows made of . . . paper. Truly! For it's

Japan. Come from lovely Lake Biwa through twisting tunnels. . . in a torch-lit boat . . . the light slipping over coppery faces of the rowers. [2]

Foreigners have been drawing attention to Kyoto for quite a long time. A travel ad in *New Yorker Magazine* of December 10, 1990, touts Kyoto as offering a glimpse of Japan's ancient glory: "In small workshops, Kyoto artisans create porcelain, fabrics, lacquerware, and pottery as they did when they served the imperial court centuries ago."[3] A lot of this is true. One of the major aspects of its antiquity that remains in the city is its crafts.

In the *Mainichi Daily News* of April 1, 1991, one reads of the Foreign Minister, Alexander Bessmertnykh, of the former Soviet Union visiting Kyoto:

> Bessmertnykh's trip to Kyoto was aimed at observing traditional Japanese culture and arranging a similar sightseeing stop for Gorbachev who is scheduled to visit Japan from April 16-19, officials said.[4]

Unfortunately, Gorbachev's visit to Kyoto never came to pass; due to lack of time he had to go directly from Tokyo to Osaka. On the one hand, Kyoto is a drawing point for ordinary foreign visitors and foreign dignitaries, and on the other hand Kyoto is pretty easily removed from the itinerary when other more important things come up.

What strikes visitors are certain natural features that can be seen by just walking around. These features, of course, are important now, but they were also important 1200 years ago. They define the city in many ways. The mountains that surround the city, the Eastern mountains, the Higashiyama, which run north to Mt. Hiei; and the mountains that circle around the north of the city, and the mountains in the west, leave only the south open. As for rivers, the *Kamo River* used to form the eastern boundary of the city and was the major water source for the people.

These mountains and rivers are mentioned in ancient Japanese literature like the *Tale of Genji*. A poetic phrase for Kyoto is "the city of purple mountains and crystal streams". Aspects of the city, allusions to Kyoto, have been worked into the total cultural tradition of Japan--the literature, the graphic arts and architecture. These natural features are a striking aspect of the city.

Another striking aspect of the city, of course, is the grid pattern of the streets. One cannot help but notice that all of the streets run north-south or east-west. In comparison, Tokyo is a real rat's nest. The streets do not seem to go in any particular direction. There actually was some good reason for this, namely security, back in the Edo period. Tokyo was laid out as a military city with no direct approaches to the castle in the center. But Kyoto, laid out much earlier, was a political city, a religious city and administrative city. It was never a military city. The grid pattern we see in the streets relates directly to the origins of the city. This is a man made feature.

So, the striking aspects of Kyoto are the natural features that surround its borders and the man made lay out of the city within these natural boundaries. These features allow you to orient yourself very easily. I lived in Kyoto for quite a long time. For many years, I walked in the city for countless hours on many occasions and have never gotten lost. You cannot get lost because anywhere you go you know the streets are going north or south, east or west, and if you look around you can see Mt. Hiei. If you walk east, you run into the river--you just can't get lost. If you get lost in Kyoto, you are doomed in Tokyo. This is one of the attractions of the city, strolling around and enjoying yourself. The only danger is you might enjoy your strolling well beyond the physical capacity of your legs.

When walking around the city, one thing you might notice is that there are no permanent monuments, no structures intended to last through the ages like great stone arches or pyramids. There is nothing like that. What you see on the streets are primarily wooden buildings that are dilapidated in some cases, often times unpainted, that will, before long, disappear if they are not renewed. Perhaps it is the idea of renewal within this grid pattern of streets and within the natural features that shows how the city itself continues to live without placing emphasis on anything permanent. Perhaps today's concrete buildings will be those monuments in the future--I don't know. Certainly, in the history of Kyoto as we know it now, the city has not been characterized by this sort of thing. I think that this makes it a little different, for instance, from European cities with their timeless monuments or even Chinese cities whose massive stone walls define their past.

Because of its antiquity, because of its association with cultural patterns, because of the general focus that Japanese have directed toward Kyoto, more than any other point on the map, Kyoto is representative of Japan. For that reason, people such as the leader of the former Soviet Union or the President of the United States, or the Queen of England, want to come here. A visit to Kyoto is a high point of their visits to Japan.

The problem is that if Kyoto represents Japanese history, as I have tried to suggest, organizing a discussion of Kyoto's history without discussing all of Japanese history is very hard. What I will do is present four topics that tend to overlap a great deal.

First, I want to focus on Kyoto as a *religious city*. This is perhaps a more "felt" than "seen" aspect of the city today, but it is important. I will spend the longest time on this topic because it is the part that interests me the most.

The second is the *political city*, as opposed to the religious city. This indicates the princely city--the political, administrative city, the focus of the bureaucracy. It is not so today, of course, but Kyoto had been so for a major part of its history.

The third topic is the *cultural city*. We might call this the aristocratic aspect because the refined arts and crafts, as they are pursued in Kyoto, even today, were originally designed to serve the aristocrats.

Finally, and very much related to this, is the *commercial city*, the city of buying and selling. We could call this the commoner aspect of the city, because it was, of course, the people who lived in the city, the commoners, who made the products for the aristocrats who controlled Kyoto. It is this aspect of the city that remains very important even today.

A guidebook for Kyoto, published in the 1780s, over 1000 pages long, demonstrates that even in the eighteenth century lots of people were coming to Kyoto on pilgrimages or to have a good time, and they wanted to know about the places in the city.[5] Today, there are no guidebooks this big for Kyoto. The standard foreign guidebook for all of Japan is smaller than this. If nothing else, this shows that Kyoto is not just a tourist city of today, but it has been the focus of attention for a long time. Pictures shown in this old book are surprisingly fresh: Mt. Hiei and Enryaku-ji; the Imperial Palace, the grounds of which function today as a park for the city; the Silver Pavilion which dates from the 1470s; and the Sanjo bridge, which marks the end of the great Tokaido Road that connected Kyoto to Edo back in the old days, and which looks pretty much today as it did when this picture was completed in the eighteenth century. You can actually find your way around some of the sites in Kyoto with these pictures. Things have not changed much.

We will now look at the city from the four points of view mentioned: the religious city, the political city, the cultural city and the commercial city.

Kyoto as a Religious City

With regard to the idea of the religious city, there is a term worth thinking about called *astrobiology*, though I am not sure how established this term is. What astrobiology focuses on is the idea that there is some sort of parallel between the mathematically precise movements of the heavens and certain biological rhythms of life on earth. The progression of the seasons and so on seems to follow a pattern related to the way the sun and stars move around. With the seasons, of course, come the growth cycles. Astrobiology postulates a relation between the precise movements seen in the sky above and the biological rhythms of the earth itself. Of course, ancient people tried somehow to guarantee that these biological rhythms, the harvest in particular, would be regular, through being able to "read" and understand the precise and more regular movements of the heavens.

The grid pattern of the city of Kyoto is an expression of that aspect of astrobiology. There was the hope that somehow, through replicating on the face of the earth where people lived the same sort of mathematically precise, regular arrangement of the heavens, the way people live and organize themselves would somehow guarantee the continuity of those rhythms throughout the rest of the land. The city of Kyoto, then, the grid pattern, would be a reflection, a statement of hope that there would always be a harvest following every planting, and so on.

So, astrobiology is one element of the very deep religious nature of the city.

Geomancy is another element of this. It postulates that the fortunes of a city or a household or wherever people are situated are somehow tied into the lay of the land, the way mountains are placed or the way the waters flow. There are currents on the surface of this earth--*chi* or cosmic breath, that waft about. Some are good, some are bad. The lay of the land affects those currents. So, you want to put yourself in a place that is most protected from the bad currents and that receives the better currents. This practice of "wind and water" or *fusui* as it is called in Japanese, is the art or science of analyzing the topography for the proper situating of a structure or city, or in some cases even altering the landscape just a little bit to block bad currents and provide protection.

Kyoto's most prominent geomantic feature is Mt. Hiei, up in the northeast, the so-called "Devil's Entrance" or *kimon* area. Mt. Hiei blocks the flow of bad currents said to come from the northeast. As for the water element of Kyoto's geomantic features, the *Kamo River* plays the most important role.

So, on the one hand there is the astrobiological idea that life on earth is somehow connected to the heavens and through proper understanding one may have some control over the course of one's life; and on the other hand there are the natural features of the earth itself to be taken into consideration through geomancy. The study of these two concepts results in the planning of a proper city.

The Chinese were the first in East Asia to develop this into a real practice, a "science". The result of this for the Chinese was that a city should be located on a cardinal north-south axis. It would be symmetrical, usually square. The perimeter should be carefully defined, usually in China by a massive wall. The focus would be on the center of the city where the leader, the emperor, would live. He then would mediate between heaven and earth as a kind of fulcrum between the precise movement of the heavenly bodies and what would hopefully be a similar precision of movement on earth. Ch'ang-an, laid out in the seventh century during the T'ang dynasty, displays these features.

It should have been square with the emperor's palace in the center. This turned out not to be practical, so the emperor was moved into the north central section facing south, thus dividing the city on a central axis. As a result the city was arrayed before the emperor to his left and right. The statements of an early philosopher, Mencius, became fundamental to Chinese political ideas. He stated that the role of the emperor was to stand at the center of the earth and stabilize the people within the four seas--not just China, but literally the whole world, a view shared by the Chinese throughout their history.

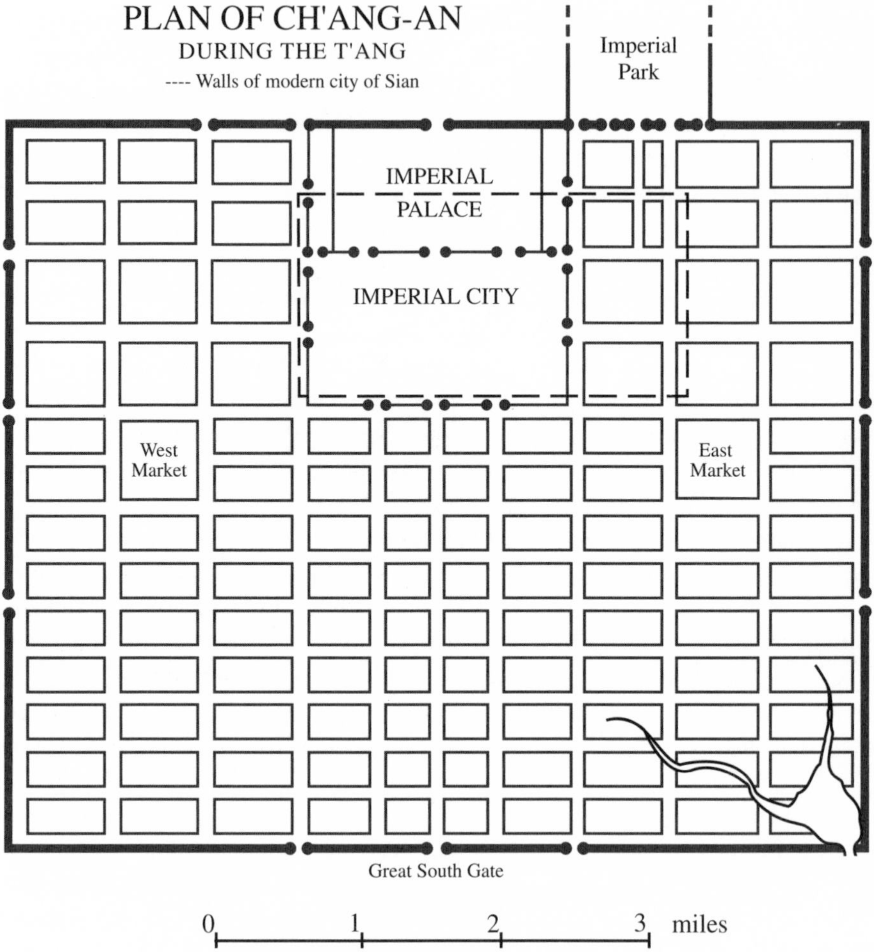

PLAN OF CH'ANG-AN
DURING THE T'ANG
---- Walls of modern city of Sian

Imperial Park

IMPERIAL PALACE

IMPERIAL CITY

West Market

East Market

Great South Gate

0   1   2   3   miles

figure 1 "Plan of Ch'ang-an"[6]

The palace structure that would be built for the emperor to "stand" in was called, in Japanese, the *Daigokuden*, the "Great Pole Hall". This suggested that there was a kind of imaginary pole running through the place where the emperor stood right up to the pole star in the heavens. As the stars seemed to move around the pole star, so too life on earth would somehow revolve around the emperor and the Great Pole Hall--the axis of the capital, the empire, and the universe.

In the area of the old Nara period capitol, archaeologists have excavated the foundations of this Great Pole Hall. It was built very much in Chinese fashion in the eighth century, with a raised platform of tamped earth and the hall itself built on top of that. There the affairs of state (of the universe, in a way) would be conducted.

The Japanese adopted these plans from China in the seventh and eighth centuries when a number of official missions were sent to China. The ambassadors and others visited the Chinese capitals and saw what a civilized state ought to look like. They brought these ideas back to Japan, and began to apply them. The city of Ch'ang-an was very much the model for the city of Nara as it was laid out then in the early eighth century. There were several Chinese style cities laid out before Nara, but Nara was larger, and it was hoped it would be a truly permanent capital

The city of Nara, of course, did not turn out to be the permanent city. The capitol was moved for several reasons, one of which was the power of the Buddhist temples. This caused the Emperor Kamo in 784 to decide to move away. It took about 10 years, but by 794 the city of Kyoto, or as it was called then, Heian, was laid out. It is significant that the name was a combination of *hei* from *heijo* (peaceful castle), the original name for Nara, and *an*, from Ch'ang-an (long peace), for Kyoto was to be a place of "peace and tranquility" as well as a celebration of its predecessor and model. There was every hope that if Nara had not been a permanent capital, then somehow this new Heian would be so. In a way it worked out very well, for Heian, or Kyoto, was regarded as the home of the Japanese sovereign from 794 until the mid-nineteenth century, over a thousand years.

The city was laid out, as the map in *Figure 2* shows, with the *Kamo River* on one side, Mt. Hiei in the top right, and the grid patterned city in the center. A great avenue led down to a ceremonial gate, a sort of triumphal arch, the central approach to the city. Heian, about 2.5 miles wide by 3.5 miles north and south, was to be the home of the emperor, of the aristocracy, of all the people who supported this group.

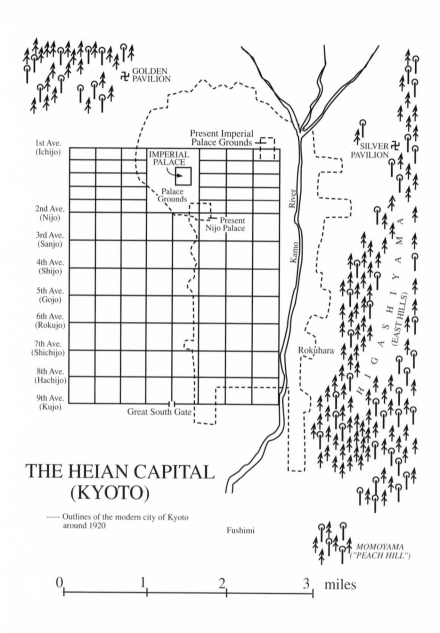

THE HEIAN CAPITAL (KYOTO)

----- Outlines of the modern city of Kyoto around 1920

Figure 2 "The Heian Capital (Kyoto)"

This city represented the Chinese ideal even more closely than the Chinese cities. However, there was one major difference in the Japanese rendition--the Japanese capital did not have a wall around it. The Chinese cities, whether they were capitals or otherwise, invariably had massive walls, originally tamped earth, later faced with stone, with towers, massive gates. This was necessary to protect the city from invading hordes of barbarians sweeping into China, usually from the north. Chinese history is marked by this sort of conflict. Because Japan is an island surrounded by water, with natural defenses, its cities have never been fortified. Castles were fortified, but cities themselves were generally unprotected. Certainly the city of Kyoto was without defenses. It did have an earthen embankment around it to suggest the limits, but the embankment was planted with willow trees. There were water courses that were directed around the city, but more to define the borders, and not to act in any way as a defensive perimeter. The gate itself was just a symbol for ceremonial use. This suggests a major difference between Japanese and Chinese history: the Chinese concern with the possibility of invasion and the absence of such concern among the Japanese.

Kyoto then, laid out in 794, represented ideas of astrobiology, which may be associated with Confucian ideas, and the Taoist ideas of the geomancy--major elements of Chinese philosophy. However, as a religious city, Kyoto reflected more than just these ideas. Buddhism and Shinto were part of the city. Buddhism colored the city from its very beginning. The capital had moved from Nara to Kyoto because of problems with the Buddhist temples, but there was no real revolt against Buddhism--only against certain institutions that had created problems in government in the eighth century. When the capitol was moved to Kyoto, although the temples of Nara were not allowed to move with it, new temples were built in the city. As a matter of fact, there were already some temples in the area before there was any significant habitation. They were worked into the design of the city itself.

Two new temples that were built at the time, built right into the capital, were two located at the southern border, the West Temple, or Saiji, and the East Temple, or Toji. The West Temple no longer exists; the East Temple, Toji, is still very prominent. A number of Buddhist sculptures in the temple date from the ninth century, though none of the structures from that period remain.

Temples were built in the city, giving it a Buddhist coloration. Mt. Hiei itself, although a mountain, by the ninth century was becoming a Buddhist monument. Saicho, a priest who had broken away from the Nara institutions, had located a small hermitage on the mountain. He struck out on his own, when the emperor was also breaking away from the old Nara capital and the Buddhist institutions there. The emperor and Saicho had a sort of "meeting of the minds," locating the new capital with Mt. Hiei up in the "Devil's Gate" area, where there just happened already to be a temple with an independently minded priest. Things seemed to fall together, which meant that Saicho received imperial support. His temple, Enryaku-ji, grew very rapidly to become Kyoto's most prominent temple, protecting, along with the mountain, the city as a whole. Indeed, Enryaku-ji prospered from its foundation in the ninth century until it was finally destroyed in the sixteenth century in the wars of re-unification. It was eventually partially rebuilt and is still a very impressive site.

The grid pattern of the city itself took on a sort of Buddhist coloration. Not only was there a Buddhist protective element in the temples scattered through the city, but it turned out that the whole grid pattern reflected a new Buddhist idea that was being introduced to Japan in the ninth century. This was Shingon, a type of esoteric Buddhism. Kukai, another dissident monk, had gone to China to study the late developments in Indian Buddhism. He brought back these new ideas that were best expressed by the *mandala*, especially the *mandala* of the "Two Worlds," the womb-world and the diamond-world, the changing and unchanging, matter and spirit. This unchanging, diamond-world *mandala* is almost an analog of the layout of the city. Instead of being laid out in a circular pattern as the womb-world *mandala*, the diamond-world *mandala* is organized as a great grid with Dainichi, the Great Sun Buddha, in the north center, which was parallel to the emperor's position in the city. All the other Buddhas were arrayed about him in regular fashion, just as the city itself was arrayed about the emperor. This parallel between the diamond-world *mandala* of the new esoteric Buddhism and the lay out of the city itself could not be missed. There was a kind of convergence, therefore, of hopes, desires, and religious developments at this time with Saicho and Kukai both becoming very prominent as protectors of the city.

To further protect the city, a great *kanji* character, *dai*, was cut into one of the peaks of the eastern mountains sometime in the Heian period. Some say this was done in the eighth century by Kukai, some say the ninth, and others say the tenth. Whenever it was made, its purpose was to protect the city from plagues. Probably it was originally made as the character for "fire" that eventually eroded into the character for "big," *dai*. The character *dai* does not make much sense as a protector, but "fire" would, for fire burns away pestilence and purifies. Indeed, every year on August sixteenth this character is burned on the mountain. Bonfires are placed through all of the stroke marks, and they are lit at about 8:00 p.m. making it a great fiery symbol. In addition, four other religious symbols were made on the mountains north and west of the city. Thus, Buddhist ideas of healing, purification, and salvation were cut into the landscape as protective devices around the city. It became, literally, a Buddhist city.

However, as I mentioned earlier, there was the Shinto aspect as well, the presence of the indigenous religion. Buddhism, Confucianism, and Taoism, were all essentially imported religions. They met with open reception, but still, the expression of these religions was largely foreign. On the other hand, Shinto was indigenous. Before the city of Kyoto was established there were already prominent features in the area that were worshipped in the Shinto fashion. The rivers themselves had shrines dedicated to them--the Shimogamo shrine and the Kamigamo shrine were, for example, dedicated to the water spirit of the *Kamo River* that was so important for the city.

Kiyomizu-dera, a Buddhist temple with Shinto origins, is located on the slopes of the eastern mountains. It is a religious complex which centers on a spring of pure water, *kiyomizu*, that gushes from the rocks. People still go there to drink the water, and some even stand in the cascade to purify themselves. Just a bit to the southeast of the city is the Inari Shrine, dedicated to the rice spirit. Many shrines, then, throughout the city, either inside or around the periphery, represent various aspects of Shinto, celebrating natural wonders like flowing waters, or the harvest.

Some shrines were founded to celebrate individuals who had been prominent in the city. One important shrine, in the northwestern part of the city, is the Kitano Tenmangu shrine. A huge flea market is held there on the twenty-fifth of each month when the death anniversary of a ninth century political figure is celebrated. He had been slandered and exiled from the city and finally died, it is said, of a broken heart. When his spirit returned to get even with his attackers, they decided the only way to pacify him was to build a shrine and make him a deity. Thus, a Heian court noble, who had been on the outs politically, became a deity after his death with a major shrine built in his memory. This became the center of a whole network of shrines all over Japan.

Although Kyoto is said to have over 2,000 shrines, perhaps the most important Shinto aspect of the city, at least in its history, is not a shrine at all but a unique ceremony that made Kyoto a truly important city. This is the festival of enthronement, the *daijōsai*, the great food harvest festival that is celebrated only in conjunction with the ascension of a new emperor. There are a number of different ceremonies that are a part of the enthronement process, the transfer of authority from one emperor to another. The *daijōsai* is the most Japanese of those ceremonies, certainly the most Shinto. It takes place late at night when the new emperor enters some specially built structures that are immediately torn down after the ceremony. In some mysterious fashion, the authorities have never been clear on this, he partakes of rice--specially grown, specially harvested rice. Somehow, through ingesting the rice he becomes the emperor. Some say that the spirit of the "Sun Goddess" Amaterasu-O-mikami enters the emperor through this ceremony, making him more than just an ordinary mortal. Others say that is not quite it. There is a lot of controversy as to just what the *daijōsai* actually means, particularly since the emperor, after World War II, declared that he was not a deity. What does it mean now? My reason for mentioning this is that Kyoto had been the site of this ceremony of making the emperor a god since it was founded in the ninth century. The palace area, where the special structures were set up and the rituals were carried out, was, in a sense, the most sacred place in Japan during the brief period of the ceremony. This ceremony was intimately associated with Kyoto and performed throughout the period that Kyoto was the home of the emperor until the Meiji Restoration in 1868. There were a few times when, for various reasons, the *daijōsai* was not held; whenever it did take place it was in Kyoto.

The new Meiji emperor moved to Tokyo in 1868, and there he performed the initial enthronement ceremonies. However, he returned to Kyoto three years later to celebrate the final ritual, the *daijōsai*. It was as if the emperor could not be the true emperor unless the ceremony were held in Kyoto. Very soon after that, the emperor promised that the *daijōsai* would be forever carried out in Kyoto. When the emperor moved away to Tokyo (Edo) in 1868 the people of Kyoto felt a serious loss. They had lost one of the main things that made the city unique and important. The emperor therefore promised that a key element of the enthronement would continue to take place in Kyoto. The Taisho emperor and Showa emperor (who passed away not long ago) had their *daijōsai* ceremonies performed in Kyoto. This important religious element of the city was therefore maintained until 1990. It was then decided that the *daijōsai* and all of the ceremonies for the new Heisei emperor would take place in Tokyo.

This may not sound like a very important point, but in looking at the whole span of Kyoto's history and the issue of Kyoto being a religious city, the final move of this ceremony to Tokyo means that an essential aspect of Kyoto as a religious city has been removed. It is still the home of many important temples and shrines, but so are other places in Japan.

Possibly a reason for moving the *daijōsai* ceremony concerned the question of whether the ceremony is really religious or just a traditional event sponsored by the government. It is hard to say. Another reason, no doubt, was security. The palace in Tokyo is a military structure--outdated, true, but nevertheless a very huge walled space with a moat--and as such it is easy to protect the imperial family from the radical groups in Japan that always threaten to create incidents on occasions such as this.

Kyoto as a Political City

The emperor in Kyoto was not only the chief religious leader but also the head of a bureaucracy. The Chinese style of government with ministers, bureau chiefs, and so on, was sort of a great bureaucratic pyramid. The bureaucracy not only administered the city but the whole country through the appointment of provincial governors, assistant governors, district magistrates and so on, right down to the person who went to the various farms and households and extracted taxes. The emperor was the head of this system.

The bureaucracy that the emperor headed was Chinese in style--Confucian in style, symmetrical, orderly. On paper, it looked as orderly as the city does, almost a reflection of one another. Symmetry represented order, order reflected the symmetry of the city.

This began to break down, however, in the tenth century and continued through the eleventh and twelfth centuries. One of the first signs of the breakdown was the change in the role of the emperor. His religious role remained, but gradually the administrative role began to slip away through the appointment of regents, necessitated because often the emperor was but a child, eight or nine years old, who could not function as an administrator. Gradually from the latter part of the ninth through the tenth centuries there developed a regular system of child emperors taking the throne with their maternal grandfathers, coming from the Fujiwara family, becoming regents for the emperor. They were regents when the emperors were just children, and remained so even when the emperors became adults with the adoption of an office, "regent for an adult emperor." The system of maternal relatives acting as regent served to insure the smooth transition of authority and kept the emperor from becoming too powerful. Indeed, eventually the regents themselves, these maternal relatives, gradually lost power as others in the court aimed for that position. Contests for power aimed at control over the emperor, or to act as the emperor's spokesperson, but never to usurp his position.

The most significant change in this situation was the movement to warrior rule, in the twelfth and thirteenth centuries. As the Heian aristocrats became more concerned with familial conflicts over who would be related to the emperor, who would actually exercise power through these familial connections, gradually out in the provinces warriors began to take affairs into their own hands. This was the setting for the rise of the *samurai*. The *samurai*, who were essentially managing the land and running the aristocrats' estates and keeping the peace in the provinces, were gradually called into the capital to settle some of the familial disputes. In time they began to see that if they were going to help settle disputes, they might as well also take a portion of the administration of the state.

By the thirteenth century, one of the provincial warriors had actually set himself up as the ruler of the city and of the court. This was a fellow named Taira no Kiyomori. He was powerful enough to have his daughter marry an emperor and thereby soon became the maternal grandfather of the reigning emperor, and thus the effective regent. Thus a warrior from the provinces took over a traditionally aristocratic position.

This lasted only a short time. The focus on the city of Kyoto alone began to shift as more astute warriors realized that perhaps Kyoto as a center of politics and administration had passed its time, and that society had changed and there was more potential in the provinces among the warriors themselves. A feeling developed that perhaps the provincial bases were more powerful and the provinces themselves would have some say apart from the city. Kiyomori's rival and successor, Minamoto no Yoritomo, became the first of the shoguns, the first of the military leaders. He then actually shifted rule from the center of the old, aristocratic Kyoto and developed a new center in the East--Kamakura, south of present day Tokyo. This became a political center in the late twelfth and thirteenth centuries.

With the split between Kyoto in the west and Kamakura in the east (and its later successor, Tokyo/Edo), we actually have a fundamental division in Japan, which continues today, between east and west, with great competition between these two areas: Kyoto,

Osaka and Kobe--the Kansai area always claiming to have its roots in tradition and the authority of antiquity behind it, representing the true Japanese spirit in competition with the newer east--Kamakura, Tokyo/Edo, where political power has actually been located off and on, mostly on, since the thirteenth century.

This split means that from this point on there was a constant battle back and forth as to which area would have the most authority. Kyoto and Kansai have always had, until very recent times, the aura of antiquity, with Kyoto as the home of the emperor, who, child though he might have been, nevertheless technically appointed the *shogun*. Thus, the legitimizing authority was in this area, versus the functional, actual authority in the other area. Whenever there was a fragmentation in the active authority in the east, when warriors fought amongst themselves, when the *shogun* was not strong, the power would shift back to this area.

The Kamakura *shogun*s themselves gave way to another system of regency rather quickly, one that arose in the east, by the end of the thirteenth century. There was political fragmentation and collapse, a brief restoration of the rule from the emperor's court in the early fourteenth century, and the rise of a new series of *shogun*s, who were weaker and could not afford to remain apart from tradition. They resettled in Kyoto in the Ashikaga period, from the 1330s to the sixteenth century. Military figures came to be prominent in the city as they tried to take to themselves part of the old aristocratic trappings to gain an aura of legitimacy.

The result of this was that the warriors became established as legitimate rulers, because they moved into the city and themselves became aristocrats. The warriors supported the arts of the nobles: literature, poetry, painting, and crafts. In addition, they patronized new art, sometimes through new contacts with China, like the arts associated with Zen, which gave them an element of independence from the old aristocratic monopoly of the arts. What developed in the fourteenth and fifteenth centuries was a merging of the warrior and aristocratic traditions. Accomplishments of the past were preserved through this merging of the old tradition, because there was never any idea of removing the old court. There was nothing similar to the French Revolution where the aristocracy was violently removed. Instead, the aristocrats were controlled by merging with them. This was terribly important to some of the stereotypically Japanese arts as we know them today: tea ceremonies, flower arranging, ink painting, and so on.

The Gold Pavilion, built by Ashikaga Yoshimitsu, one of the *shogun*s, a culturally oriented but politically powerful man, came out of this. The gilded hall is the centerpiece of a great palatial complex to which he would invite the emperor and other court nobles. The structure we see today is a reproduction, for the original was burned down in 1950. Nevertheless, it reflects well the merging of the aristocratic and warrior traditions.

The Silver Pavilion, on the other side of the city, was built by the eighth *shogun*, Yoshimasa, and was also a reflection of the merging of traditions at a point when control by the *shogun*s was rapidly weakening. The city experienced devastating battles during the 1450s and 70s when a huge civil war took place. Virtually all of the city was burned. Great armies, located in various parts of the city, fought for about 10 years and, during the course of the fighting, destroyed virtually everything in the old city. There is nothing in the area of the old city until one gets way down by the National Museum, that predates the wars. It was the most destructive, devastating period in the history of Kyoto.

However, the grid pattern remained, the river remained and the mountains remained, so the fundamental aspects of the city remained. None of the man-made elements survived. For quite a while after this, through the late fifteenth and early sixteenth centuries, Kyoto existed as a kind of backwater town. The whole country was in a period of chaotic warfare. For historians this was a period of high feudalism, with complete fragmentation of politics. There was an emperor in the city but he had absolutely no power, no authority at all. There was even a *shogun*, a military leader, but he had no power either. No one listened to anyone during this period. There was only the aura of the past, vestiges of tradition, which remained in this area during this period. Still, it was possible for someone to come along and restore order by utilizing culture and tradition as a focus for rebuilding.

This is, of course, exactly what happened. In the latter part of the sixteenth century came the Great Unifiers, Oda Nobunaga, Toyotomi Hideyoshi, and Tokugawa Ieyasu. The latter two, who completed the re-unification, had very different attitudes toward Kyoto. Hideyoshi, in the 1580s, a comparatively weak ruler without much tradition or background (having been a peasant who rose to the top), needed the city and the aura of the old emperors to help legitimatize himself. Hideyoshi rebuilt Kyoto after the long period of devastation. He had completed the process of unification to the extent that all the various power holders, the warlords (*daimyō*), paid him homage. Because of this he had the time and wherewithal to cause the city to be reconstructed. It was rebuilt largely following the original plan, but with modifications in that the whole western side was sort of abandoned, and the east side expanded across the river, with the palace occupying an area a bit to the east of the original palace. The *Kamo River* now came down through the city instead of forming one of its borders. He built a wall around the city, again more for ceremony than protection. He worked on controlling the *Kamo River*. Much of what you see there now in terms of flood control devices, like the channels along the side to control flooding, started under Hideyoshi.

He relocated many of the temples in the city. In what is now the tourist district, there is a street just off of Kawaramachi called Teramachi, meaning "temple street". Hideyoshi had many of the major temples relocated here, a sort of temple ghetto. If you go up high in one of the department stores and look down you will see graveyards behind the curio shops. In this area you can see a most curious sight: one temple decided to build a parking lot, so the temple buildings were raised up one story and the parking lot put underneath. The point is that the cluster of temples, though a bit strange today, derives from an arrangement dating to Hideyoshi's time. The north-south grid pattern remains.

The Sanjo bridge, mentioned earlier, is still one of the sights of the city. This also resulted from Hideyoshi's efforts. Much of what we see in the city today dates from the reconstruction of 1580-1590, reconstruction that was carried out mainly to legitimatize the new power holder, Hideyoshi.

At about this time there were visitors who came to Kyoto from Europe, who talked about the city. Their written accounts give a vivid description of the changes that the city experienced in this period. St. Francis Xavier visited Kyoto in 1551 and described the city in this fashion: "On account of the wars, it is now very much destroyed."[7] Xavier had come looking for a center, an emperor, someone from whom he could obtain permission to establish a church in Japan. No one could give it to him. Kyoto was destroyed.

Fifty years later after Hideyoshi's rebuilding, João Rodrigues also a part of the Jesuit mission, wrote:

> The city of Miyako is extremely clean, and in each of its broad streets is to be found water from excellent springs and streams which flow along the middle. The streets are swept and sprinkled with water twice a day and are thus kept very clean and fresh, for every man looks after that part in front of his own house. As the ground slopes there is no mud, and when it rains the water dries up in no time. The inhabitants' houses lining the streets are usually offices, shops and workshops of many crafts, and the people have their living quarters and guest rooms inside. Some streets are very long and wide, and on either side they have arcades under which people walk to avoid the rain or the sun or to look in the shops; in these streets they sell only bolts of silk and silk articles, supplying the entire kingdom.[8]

What he meant was that the streets were organized, each arcade selling a special article. He further says:

> There are also all over the city a great number of inns and taverns which provide food for travelers, and there are public baths where a man blows a horn and invites people to the baths, for the Japanese are much given to this.[9]

What Rodrigues described in 1600 is a city which is recognizable today. In a mere fifty years, Kyoto had gone from its lowest point to a very livable city. This resulted from Hideyoshi's rebuilding.

Ieyasu, who took over after Hideyoshi died, was a much stronger leader, a very powerful *shogun*. He had the proper background and lineage to gather a very strong following of *samurai*. His strength was such that he could move his political center to Edo, the eastern area. He did not have to stay in the west. He could then establish a clear separation between the politically active administrator of the country, the *shogun*, in Edo, and the old traditional legitimatizer, the emperor, who remained in Kyoto. Ieyasu felt that this would be better for his power structure, and it continued to function for the next

250 years--Edo, the *samurai* capital, the effective capital of the country and Kyoto, the home of the court, the emperor, a sort of legitimatizer.

In order to make sure that this old court did not try to reassert itself while the *samurai* and the *shogun* were busy in the east, Ieyasu left administrators in Kyoto to watch over it. He organized the city to make sure that there would be no rebellion. One of the things that was done was the construction of Nijo castle. It is not really a proper castle, because although it does have moats and walls, it could not have withstood a proper attack. It was given moats and walls more to suggest the military nature of the occupant, the martial virtues of the Kyoto deputy who was stationed there to watch over the imperial court.

The court itself was largely confined to the palace area. Today, when you walk into the palace grounds you will find them very spacious--grassy parks, graveled avenues, baseball fields, tennis courts, people practicing karate and so on--a very pleasant park-like atmosphere. However, in the Edo period the park area we now see was filled with aristocratic mansions, where the old aristocrats with their long traditions and close association with the emperor were confined, walled in, so their movements could be carefully watched by the military guards posted around the palace. It was not that they were exactly in jail, they were under a kind of house arrest, soft jailing if you like. They had plenty of money, and they lived a comfortable style of life, but they were kept from any political activity. Furthermore, anyone in Japan who might want to operate against the *shogun* would be kept from contacting them. The various feudal lords who were vassals of the *shogun*, some of whom harbored great resentment dating to earlier rivalries, were carefully prevented from ever having any contact with the old imperial court.

Ieyasu was strong enough to center his administration in Edo, and he was astute enough to make sure that the emperor and the court were maintained to legitimatize himself and his descendants alone, and no one else. This is the role of the city then. Politics were removed from the city in the early seventeenth century.

When the restoration of the emperor occurred in 1868, the emperor moved to Edo/Tokyo. He did so because the political administration of the country had been located there for centuries, and the lines of communication for administering the country focused on Edo. The emperor, if he were going to become the real head of state and government again, would have to rule from the place that was most practical. So he moved to Tokyo. The people in Kyoto were very upset with this, and there were all sorts of things the emperor had to do to placate them, which I will mention later. Interestingly enough, when in the 1870's it was felt certain that the emperor would not be returning to Kyoto, all of the aristocratic mansions in the palace grounds were torn down. The aristocrats were forced to move to Edo, where they would then be under the watchful eye of the emperor and his new assistants. They did not want to allow the old mansions to remain in the palace grounds in Kyoto as a possible focal point for dissenting opinion.

Therefore, not only did the emperor move, but any possibility of the city again becoming a focal point of politics was removed. The core element of the religious city was gone and with it the core political element went too.

Kyoto as a Cultural City

Ever since its founding, Kyoto has had an important role in the culture of Japan. The mere fact that the aristocrats lived in the city and had to be supplied with their needs meant that many arts would be developed in the city. Prominent residents, like Lady Murasaki and Sei Shonagon, authors of the Heian period, wrote about aspects of the city. In the Heian period, literature that mentions activities outside Kyoto always does so by saying how sad it was that this or that person had to leave the city for even a week or two. The poor provincial governor who has been posted off to northern Japan, one hopes he will survive. When anyone returned to the city, the return was always preceded by much anticipation. Kyoto was a great magnet for the aristocracy. This continued even through periods of devastation.

When Ieyasu moved to Edo and established his castle there, he was very much in need of people to make it a real city: it was just a muddy village and his castle not even completed. He needed the arts, crafts and services that were present in Kyoto. He tried to bring people up to make Edo livable, but some of those he asked refused to go. One prominent figure in the history of Japanese art, Honami Koetsu, was skilled in laquerware and calligraphy, paper making, painting, so skilled in the arts that he drew a whole group of artists around him and created an arts community. Koetsu refused to go to Edo. Ieyasu, much to his credit, understood this and allowed him to remain in Kyoto, and saw that he was given a plot of land in the northwestern area just outside of the city for his artists' colony. Koetsu, with his artist disciples around him, maintained direct contact with his old aristocratic traditions that had been modified by the military presence in the city. Ieyasu, though not pleased, nevertheless recognized that he could not remove the cultural aspect of Kyoto and, instead, decided he would help cultivate it.

As for the aristocrats themselves, who remained in their plush ghetto, Ieyasu issued a series of laws for governing the noble households, the *Kuge Shotatto*. These laws emphasized that the old nobles should confine themselves to aesthetic pursuits, to the arts. This was their only area of legitimate activity. While they were in this hothouse atmosphere, this aristocratic ghetto, the government in control enjoined them to continue the traditional practices to keep them alive. This explains to some degree why they survive today. In short, Kyoto has been designated as a cultural city from the seventeenth century on.

Because it was a cultural city but not directly under the thumb of the government, Kyoto was comparatively liberal in its culture. A lot of new arts arose, arts that might have offended, to some degree, at least in their initial stages, some of the more prudish *samurai* leaders. The Kabuki theater started in Kyoto along the banks of the *Kamo River* with prostitutes dancing to entice their customers. Had this been done in Edo, Ieyasu and his followers would have clamped down on it right away. Rodrigues, the Jesuit visitor quoted above, wrote about the theater in Kyoto:

> At certain places on the roads at the entrances to the city there are gated wooden enclosures in which are held continuous performances of comedies, farces and other plays which recount ancient legends to a certain singing and tone accompanied by musical instruments, and these provide much recreation for the Japanese. The gates are always kept closed and the people who enter each pay a certain sum, and the actors earn their living with the money thus collected because a goodly number of people attend each performance. When the play is over, they leave and others enter, and there begins another play or drama, in which the actors wear rich silk costumes suited to each character.[10]

As a point of reference, this was the time of Shakespeare. In terms of entertaining the public, much the same thing was occurring in Japan as in Europe and Rodriguez focused on this.

The most striking artifacts of this period are paintings of the city--great screen paintings, paintings that focus on various sites that had been rebuilt, temples, streets, and so on. These great screen paintings are full of gold: in order to divide the space, golden clouds waft about the city, revealing and highlighting the various structures glimpsed from a bird's eye perspective, and the streets that also help divide the space are painted with gold. Gold sky, gold streets, it is as if Kyoto was seen as a kind of golden city, a jewel box, if you will, an aesthetic city promoted as such by the government, and seen as a cultural city by the populace--not just the populace of Kyoto but increasingly the whole of Japan. The guide books of the day emphasized this, and many were published in the city, like the massive guide book I mentioned earlier, for Kyoto was the center of publishing well into the eighteenth century when Edo began to surpass it.

When the emperor moved away in 1868 he took away, of course, the religious and political aspects of the city, but the cultural aspect was to remain. As a kind of "payoff" to the citizens of Kyoto, the city became a place where many "firsts" of modern Japan occurred.

The first elementary school in Japan was established in Kyoto in 1869, followed by the first middle school or junior high school. A tunnel from Lake Biwa, the tunnel mentioned in the *National Geographic* ad cited earlier, that brought water in from Lake Biwa to the city to increase the water supply, was constructed between 1885 and 1904. This tunnel was one of the wonders of the world at that time. A 1904 issue of *Scientific American* mentioned the tunnel as a magnificent achievement of engineering. It was not only used for water but also for boats and shipping for quite some time, as well as for the sort of tourist experience mentioned in the ad. Because of the water the tunnel brought from lake Biwa, Kyoto was the site of the first hydroelectric generators, which gave

Kyoto the first electricity in Japan. Electricity meant that Kyoto had the first street car, the first electric street lights. These were all promoted, then, by the emperor as a sort of "payoff" for the city for having lost his presence.

Arts and crafts were promoted through government projects, like revitalizing textile production with the introduction of new weaving machines while at the same time preserving the old traditions of Nishijin brocade.

Because of the cultural nature of the city, which was established in the seventeenth century and was reinforced in the late nineteenth century, Kyoto was spared from bombing during World War II. It emerged from the war years with its antiquity intact, unique among the major cities of Japan. Edo, or Tokyo, with three hundred years of history prior to the war, had been devastated. Only the palace was spared. Osaka, an old city as well, now has only one structure dating to the Edo period. Even the Allies decided that the aesthetic nature of Kyoto was worth preserving.

Kyoto as a Commercial City

A great many people lived their daily lives in the city, producing things not just for the aristocrats and themselves, but eventually for the country as a whole. It was in the Edo period that Kyoto became a truly important commercial city. As the economy in Japan expanded with the long period of peace and relatively unrestricted travel, Kyoto became a great source of manufactures that improved the lives of those in various parts of the country. Hideyoshi, through his rebuilding the city, was partially responsible for this because, as he rebuilt the city and it grew, he freed the old artisans from their religious and aristocratic patrons. Everything had been divided up, locked in, monopolized. Hideyoshi broke down all these relationships and made the merchants and artisans largely independent. They repopulated the city and began to make it a center of commerce. By the late seventeenth century Kyoto had become just such a center. One of the European visitors at that time, Engelbert Kaempher, a German doctor attached to the Dutch mission based in Nagasaki, passed through Kyoto four times in 1691 and 1692. He wrote about the city in glowing terms:

> Miyako is the great magazine of all Japanese manufactures and commodities, and the chief mercantile town in the Empire. There is scarce a house in this large capital, where there is not something made or sold. Here they refine copper, coin money, print books, weave the richest stuffs with gold and silver flowers. The best and scarcest dyes, the most artful carvings, all sorts of musical instruments, pictures, lacquered cabinets, all sorts of things wrought in gold and other metals, particularly in steel, as the best tempered blades, and other arms are made here in the utmost perfection, as are also the richest dresses, and after the best fashion, all sorts of toys, puppets, moving their heads of themselves, and numberless other things, too many to be here mentioned. In short, there

is nothing can be thought of, but what may be found at Miyako . . . nothing, though never so neatly wrought, can be imported from abroad, but what some artist or other in this capital will undertake to imitate.[11]

Statistics on trade within Japan during the Edo period are interesting. Most areas were self-sufficient in basic needs, but there are lists of almost 2,000 products that were traded interregionally. About forty percent of those products came from this area, either from Kyoto directly or the area right around the city. We are talking about manufactured goods--brocades, textiles, lacquerware--the things that Kaempher was mentioning. Kyoto was the great magazine, the great factory of the empire through the Edo period.

In the Meiji period, when more foreign visitors came to Japan and were finally allowed to visit the city of Kyoto freely, they, too, focused on the manufactures of the city. The guidebooks, diaries and journals of the time constantly mention bronzes, lacquerware (or Japanware as it was called), textiles, and so on. Visitors marvelled at the low prices.

Today, these crafts are still practiced in Kyoto. Kyoto does not have any heavy industry despite the desires of some industrialists. The powers that be and the residents have not wanted smoke-stack type industry, so the city does not have it. Instead, the traditional crafts have been promoted. If you go to Okazaki Park where the city museum and Heian Shrine are located, you will find the Museum of Traditional Arts and Crafts, celebrating all of the arts and crafts traditionally practiced in Kyoto. Demonstrations go on daily. You can get a quick overall view of what the city produces. If you choose to walk around the city, down the narrow streets, here and there you will hear the sounds of craft related activities, the sound of looms, etc.

Much of this tradition is important as the basis for modern developments. Tradition does not mean just preserving old things, but bringing the old into the new developments. For instance, Kyoto has been the center of *sake* brewing, particularly in the area just south of the city. One of the brewers decided that beer and whiskey were destroying the *sake* market, so the company came up with *chu-hai*, a kind of cocktail using lemon and a mild form of *shochu*, a vodka-like drink it had developed. It thus originated a new Japanese-type drink that could be marketed through automatic vending machines on the streets, a fruity sort of high kick cocktail. The same company is also interested in biotechnology, and is using its brewing background to make advances in this area. Kyocera, which makes ceramic bases for computer chips, is based in Kyoto with its long tradition of fine ceramics. Kyocera has developed ceramic knives, and is working on a ceramic automobile engine. In an environmentally conscious move it has developed a high-tech ceramic material to use for personal seals which up to now have been made of ivory. Since it is the expense that makes these seals desirable, plastic would be frowned upon, but expensive high-tech ceramic would be acceptable, and thus replace the desire for ivory.

Another company that makes automatic ticket machines for train stations as well as electronic goods has been looking into the area of making artificial limbs for amputees. Engineers have focused on the puppets mentioned by Kaempher, examining how the puppets are made to move in order to help design the artificial limbs. There are all sorts of dimensions to this use of traditional practices as the basis for truly modern developments. In short, Kyoto's antiquity in no way limits its ability to be modern.

The major income of Kyoto is from tourism, 33 million visitors a year. Tourists demand services that the city is hard pressed to provide: parking spaces, hotels, etc. It was decided a couple of years ago to tax the tourists to pay for the necessary improvements. This was to be done by taxing the temple admission fees. The temples did not like this, as it involved the government looking at their financial records, so they closed their doors. The result was that the tourist shops around the temples lost business. This caused a terrific problem for the city government. Eventually, the tax was rescinded. Thus, the impact of tourism is multidimensional, with benefits as well as problems. The city leaders have to be very careful in how they solve these problems, watching out for the toes of tradition.

The issue now is, what is the future of Kyoto? How will these problems be solved. The serious threat today is to the nature of the city, its very appearance. This threat revolves right now around the issue of high buildings. You have seen Kyoto Tower, 131 meters tall. There was much controversy when it was built, because it was to be taller than any other structure in the city. It is taller than the pagoda at Toji, which had for centuries been the tallest structure in Kyoto and a major symbol of the city. People were afraid that the tower would be an eyesore. Well, it was built and until recently it was the only thing that broke the traditional skyline of the city, a city characterized by low wooden buildings. Gradually, more and more concrete buildings were built. Owners of small plots of high-priced land want to get the most out of their property, and this can be done with multistoried concrete buildings. The question right now is, how high these buildings should be.

Until recently forty-five meters, the height of the Toji pagoda, was the height limit, a kind of unofficial, accepted limitation. The city council passed a resolution that raised it to sixty meters, 180-190 feet. This was to be the new limit. Of course, people began to think about building more tall buildings. One of those buildings is going to be the Kyoto Hotel, on Kawaramachi, close to the *Kamo River*, on the eastern side of the city. This construction proposal has met with great opposition, because if the whole area of the city along the river suddenly becomes a wall of sixty meter tall buildings, it will look something like Miami. The Higashiyama mountains, celebrated since Heian times, will be cut off from view except from the windows of those buildings. Right now, it seems that the Kyoto Hotel will be forced to back away from its plans. There will be a compromise.[12] The Kyoto train station will be rebuilt, to celebrate the 1,200th anniversary of the city. It will be at a height just below the sixty meter limit.

I mentioned before that one of the important characteristics of Kyoto was that it did not have permanent monuments--no great stone structures designed to last through time. This is changing. In the process of renewal, more is being made of concrete and being made larger. The city may change very seriously indeed. Will Kyoto be able to protect itself better than other areas? This will depend on something other than the mountains and waters, it will depend on the people, perhaps the most enduring aspect of this marvelous city.

III
Some Themes in the Christian
Experience in Japan
Hakan Eilert

Others, neither merchants nor soldiers, neither academics nor sightseers have come to Japan seeking to bring about changes following normative paradigms originally formulated elsewhere. These persons, whom we call missionaries, gave enormously of their time and effort and were recipients of more from their experiences in Japan than they initially might have thought possible. Dr. Eilert completes our initial orientation by demonstrating creative developments within core structures of two cultures while also launching us into a consideration of key themes of our study: the attempt to understand another in his or her religious living, which involves also the matter of reflective reciprocity in colloquia about what concerns us most -- the purpose of our lives and the ground of meaning.

My story goes back a long way, in fact to a Norwegian missionary, Karl Ludvig Reichelt (1877-1952), who came to China in 1902. After a couple of years, he found that it was not easy to succeed as a missionary in China. Chinese ways of understanding are very different from the structures of European thought. He felt this way particularly after having met some Chinese Zen monks in the mountainous areas. Reichelt became convinced that in order to succeed as a missionary in China he had to know Chinese and Chinese ways of reflection--especially the Buddhist and Confucian traditions.

Thus Reichelt engaged in a study of Chinese religions--a work which became a life-long preoccupation. Eventually he became quite an authority in his field in which he published several books. But one result of his efforts was that his home mission board in Norway became unhappy with him. Reichelt was reprimanded and told that it was his task to preach the Gospel in the traditional way and not to engage in religious dialogue with Buddhists and others. He was told that the truth was Christianity and all other religions were wrong. He was more or less asked to leave the missionary society.

At that time, in Sweden, my home country, the Archbishop was Nathan Söderblom. He was a historian of religion, having studied in Paris. He published his thesis on Persian religion. He was a person of considerable standing and vision. He understood the Christian mission in a dynamic way. Söderblom was convinced that God is at work within humankind's religiousness as such.

From such a perspective Söderblom encouraged the missionary movement, and people in the northern countries of Sweden, Norway, and Denmark came together and started, in 1925, a new missionary society called the Nordic Mission to the Buddhists. Luckily, Karl Ludvig Reichelt was at hand. He accepted the calling to return to China, and a Center, called Tao Fong Shan, was established in Hong Kong in 1925. Buildings in

Chinese style were built later, in 1930. Reichelt could continue his work. He died in 1952 and was buried in Hong Kong. On his tombstone is inscribed a quotation from the New Testament: "He saw the glory of the Lord."

Reichelt also met Japanese Buddhists. He went to Japan and visited Kyoto, where, in 1927, he met D. T. Suzuki. He was very impressed with Suzuki. Reminiscing he said that Suzuki was a man of vision and insight:

> It does not strike one that he [Suzuki] is a Buddhist, because he is well versed in the various views, and he knows that it is not a question of words and definitions, but of spiritual realities. He is entirely foreign to narrowness and zeal to propagate. His mind abundantly filled with reverence moves freely on the highest stage of religious life.[13]

In Kyoto, Reichelt lectured at Otani University and discussed religious issues with Suzuki and other famous Buddhists. He was encouraged by Suzuki to set up a Christian study center in Kyoto, in order to pursue an open minded way of understanding religion. Reichelt, as well as many others in various parts of the world, was seeking for new approaches. But Reichelt's dream never came true until after his death in 1952. That same year a Christian study center was established in Kyoto by the Nordic Christian Mission to the Buddhists.

However, the basis was not broad enough. We found that this kind of work had to be much broader in scope. The same feeling was prevalent among Japanese Christians. So, in 1958 the National Christian Council opened the Center for the Study of Japanese Religions in Kyoto. Since then, the Center has been through many ups and downs. Gradually it has gained strength, being involved in many interesting developments. In the 1960s, the Christian churches launched new standpoints, gradually changing the "black-white" scenario as far as judgments of other religions are concerned. Recall the Vatican council in the 1960s, and the way the World Council of Churches slowly changed directions. The same kind of signal sounded within the World Council of Churches: understanding, openness, dialogue, a desire to meet and become friends together in one world. This was not for the sake of streamlining religions, but in order to understand religion in a new way. It was felt that opening up dialogue would be helpful and stimulating for each partner.

Now, I am not going to present an historical account of what happened within the Christian tradition in Japan. I have been trying to "put the pieces together" for quite a number of years, actually since the 1960s when I studied in Kyoto, and during the last eight years that I have been here in Kyoto. I will be leaving Japan soon and these comments will be part of my "swan song," an attempt to put some pieces together and make some sense of the dialogue between Japan and the West, between Christianity and Japanese religions.

First of all, let us turn to Francis Xavier, who came to Japan in 1549. He was one of the founding fathers of the Jesuit order and also one of the foremost missionaries of the Roman Catholic Church. He landed in Kagoshima in a Chinese junk in 1549, and his mission, his cause, was to plant the Christian Gospel in Japan. He was eminently equipped for such a task. He had met some Japanese outside Japan and held a high estimation of them. He liked the Japanese people. In a letter to his people in Rome, he wrote "If asked if I value the Japanese people, I do very highly indeed, probably higher than my own people."

When he came in contact with Japanese religions, he was not equally happy. We must bear in mind that Xavier was a child of the counter-reformation which had been launched within the Roman Catholic Church in Europe. He came to Japan with certain ways of reflection and thinking with a distinctly European shape. How could he possibly understand religious people in Japan? Perhaps you have heard of his encounter with the Jodo Shinshu sect. He was stunned, to say the least, and wrote back to his people in Goa, on the western coast of India, that it seemed that the Protestant heresy had already come to Japan.

Xavier also met Zen Buddhists and made several visits to a temple not far from Kagoshima. The name of the abbot was Ninshitsu. They had a number of encounters and talks with each other, dialogues, we can say. One day Xavier happened to be in the temple while the monks were meditating in the meditation hall (*zendō*). Xavier was amazed. He did not understand the method at all. He asked the abbot what the monks were doing, sitting motionless on the floor. The abbot told him, smiling:

> Some are calculating the contributions received from their followers during the past months. Others are thinking about how they might get better clothing and personal care. Still others are thinking of vacation and pastimes. In short, no one is thinking of anything important.[14]

It was difficult for Xavier, getting such a response, to figure out what it was all about. We gather that Xavier did not understand Buddhism. He could not see that there are different ways of reflection. He was a child of his own background, his Western way of understanding. He took the answer of the abbot seriously. But in Zen Buddhism, there *is* no particular thing to think on, is there? Zen has to do with letting go, with open-mindedness, allowing the Buddha mind to function freely. In the process of letting go, all sorts of odd thoughts crop up. The abbot was well aware of the working of the human mind. He knew what is involved in meditation -- settling the mind. Xavier did not know much about such things. Thus the different ways of reflection between East and West stand out.

In the West, a certain kind of theological positivism believed it was possible to understand this world: soul, mind, God, world, man. Neat! By studying scripture, one comes to certain conclusions, through logic. Xavier could not grasp the meaning of Zen.

He was perplexed. He was convinced of the superiority of the Christian way. There are many incidents proving his failure to come to terms with Buddhism. Listen to another extract from Xavier's letters which speaks for itself:

> I have spoken often with some of the most learned monks, especially with one who is held in high esteem here by everyone, as much for his knowledge, conduct, and dignity, as for his great age of eighty years. His name is Ninshitsu, which in Japanese means 'heart of truth.' He is among them as a bishop, and if he measured up to his name he would be blessed. In the many conversations I had with him, I found him doubtful and uncertain as to whether our soul is immortal or whether it perishes with the body. Sometimes he would say 'Yes,' but again, he would say 'No.' I fear that the other learned monks are like him. But it is a marvel how good a friend this Ninshitsu is to me.[15]

Different ways of reflection appear. A Buddhist sense of "being-non-being" is set in contrast with Xavier's sense of a polarization between two extremes. The dual vision of Buddhism, a way of abstaining from statements, the non-objectifying way of understanding -- Xavier found that nothing was said about an Ultimate Reality.

The encounter between Xavier and Ninshitsu has traits that continue to appear in the ensuing story of encounters between Christianity and Japanese religions; inability to understand, harsh judgments, often from the Western side, conviction that "we" know how to explain humankind's existence and pass judgments. From a Japanese standpoint, there has been a reluctance to spell things out. It is thought provoking to keep in mind the failure of Christianity to get into true contact with Buddhists at that time.

Of course, there are many other aspects to the encounters between East and West in the 16th and early 17th centuries in Japan. These were mainly on the political level.

Take a look at what happened at the beginning of the 17th century when the Tokugawa Era started. To the Japanese the situation was difficult to assess, that is, to appreciate Christianity because it was itself in turmoil, as seen in the conflicts between various Catholic orders and between the Portuguese and the Dutch. There was also a growing suspicion that Christianity was not in line with Tokugawa ideas concerning the dominating role of the social order itself, as a necessary framework for a peaceful and harmonious existence. Christianity talked about the God of heaven, a message which came across as undermining the Japanese way of endorsing the authority of the emperor and the *shogun*.

Before and after the Meiji Restoration, which took place in 1868, many Westerners came to Japan with a mission. Many of them were highly educated, like the American consul, Townsend Harris. He was a fervent Christian and, like many of his compatriots who came to Japan, he hoped to introduce Christianity to the people. The missionaries who came here, mostly from the United States, had this kind of mission of conversion in mind. They were pioneers, characterized by American revivalism, even "biblicism" perhaps. They were consumed with morality and zeal. There were persons like James Curtis Hepburn (1815-1911), James Hamilton Ballagh, Leroy Janes (1838-1909), William Smith Clark (1826-1886), Jerome Davis and many others. They talked about the need to go through a certain period of personal struggle, breaking through the darkness of the night into the truth of light. One can come to such a breakthrough by studying the Bible, through prayer, and attending worship services.

The revivalists were influenced by certain ways of understanding Christianity. They had a limited understanding of Japanese ways of reflection or of Japanese religions. The indigenous religions were considered to be outdated. The missionaries looked upon the process of modernization in Japan as part of Christianization, the uplift of Japan, the need to introduce new ways of understanding, new methods in education, etc.

Likewise, many Japanese were interested in changing the conditions in Japan. Some pondered why the Western world had made progress in so many areas. Some came to the conclusion that the answer was Christianity, which was the dynamic force behind the technological prowess of the West. Many of the Japanese who felt this way became Christians. More often than not these Japanese had been Confucianists. It has been pointed out that many of the Japanese who turned from Confucianism to Christianity did so without difficulty. In Confucianism the Will of Heaven is a major theme. Heaven could sometimes be personified. Many of the previously-Confucian Christians later became prominent persons in the nation's life.

However, a split between the missionaries and the Japanese Christians developed. The argument was about different ways of understanding how Christianity should be interpreted in Japan. More often than not, the missionaries said that it was a matter of presenting and maintaining the Christian faith like we have it in the West. There was a dogmatic package which has been practiced and cannot be changed, only transferred.

Many Japanese Christians were unhappy with such a takeover. They wanted to retain their own "face," so to say, their own identity. They believed that Christianity must have a Japanese face in order to be accepted. This issue is still discussed within the churches today -- the issue of indigenization. Some Japanese Christians were more outspoken than others. I mention three: Danjo Ebina (1858-1937), Kanzo Uchimura (1861-1930), and Masahisa Uemura (1858-1925). These three persons played a prominent role in the growing uneasiness which occurred between the missionaries and the Christians of Japan. In a sense, it all started in Kyoto. This city has always been the vital place for the study of Japanese religions. Doshisha University invited some non-Christians to speak. The students wished to hear about other religions, to know more. The Christian missionaries vehemently objected.

This event illustrates the pattern of what often occurred. The Japanese Christians seemed to have a much broader vision of dialogue than many of the missionaries.

Also, Danjo Ebina, who died in 1937, was a towering personality in Japanese Christianity. In my estimation he has often been neglected, not given due appreciation.

Ebina was one of those young Christians who had been formed by the Confucian way of thinking. He went to a school in Kumamoto. His aim was to learn English, because he knew that English was helpful in the new developments of Japan. Soon, he was fascinated by his teacher, Leroy Janes, who used to be a captain in the American Armed Forces. Janes had a certain magnetism about him for Ebina, the kind that certain teachers have. The Japanese students loved him. Janes had a moral strength and other qualities which endeared him in the eyes of the Japanese. Ebina could not withstand his influence, and ended up a Christian. Still he had no wish to give up his loyalty to Japanese values. Robert Bellah, in *Beyond Belief,* has written about Ebina's conversion. Bellah points out how Ebina shifted his loyalty from the emperor to God, the God of heaven, because no emperor, *shogun,* or territorial lord (*daimyō*) can lay claim on his loyalty. Ebina went through a conversion experience finding that the God of heaven is God alone. "Hearing God's command I became a changed person," he wrote.[16]

But after some time Ebina became unhappy with Christian life. It seemed that something was left out. Ebina went through a second conversion realizing that God in heaven is not to be understood as Lord in the sense of a dominating father figure. God does have the meaning of power; but first of all God is love and mercy. Following the second conversion, he said, "From that day on I have had peace with God. I have been his blessed child. At the same time, as a child of God, I grow into manhood in Christ."[17] This growth meant that much of the things he left behind came back to him, for re-evaluation: reading, studying, knowledge, and so on. He had rejected all that before. Now he knew that to become a full person, to attain wholeness, has to do with accepting the world as it is, God's world.

In such terms of understanding, Ebina also turned to Japanese religions and became eager to include Japanese religious insights in his Christian understanding. He referred to a statement of Jesus: "I have not come to destroy but to fulfill." Ebina became a representative of a multi-dimensional interpretation of Christianity. Christianity can be identified with a global, universal development of the divine spirit. It functions like a prism; it is reflected in many different stages. In this way, Ebina could include Japanese ways of thinking and Japanese history as preparatory stages for an important task to fulfill in the world. He claimed that Japan was a bridge building society. The Japanese people had been given a special task in the kingdom of God, to usher in a new era in humankind's religious development. Remember that he was talking in the early 20th century when the Japanese had recently struggled with Russia and came out victoriously, in 1905.[18]

There was an uproar in Christian circles in Japan. How could Ebina say such things? He was challenged. Like when he said, "I offered up the seat of my sin--self--on the cross of Christ and have the awareness of being raised up again in Christ's God-centeredness."[19] Ebina was accused of taking the doctrine of sin too loosely. His defence was that Christians talked too much about sin. He himself felt he had laid down his entire self before Jesus, and that was that.

Kanzo Uchimura was another representative of contemporary attempts to give a Japanese face to Christianity. Uchimura studied in Hokkaido and became a Christian. Later he became disappointed with official Christianity because there was a difference between word and deed. A famous incident occurred in Tokyo when Uchimura refused to bow before an image of the Emperor. This incident created quite a stir. He would not bow. It was a *cause célèbre*. Uchimura's understanding of Christianity involved a broad vision, including his own Japaneseness.

> I have not learned from Christian missionaries what religion is. Nichiren, Honen, Rennyo and other pious, worthy men have already given to my fathers and forefathers and to myself knowledge about the essence of religion before I was called to worship at the feet of the divine man from Nazareth.[20]

He felt that religion had been misused and did not help people to develop a sincere worship that complied with the intentions of the Gospel. "Churches--no, Gospel--yes."

His intention was to form a "non-church church." With such an aim he became the founder of the non-church-Mukyo-kai movement in Japan. It still exists, even in Kyoto, but has not become very strong, perhaps there are approximately 35,000 followers.

Kanzo Uchimura is an interesting person in the meeting of Japanese and Christian religions.

Emil Brunner, a Swiss theologian who came to Japan in the 1950s, said that the Mukyo-kai movement is purely Japanese in its form of Christianity, which responds to and understands the Japanese spirit. I think this kind of movement has not been sufficiently appreciated and still raises questions for us even today. As a person, Uchimura was thought-provoking.[21]

The third person mentioned above, Masahisa Uemura (1858-1925) developed the Japaneseness of Christianity in his own ways. He accepted a way of theologizing which was introduced from the United States and Europe. He became a representative of Christian orthodoxy. Somehow, he managed to combine Japanese history with this orthodoxy. He did give a Japanese "face" to the work of Christ. He found that the way of the warrior, *bushidō*, could be used in a Christian context. "There is a Christian *bushidō* ideal which could give a much deeper understanding to the Christian ideal."[22] God has wanted to educate the Japanese people and the *bushidō* ideal was the way. But Uemura became, in many ways, a conservative.

I must also mention Toyohiko Kagawa (1888-1960), an eminently gifted theologian, social worker, preacher, and pastor from Kobe. Kagawa felt urged to take a stand for the "marginalized" people, the sick, poor, and oppressed. He felt that it was the calling of a Christian to live in *ishiki*. This word *ishiki* means God consciousness. But not in the sense of being in complete command of our faculties. *Ishiki* has to it a God-ward relation. It seems inborn in each person, a longing for God, a compassion-like orientation. True religious life requires that a person's *ishiki* comes alive in a union with God. *Ishiki* is a mystical state, a stance where true God consciousness reigns supreme.[23] There is a kind of mysticism in Kagawa. He often talked about the Christian's life as one of sacrifice and redemptive love. Throughout his own life, he was always active, always on the go, trying to find new ways to interpret God's will and presence in the world. Yet, he was very much a Japanese. It has been said that he did not have a theology. He said he did not need one. He believed that being a Christian means to stand in the presence of God acting out the will of God in the world. Still, in his thinking he was well informed about his native country. His understanding of Christ had a Japanese flavor. The Japanologist Ivan Morris believes that the Japanese have always taken a stand for the "underdog," as did Jesus. Jesus was the kind of person the Japanese would understand, would side with.

I have attempted to show how some of the Japanese Christians attempted to work out a Japanese profile for Christianity. To find such a profile is an ongoing challenge among Christians in Japan. Perhaps several profiles are needed, since Christian faith requires a multidimensional interpretation. In studying Christianity in Japan, one becomes aware of the fact that it has to wear many faces. Therefore persons like Uchimura and Ebina had a hard time in the churches. They opted out of the churches and took on work in Christian education. This has happened frequently in Japanese history. Christianity as a challenge is not always dealt with within the churches. There are other and more radical ways of learning about Christianity outside the churches.

From the "other side," particularly among Buddhists, there was little cheerfulness when the missionaries arrived in the 1860s. Buddhists were ridiculed and often basely discussed by Christians. Christians felt that Buddhism belonged to the past. For some Japanese, the Meiji restoration set things right. They affirmed that the Japanese tradition is Shinto. This led to the development of the so-called Kokugakuin National School, a disastrous course, which we will not go into here.

Buddhists felt morally neglected. They finally realized that it was not possible to make a frontal attack against Christianity. Somehow they had to compromise. Buddhists found that Christianity had contributed to certain significant and necessary changes which should be endorsed: for example, the appreciation of education, and the critical examination of scriptures, etc. They sent some of their students to London and other places to study. Max Müller, a famous philologist, received two Japanese students who learned Sanskrit and Pali and upon returning to Japan introduced ancient Buddhism to the Japanese. Previously, the Japanese mainly had been informed about Buddhism from China. Now, a new horizon opened up and it was for the good of Buddhism in Japan.[24]

Christianity acted as the merciful Samaritan for the Buddhists. In its own way, Christianity helped Buddhism to recover from the impact of Western influence and the rise of Shinto nationalism. There were some eminent teachers of Buddhism who made a deep impression not only in Japan but perhaps even more so outside the country. One such person was D. T. Suzuki. Another was Kitaro Nishida. Both came from Kanazawa, a five hour train ride from Kyoto, in northwest Japan. Suzuki studied in various schools but, it seems, he never took an examination. He was a prolific writer, introduced new books from Europe, made translations. His research into Buddhism, religion, and the existential issues awoke dear respect. Suzuki dealt with existential problems in a new way. He lived in Tokyo as a young person, but spent most of the time in Kamakura. Since he knew English he was sent to the United States where he became involved in Buddhist translation work. He spent twelve years in the U. S. and returned to Japan in 1910. For several decades he was the most prominent spokesperson and interpreter of Zen Buddhism. He was highly respected, even in the West, where he spent most of his latter years. He died in 1966.

What was his message? I think his message was to transcend religion in the name of religion. This has sometimes been called "Suzuki Zen." What he said was very much needed at that time--to transcend religion in the name of religion. He read Meister Eckhardt, the German mystic, and claimed that mysticism transcends the border lines between the religions. There are different ways of expressing the same message: Jesus and Buddha walk together.[25]

D. T. Suzuki loved people and cats. He was very much alive, outgoing, and deeply religious. He believed in an inner world--a way which united people from all religious traditions. World religions come together in a kind of mysticism, but move beyond mysticism, to point to the creative spirit. Many people all over the world read his books. There was a demand for such a message especially after World War II.

Kitaro Nishida (1870-1945) was very different--mindwise, personwise. I wonder whether or not he was a happy man. One can become so involved in the study of religion and philosophy that it overshadows the joy of life. Nishida was an eminent philosopher. Probably his most famous book was *The Study of Good*. It offered wide horizons trying to broaden Japanese ways of reflection, introducing Western ways of philosophy, such as Hegel, and a Buddhist sense of *mu*, "nothingness." Nishida aspired to become a broker between Buddhism and Christianity. His conviction was that essence precedes existence, precedes thinking. It was a way of Zen thinking, *mu* thinking, nothingness thinking. He struggled all his life to come to terms with existential questions.

Another person who used to talk a lot about Christianity is Keiji Nishitani (1900-1990). We saw him quite often at the NCC Center in Kyoto. When he got older, in recent years, he had given up teaching and had ample time to spare. We used to call him, inviting him to come over to the NCC Center. He would come in his down-to-earth Japanese clothes, begin speaking, like pressing a button. It seemed that to Nishitani *sensei* speaking was a natural function of the body, like breathing or digestion. His philosophizing came to him that way, too. His insights were very striking at times. His personal way made a deep impression on many of us. His *magnum opus* was *Religion and Nothingness*, an outstanding book.[26] In conversations he would ask, Am I a Christian? Am I a Buddhist? I don't know. That is not at stake. I am transcending labels. To find one's way in life is a deeply personal matter. Perhaps I am on my way to become a Buddhist.

People came from all over the world to meet and enter dialogue with these illustrious Japanese teachers and to get involved in the study of Japanese religions and Christianity.

Paul Tillich, a very influential Christian theologian, spent some months in Japan in 1960. When he returned to Chicago he said to his friend, Mircea Eliade, that the voyage to Japan had a tremendous impact on his entire life and thought. In his monumental work, *Systematic Theology,* he had dealt with themes having to do with Europe. Japan had introduced him to Eastern ways of reflection, showing that he needed to broaden his horizons. He died five years later and never had the chance to rewrite his *Systematic Theology*. But he had a vision and a hope for a universal theology, which will penetrate and go beyond Western frameworks.

On October 12, 1965, he gave a lecture in Chicago, "The Significance of the History of Religions for the Systematic Theologian."[27] His last words were concerned with openmindedness, generosity, and the spirit of freedom. Ten days later he died.

One of the most important and thought-provoking Japanese theologians is Katzumi Takizawa (1909-1984). He studied with Nishida in Kyoto and became a philosopher in his own way. Nishida said to him: "You must go to Europe and study Western philosophy. Don't study with Heidegger because he has no God. You must study with Karl Barth." Takizawa went to Bonn and studied with Karl Barth. Here, to his amazement, he found that there was a similarity between what has come to be called the Kyoto School of Philosophy and Christian thought as it has been exposed by Barth. This was Takizawa's greatest discovery -- humankind is a primordial fact which we cannot deny. The now, the givenness of existence in itself, cannot be deduced and worked out. From there on he went to the emptiness idea in Buddhist thinking. In Christianity, there is also discussion of the empty "I." There is no self-sufficient ego. Like the prodigal son in Luke, we need to come to ourselves, to our true self. Takizawa felt that way. Self has a double meaning, it could be spelled with a capital or a small letter. Self is the merger between God and man. It is not the kind of merger where God and man are one, not "I am God," but "I am with God."

Takizawa was thrilled with this way of thinking, and returned to Japan with a new insight. He did not really know if he was a Christian or a Buddhist. Perhaps he was both. He had to work out his dilemma: whether to become a full-fledged member of the church or not. The church required baptism. He finally decided to become baptized in 1958. Katzumi Takizawa is one of the most radical and most thought provoking Japanese theologians.

There are many Japanese Christian and Buddhist thinkers on the scene today; some more radical, more creative, than others. What interests me most, however, are those who struggle to overcome the encounter between Buddhism and Christianity and to arrive at a primary standpoint where religion breaks through its own provincialism in the name of religion.

Some of us wonder if Japanese Christians and Buddhists will usher in a new era in humankind's religious development, an era characterized by unity in diversity.

IV
An Introduction to Shinto
Naofusa Hirai

Seeing that we too are continuing a process of cross-cultural reflections, as Americans and Japanese have done before, noting also the pluralistic context of our study in Kyoto, and seeing how Christians from the West and within Japan are reformulating a sense of Christian self-understanding, we now make our move to consider in a sustained way the older religious traditions that have contributed to the religious experience of Japanese. Long a central part of what Japanese men and women have found to be most integrative in human living, in forming community, in finding coherence in purity and honesty, in discovering the dignity of the human personality to be inseparably related to the divine, Shinto, in its impressive antiquity and amorphous pervasiveness, remains an important dimension of Japanese religiousness. Professor Hirai introduces us to this rich and variegated tradition.

Shinto is the native, national religion of Japan with a history of over two thousand years. It is incorporated with old traditional religious practices in Japan as well as the life attitude and doctrines which support these practices. Modern Shinto can be divided into three types: (1) Shrine Shinto, (2) Sectarian Shinto or Sect Shinto, and (3) Folk Shinto.

Shrine Shinto, which has been in existence from the prehistoric ages to the present, constitutes a main current of Shinto tradition. It seeks for the ultimate meaning of life based on the relationship between humankind and *kami*, deity. Shrine Shinto wishes to promote the practice of basic life attitudes of Shinto to enrich human life and to fulfill the ideal of Shinto in this present world. Shrine Shinto has no founder; its three foundations are: (1) the spirit of Japanese myth, (2) tradition of Shinto Shrines, and (3) individual, pious, religious experiences. Through the reinterpretation and the reevaluation of these three elements, Shrine Shinto has its own doctrine, involving ritual practices and the good works of believers.

Sectarian Shintō is a relatively new Shinto movement based on the Japanese religious tradition, and it is represented by the thirteen major sects which originated in Japan around the nineteenth century. These major sects share the following common characteristics.

(1) Each of them has either a founder or a systematizer who organized the new religious body in accordance with the particular principles drawn from the Revival Shinto school or from an individual's religious experience. Revival Shinto started around the eighteenth century to reinterpret Shinto and aimed to go back to the so-called genuine tradition of Shinto.

(2) Emphasis has been put on the practical side of religious activities rather than

on speculation on philosophical problems.

(3) The followers, at the beginning, consisted mostly of common or ordinary people.

(4) Each sect was independently organized before World War I. New Shinto sects which appeared in Japan after World War II are conveniently included in this type.

Folk Shintō is an aspect of Japanese folk belief which is closely connected with Shinto. *Folk belief* refers to the so-called natural, that is, non-dogmatic, non-revealed, and usually but imperfectly organized religions of semi-civilized people, and is of classical antiquity. Folk Shinto is at the base, is the understructure, of Shrine Shinto and Sectarian Shinto.

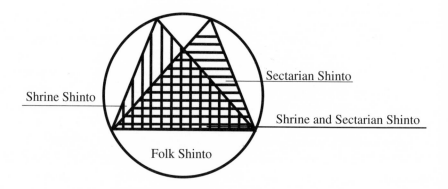

Except in the case of some Sectarian Shinto sects, there is no founder in Shinto. When the Japanese people became aware of themselves and of their culture Shinto was already there. There is no official or authoritative scripture in Shinto which can be compared to the Bible of Christianity or perhaps to the Qur'an of Islam. The *Records of Ancient Matters* (*Kojiki*) and the *Chronicles of Japan* (*Nihon-shoki* or *Nihongi*) are regarded, in a sense, as sacred books of Shinto. They were written in 712 and 720 respectively. They contain the traditions of ancient Shinto and, at the same time, they are sources for the history, topography, and literature of ancient Japan. It is not impossible, however, to form Shinto doctrines by interpreting myths and religious practices described in them.

The core of the myths consists of tales about Amaterasu-O-mikami, the so-called "Sun Goddess," the ancestress of the Imperial Household, and tales of how her direct descendants unified the Japanese people under their authority. At the beginning of Japanese mythology a certain number of *kami*, like the *kami* of *musubi* (mystical power of growth, creation or harmony), revealed themselves. Then a couple of *kami*, Izanagi and Izanami, gave birth to the Japanese islands as well as to the *kami* who became ancestors of various clans. The Sun Goddess (the ruler of the Plain of High Heaven), the Moon Ruler and the Ruler of the Nether Regions, were the most important of the *kami*. Ninigi-no-Mikoto, who was sent down to the Japanese islands to reign over the country, was a grandson of the Sun Goddess, and his grandson, Emperor Jimmu, was said to have become the first emperor of Japan.

The Three Sacred Treasures, which are still the most revered symbols of the Imperial throne, were first given by the Sun Goddess to her grandson, Ninigi-no-Mikoto. The Grand Shrine of Ise is dedicated to this ancestral Sun Goddess and is the most highly respected shrine in Shinto. The Japanese classics also have myths and legends of many *kami*, as many as eight million. Some of them are tutelary deities of clans who later became the tutelary *kami* of respective local communities. Many others, however, were not enshrined in sanctuaries and had no direct connections with the actual Shinto tradition. Little attention had been paid to Shinto mythology until the development of Revival Shinto, and even today the myths are not necessarily well-known except by Shinto priests and scholars.

At the core of Shinto there are beliefs in the mysterious power of *kami* (*musuhi*--creating and harmonizing power) and in the way or will of *kami* (*makoto*--truth or truthfulness). Since the nature of *kami* transcends our cognitive faculties, it is impossible to provide generalized definitions in words. Devoted followers, however, are able to understand *kami* through faith. They usually recognize *kami* in polytheistic ways.

Parishioners of a Shinto shrine believe in their tutelary *kami* as the source of human life and existence. Each *kami* has a divine personality and responds to truthful prayers, revealing to humankind the way of truth or truthfulness (*makoto*) and providing guidance in living in accordance with this truthfulness. According to a traditional way of Japanese thinking, truth, *makoto*, which is not an abstract ideology, manifests itself in reality in an infinite variety of forms, times, and places. It can be recognized every moment in every individual thing in the encounter between a person and *kami*.

In Shinto, all the deities are regarded as being cooperative with each other, and a life lived in accordance with *kami*'s will is believed to produce the mystical power that gains the protection, cooperation and approval of all *kami*.

As a basic attitude toward life, Shinto emphasizes a heart of truth (*makoto-no-kokoro*) or a true heart (*magokoro*), phrases also expressed as sincerity, pure heart, or uprightness. This is the revelation of *kami*'s truthfulness in us. Commonly speaking, this refers to one's sincere attitude of doing one's best in the work one has chosen or in one's relationship with others, knowing that the ultimate source of such a life attitude is in the awareness of the divine.

Although Shinto ethics do not ignore individual moral virtues like loyalty to the nation or filial piety to parents, or love for neighbors, or faithfulness to friends, it is generally considered more important to seek for a pure heart, *magokoro*, which would constitute the fundamental dynamic life attitude to bring forth these virtues. True heart, *magokoro*, was interpreted as a "bright and pure mind," or "bright, pure, upright and sincere mind," in ancient scriptures dating from the eighth century. In other words, it is the pure state of mind. Purification, physical and spiritual, is stressed in Shinto, even today, to produce such a state of mind. It is a necessary means to make possible our communion with *kami* and to enable us to accept *kami*'s blessings.

In Shinto it is commonly said that "Man is *kami*'s child". First, this means that men and women were given life by *kami* and their nature is therefore sacred. Second, our daily life is made possible by *kami*. Accordingly, one's personality and life are worthy of respect. One must revere the basic human rights of everyone, regardless of race, nationality, etc., as well as one's own. The concept of original sin does not appear in Shinto. On the contrary, humankind is considered to have a primarily divine nature. However, in actuality, this sacred nature is seldom revealed. Purification is considered symbolically to clear the dust and impurities that cover one's inner mind.

Shinto is described as a religion of continuity or communion (*tsunagari*). The Japanese, while recognizing each person as an individual personality, do not take that person as a solitary existence separated from others. On the contrary, one is regarded as a bearer of a long history which continues from one's ancestors and on to one's descendants. One is also considered a responsible constituent member of various social groups.

Norinaga MOTOORI (1730-1801), the founder of the Revival Shinto, said that our human world keeps on growing and developing while continuously changing. Similarly, Japanese speak in myths of an eternity of history in the divine edict of the Sun Goddess. From the viewpoint of finite individuals, Shintoists also endorse the notion of "middle present" (*naka-ima*), which repeatedly appears in the Imperial edicts of the 8th century. This is the idea that the present moment is located in the middle of an endless development of human history from the past to the future. As a way to participate directly in the eternal development of the world, it is required of Shintoists to live fully each moment of their lives and make each moment as worthy and significant as possible.

Historically, the tutelary *kami* of each local community (*uji-gami*) played an important role in combining and harmonizing different elements and powers. The Imperial system, which has been supported by the political philosophy of Shinto, is an example of unity and harmony assuming the highest cultural and social position of the nation. After the Meiji restoration (1868), Shinto was used as a means of spiritually unifying the people during the period of repeated wars. Since the end of World War II, the age-old desire for peace has been reemphasized. The *General Principles of Shintō Life* (*Keishin-Seikatsu-no-Kōryō*), proclaimed by the Association of Shinto Shrines (Jinja Honcho, in which about 99% of Shinto shrines are included) in 1956, has the following articles:

(1) Let us be grateful for the grace of *kami* and our ancestors' benevolence, and with bright and pure *makoto* (sincerity or true heart) perform religious services.

(2) Let us work for people and the world, and serve as representatives of the *kami* to make the society firm and sound.

(3) In accordance with the Emperor's will, let us be harmonious and peaceful, and pray for the nation's development as well as the world's co-existence and co-prosperity.[28]

Shinto does not have a custom of Sunday services. People visit shrines at their convenience. Some may come to the shrines on the first and fifteenth of each month and on the occasions of rites or festivals (*matsuri*), which take place several times a year. Devotees may pay respect to the shrine every morning. For example, devoted Shinto followers go to worship at the Meiji Shrine every day, and have done this for more than fifty years.

Various Shinto rituals, such as rites of passage, are observed in Japan. The first visit of a newborn baby to the tutelary *kami*, occurring around thirty or one hundred days after a child's birth, is an initiation of the baby who has become accepted as a new parishioner. The "seven-five-three" (*shichi-go-san*) festival on November 15th, is the occasion for children of three, five, and seven years of age to come to the shrine with thanksgiving and to pray for *kami*'s protection for their healthy growth. January 15th is Adults' Day. Youth in the village used to join the local young men's association on this day. Nowadays, it is the commemoration day for those Japanese who attained their twentieth year. According to some statistics, about eighty percent of Japanese wedding ceremonies are held in the Shinto style. (The rest of them are in Christian or Buddhist or non-religious styles.) At the Shinto style weddings, vows are made to *kami*. Shinto funeral ceremonies are not popular. The majority of Japanese are Buddhist and Shintoist at the same time and have their funerals Buddhist style. A traditional Japanese house has two family altars: one is Shinto for their tutelary *kami* and Sun Goddess, the other is Buddhist for their family ancestors. Pure Shinto families, however, will have all ceremonies and services in the Shinto style. There are other Shinto rites (*matsuri*) concerning one's occupation and daily living, such as the ceremony for purifying a building site or for setting up the framework for a new building, a purifying or firing ceremony for new boilers in a factory, a completion ceremony for construction work, a launching ceremony for a new ship, and so forth. Even in the case of nuclear power plants, there is an opening ceremony, Shinto style.

Each Shinto shrine has grand festivals every year, like the Spring Festival, mainly for a good harvest, the Autumn Festival for thanksgiving, the Annual Festival and the Divine Procession. The Divine Procession usually takes place on the day of the Annual Festival, and the sacred palanquins go through the parish. The rough order of the Shrine Shinto rituals at the grand festival is as follows:

(1) Purification. Commonly this is held at a corner of the precincts for participants before they come into the shrine. Sometimes, they are held in the shrine before the opening

ceremony.

(2) Adoration. The chief priest and the congregation bow to the altar.

(3) Opening the door of the inner sanctuary by the chief priest. This symbolic action means the *kami* is now within us.

(4) Presentation of the food offerings. Rice, *sake* wine, rice cakes, fish, bird, seaweed, vegetables, salt and water are offered. No animal meat is offered because of the taboo on shedding blood in the sacred area. Generally, cooked food was usually offered to the *kami* in ancient Japan; nowadays, uncooked food is more often used. In accordance with this change, the idea of entertaining the *kami* changed to that of thanksgiving.

(5) Prayer. The chief priest recites prayers (*norito*). The ancient Shinto prayers which were compiled in the early tenth century form the model for *norito* and are based on the old belief that the spoken words would have spiritual potency.

(6) Sacred music and dance. I will refer to this later.

(7) General offering. Participants in the festival make symbolic offerings using little branches of the sacred evergreen tree, with strips of white paper tied on them.

(8) Removing offerings. The food and symbolic offerings are taken away.

(9) Shutting the door of the inner sanctuary.

(10) Final adoration.

(11) Feast (*naorai*). In the olden days, *naorai* was held in the middle of the festival ceremony. The feast was a symbolic action for participants to communicate with the *kami* by having the same food offered to the deity. This custom is still observed at the Imperial Household and some old shrines. Most of the shrines, however, today have the communion with the *kami* by drinking rice wine which was offered to the *kami* after the festival instead. Since World War II, it has become popular to give a brief sermon or speech before the feast.

Generally, most Shinto festivals are observed in accordance with the above-mentioned order. On such occasions as the Annual Festival, various special rites are held, also. To list some of them: special purification, abstinence, divine procession of a sacred palanquin or of boats, ceremonial feasts, *sumo* wrestling, horseback riding, archery, a lion dance, a rice planting festival, and so forth.

At the entrance of the shrine precincts a single *torii* gate stands. After proceeding on the main approach, a visitor will come to an ablution basin where one is to clean one's hands and rinse one's mouth. Usually one will make a small offering at the hall of prayer (*heiden*) and pray. Sometimes a visitor may ask the priest to arrange for rites of passage or special prayers.

The most important building is the inner sanctuary (*honden*) in which a sacred symbol (called *shintai*, "*kami*-body" or *mitama-shiro*, "divine spirit's substitute") is enshrined. Usually, it is a mirror but sometimes it is a wooden image, a sword, etc. In any case, it is carefully wrapped and placed in a container and it is forbidden to see it. Only the chief priest is allowed to enter into the inner sanctuary. When the chief priest needs to see the divine symbol, he can do so after getting approval from the Association of Shinto Shrines and after having three days purification.

At the beginning, Shinto did not have any shrine buildings. At each festival people placed a tree symbol or a stone symbol at a divine site to invite the *kami*. Later they began to construct permanent Shinto buildings and the *kami* were considered to stay there always. The inner sanctuary of the Grand Shrine of Ise and Izumo Shrine, in Shimane Prefecture, illustrate two representative archetypes of shrine construction. The former style probably developed from a storehouse for crops, especially rice; the latter, from ancient house construction. In the process of time, different variations of shrine architecture were adopted and additional buildings were attached in front of the hall of worship.

The inner sanctuary and the hall of worship are in many instances connected by the hall of offering, where prayers are usually recited. A large shrine will also have a hall for liturgical dancing.

Belief in the ancestral or tutelary deity, *uji-gami,* is the most popular form of Shinto in Japan. The term *uji-gami* originally meant the *kami* of an ancient clan. After the fifteenth century, the term was used in the sense of tutelary *kami* of local communities and all the members in the community were considered to be that *kami*'s parishioners (*ujiko*). Even today, a parishioner group consists of the majority of the residents in the community. Shintoists can also believe in shrines other than their own parish shrine at the same time. Such believers, other than parishioners, did not form any groups before World War II, but after the war some big shrines started to organize believer groups. The Believer's Association of the Meiji Shrine numbers approximately 250,000 members living around Tokyo. A branch of this association is also in Brazil.

Kokugakuin University in Tokyo and Kogakkan University at Ise are main training centers for Shinto priests. Although any Shinto believer can be a priest or priestess if one goes through a certain training process, many are from the families of hereditary Shinto priests.

The Japanese, from of old, valued intuition from their emotional and aesthetic senses in appreciating and expressing religious experiences. They detected symbols of *kami* in natural beauty and power, and they developed religious poetry, architecture, visual arts, and the like. Shrine precincts are covered with beautiful green trees and are places of a serene and solemn atmosphere. These settings are effective in calming down the visitor's mind. In the case of the big shrines, they are surrounded by expansive woods, with mountains in the background, achieving a harmony of nature and architecture. The Grand Shrine of Ise and the Izumo Shrine still retain the ancient harmonious architectural styles.

After the ninth century, complicated shrine construction was developed, adopting Buddhist and Chinese architectural styles and techniques. The curving roof style of the shrine is an example. Usually, unpainted timbers are used, but wherever Buddhistic Shinto was popular, Chinese vermilion-lacquered shrines were built. In the case of the Nikko Toshogu, the shrine dedicated to Ieyasu TOKUGAWA in Nikko, you can see a good example of a vermilion-lacquered shrine.

A *torii* gate always stands in front of a shrine. It is not known whether it originated in Japan or is somehow related to the *torana* in India as, for example, the gates at

Sanchi, or the *hua-piao* in China, or with such continental gates like those in Manchuria. Various kinds of *torii* can be seen in Japan. Their function is always to divide the sacred from the profane. A pair of sacred stone animals, dogs (*koma-inu*, dogs of Kokuryo, an ancient Korean kingdom) or lions (*karajishi*, lions of T'ang), are placed in front of a shrine. These obviously came from Central Asia or India. Originally, they were to protect the sacred buildings from evil and defilements. After the ninth century they were used for ornamental purposes on ceremonial occasions at the Imperial Court and later came to be used at various shrines generally. Some of the stone lanterns (*ishi-dōrō*) are impressive works of art. The dedicator's name and year of donation are inscribed on the lanterns, bearing witness to the long tradition of faith and urging people to maintain it.

Compared with fine Buddhist statues, images of *kami* are not outstanding, both in quantity and quality. There was no habit of making *kami* images in ancient Shinto. But after the introduction of Buddhism in Japan, and due to its influence, some *kami* images were made. They were placed in the innermost part of the inner sanctuary and were not the objects of direct worship by the people. *Kami* icons are not worshipped at shrines. During the period when Buddhist Shinto was popular, Shinto diagrams or pictures (Skt.: *mandalas*) were made at some shrines, which are today kept at museums and are no longer connected with living faith.

The history of the shrine, its construction arrangements, ritual processions, are recorded in picture scrolls and they also have valuable historical and artistic materials. At all the shrines, one can see many votive pictures, which have been dedicated by the populace from the olden days. Also at the shrines are kept articles such as calligraphy, sculpture, swords, arms, and the like which were dedicated by the Imperial families, nobles or feudal lords. Several hundred such artistic items and records of shrine constructions were designated by the state as national treasures and important cultural properties.

In ancient Japan, traditional religious music and dance of the shrines were performed for the purpose of entertaining and appeasing the *kami* rather than praising them. Japan had its native music and dance. Well-known "elegant music" (*gagaku*), which originated in Central Asia and India, from Persia mainly, came into Japan after the 6th century from Kokuryo, in Korea, and T'ang separately. The music was combined with Japanese music and dance and in the latter half of the ninth century the Japanese *gagaku* was established. In *gagaku*, there is vocal and instrumental music. Wind, percussion, and stringed instruments are used. *Gagaku* was protected by the Imperial Household as court music and was much appreciated by the upper classes in the ninth to the eleventh centuries. Later, some solemn and graceful pieces were used as ritualistic music by Shinto shrines and Buddhist temples. Today, *gagaku* is widely performed at relatively big shrines. The authentic tradition of *gagaku* has been transmitted by the Institute of Music of the Imperial Household, established in 701.

There is also a gay music with flutes and drums to accompany the divine procession (*matsuri-bayashi*) and is effective in producing a festival mood. Some organizations of Shrine Shinto and Sectarian Shinto recently began to compose some of the religious songs, making use of Western music, to praise the *kami*. Such songs will be used in the future along with traditional music.

Until the end of World War II, Shinto had been closely and deeply related to the state. Offerings had been made to *kami* annually by the government and the Imperial Household. Persons prayed for the safety of the state and the people. The affairs of worship (*matsuri-goto*) offered by the emperor from olden days included not only ceremonies for *kami* but also for ordinary matters of the state. "Shinto ceremonies and political affairs are one and the same" was the motto of official administrators. In other words, they were required to have a religious conscience and to develop impartial true-hearted political activities. This tradition was maintained as an undercurrent of history in spite of the disorder in the middle ages. *Shogun*s, including the Tokugawa shogunate and feudal rulers also, respected Shinto shrines. Villagers prayed to the tutelary *kami* of the community for their peace and welfare, and promoted unity among themselves through village festivals.

After the Meiji Restoration, the government treated Shinto like a state religion, and revived the system of national shrines, dating from before the eighth century. In order to propagate Revival Shinto as the foundation of the national structure, they initiated the "Great Promulgation Movement." The emperor was respected like *kami*. And although the Japanese constitution enacted, in 1889, a guarantee of freedom of faith under certain conditions, priority was still given to Shinto.

At elementary schools Shinto was taught to children. Most of the national holidays were related with Shinto holidays. Thus, Shinto created a role of unifying the people throughout the period of confusion and war. Shinto of this nature was called State Shinto, and came under the control of the Bureau of Shrines, Ministry of Home Affairs. State Shinto was regarded as a state cult and a national ethic, and not as "a religion." Free interpretations of its teachings by individual Shinto priests was therefore not welcome. In fact, priests of the national shrines were prohibited from preaching and presiding over Shinto funerals. As of 1945, there were 218 national shrines and approximately 110,000 local shrines. The number of Sectarian Shinto groups was limited to thirteen after the organization of Tenri-kyo and since then, the formation of new groups was prohibited. Legally, these thirteen sects were treated as general religious bodies, the same as Buddhism and Christianity, and came under the supervision of the Ministry of Education. This was the situation before the war.

After the end of World War II, the Supreme Commander of the Allied Powers ordered the Japanese government to disestablish State Shinto. All financial support from public funds and all official affiliation with Shinto and Shinto shrines were discontinued. State rites performed by the emperor now tended to be regarded as private religious events of the Imperial family. After the end of the war, Shinto faced a great crisis, politically and financially. However, shrines destroyed during the war have been reconstructed by the private support of the people, and the festivals and various rites of passage also have been revived.

Presently, Shrine Shinto is faced with two serious problems. First is to determine how the traditional unifying function of Shinto can be promoted in local communities or in the state, as in the case of the Anglican Church in England, without interfering with freedom of faith. The second problem is to determine how to harmonize Shinto with rapid modernization both in organizing believers and dealing with human problems or the meaning of life.

Shinto, together with Buddhism, is deeply related culturally and socially with the life of the Japanese people. Shinto's relationship with other religions in Japan is generally cooperative and harmonious. In accordance with the increase in international contact with nations, Shinto has occasions to be in dialogue with world religions. Most Shintoists believe that cooperation of the different religions would contribute to world peace. This, however, should not suggest casual religious syncretism. While genuinely keeping its characteristics and inner religious depth, each religion is to work toward the peaceful coexistence of human beings. This is considered to be the ideal way to be followed by Shintoists.

V

What is Shinto?
Masahiko Asoya

Leading us into a brief consideration of recent attempts to establish normative definitions of Shinto, of different interpretations drawn from ancient texts, of various kinds of shrine and modes of shrine rituals, Professor Asoya pushes to the core of the Shinto heritage and finds there the matter of trust and faith in *kami*.

It is very difficult to provide an answer to the question, "What is Shinto?" It is probably not an overstatement to say that this is the most crucial theme for any student of Shinto studies. Even a renowned scholar of Shinto studies who recently passed away reflected upon the difficulty of grasping what Shinto is.

It is said that there may be as many answers as there are respondents to questions such as "What is a human being?" or "What is philosophy?" or "What is religion?". One can conclude that the question, "What is Shinto?" possesses a similar characteristic. But that alone cannot be the reason for the difficulty.

1. *The Definition of Shintō*

The first reason why it is difficult to explain Shinto is because Shinto phenomena are deeply related to the daily lives of the Japanese. Put another way, it is a "Japanese way of living"--ever since Japanese culture started to formulate itself Shinto has found its way into the very lives of the Japanese people and the way of life is "something that needs no explanation in words." That Shinto is deeply related to the lives of the Japanese is not something of the past. It still continues in the present. For example, most Japanese visit the shrines on New Year's. According to newspaper reports, more than half of the Japanese population pays respect to the shrines on the first three days of the New Year. Considering the seasonal *matsuri*, the *shichigosan* (to be celebrated when a child becomes seven, five, or three years of age) and other festivals, Shinto style marriages, visits to distant shrines, and household practices, it is probably safe to say that close to 90% of the Japanese are related to Shinto in some way. But, according to a survey conducted by the Yomiuri newspaper, only 33.6% of the Japanese replied that they have some religion they believe in, and among them only 4.3%, or less than 10% of the population, gave "Shinto" as the answer to the question, "What is your religion?" Considering that over 90% of the people are estimated to pay respect at Shinto shrines, what does the phenomenon that only about 1.3% of the Japanese say they believe in Shinto mean? This Shinto phenomenon of shrine worship is a constituent of the life style of the Japanese, and is proof that this action is not considered a voluntary, conscious action of believing in something. It should be understandable that a sufficient answer to the question, "What is Shinto?" could not be attained by the Japanese who relate with Shinto in such a manner.

Anyone who has lived in the West for several years must have experienced this. For example, in the United States of America it is not surprising that an ordinary person engaging in an ordinary job will preach to you about the importance of Christianity for hours on end. In contrast, it is very difficult to find someone, even a Shinto priest, who will explain Shinto in a comprehensive manner. When one compares these two cases in the realm of *words*, it is obvious that there is a great difference. The reason is as suggested before, because Shinto is not something that spreads through someone's preaching. It follows a completely different development from religion which is established by the use of words.

The second reason why it is difficult to provide an answer to the question, "What is Shinto?" is derived from the first reason. Because Shinto is a way of life of the Japanese, it is not necessary to develop doctrines and to preach them. In other words, the traditional attitude of Shinto is that "no words are necessary." This has also been emphasized as a characteristic of Shinto. Even today, there are Shintoists who insist that this is the proper way of Shinto.

The Shinto tradition can be divided into four groups: (1) the *matsuri* tradition, (2) the history of Shinto shrines, (3) Shinto classics (including *Kojiki* and *Nihon-shoki*, edited around the eighth century) and (4) the history of Shinto thought. Groups one and two represent aspects such as ritual and worship and are deeply related to each other. Groups three and four are also deeply related to each other in that both represent words as a medium for Shinto. From the point of view of Shinto history, the history of *matsuri* and shrines (though there was no man-made architecture in ancient times) is the oldest. In contrast, the Shinto classics were established in the 8th century and it is assumed that Shinto theology was formulated only during the Kamakura period around the 13th century. Therefore the verbalization of the Shinto faith is a relatively recent phenomenon in the history of Shinto. Furthermore, the development of Shinto philosophy, including theology and doctrine, only took place among a limited few in the context of the general history of Shinto. Preachers of the Ise and Yoshida schools of Shinto, which started to appear in the Chusei period (twelfth to sixteenth century), were reluctant to open Shinto doctrines to the public due to the custom of secret oral tradition (*hiden-kuden*), and even during the Kinsei period (sixteenth to nineteenth century; also known as the Edo period) Shinto philosophy rarely was diffused to the public until the popular Shinto movement in the latter seventeenth century, or the National Learning Movement formulated in the middle of the eighteenth century. This does not mean, however, that I am underestimating the influence of the Shinto scholars.

The *matsuri* practice and shrine worship have been maintained constantly since ancient times. It is well known that trips to worship distant shrines, such as the Ise Shrine, were extremely popular due to the development of means of transportation. It should be obvious that there exists a gap between the verbalization of the Shinto faith and Shinto action, as in shrine worshipping. There seems to be a major difference with Christianity, where rituals and organization developed along with the doctrine and faith. For this reason, it is highly unlikely that a Christian religious leader would not preach Christian doctrines. But in the case of Shinto, it was not a mandatory criterion for Shinto priests to be able to preach the Shinto doctrine properly. To give you an extreme example, in 1883, the Shinto priests of the highest ranking Shinto shrines (*kansha*) were prohibited from preaching Shinto doctrine to the population. In other words, the period in which a Shinto priest's major role was to perform the religious rites and maintain the shrine continued until very recently, namely until the mid-1940's. It is inevitable that Shinto priests themselves cannot give a straight answer to the question "What is Shinto?"

Because of this situation, it is certainly understandable why Shinto priests, who should be the most acquainted with Shinto, were not particularly interested in verbalizing the content of Shinto.

2. *Various definitions of Shintō by Shintō theologians*

The first instance of the Shinto faith being logically organized by Shinto scholars is in the case of the Ise Shinto School (the Geku Shinto School). This establishment of the Ise Shinto theology is estimated to have occurred around the Kamakura period (thirteenth century). Here I would like to mention a number of definitions which are common in the Shinto of the early and late Chusei Period (around 1280), as well as in the Kokutai Shinto of the late Meiji Period (1900-1912).

There will probably be no argument in calling the Ise and Yoshida Shinto schools the mainstream of Shinto in the Chusei period. Since Ise Shinto considers the so-called *Shintō-Gobusho* its venerated texts, the definition will be based on this revered work. But, there is no section which gives a straight answer to the question "What is Shinto?" The following quotations suggest the meaning or content of Shinto:

> To be visited with the blessings of the *kami*, one must first direct one's mind wholeheartedly to prayer; to be granted the protection of the *kami*, one must make a foundation of honesty. In this way, the person's pristine, undefiled mind will be awakened to the original profound way.[29]

This passage can be found in the section "Records of the Enshrinement of the Two Imperial Deities at Ise" (*Ise Nisho Kōtaijin Go-chinza Denki*) and "Records of Yamatohime no Mikoto" (*Yamatohime No Mikoto Seiki*) of the "Five Sacred Books of the Ise Shinto School" (*Shintō-Gobusho*), and is known to have influenced Yoshida and Suika Shinto in later years. Its meaning is that serious prayers and honest actions are essential in winning the blessing and protection of the *kami*, and that this is interpreted as the proper way of human life. It is believed that prayers to the *kami* and honest behavior were thought to be the essence of Shinto in the Ise Shinto School.

YOSHIDA Kanetomo (1435-1511), who brought Yoshida Shinto to completion, wrote about what Shinto is. He frequently uses the word *Shintō* in his books. One example related to our topic is: (1) "True Shinto is *genponsōgen shintō*."[30] YOSHIDA Kanetomo divided Shinto into three groups and preached that *genponsōgen*, which originates from Yoshida Shinto, is the true Shinto. Its main idea is that Kuni-no-Tokotachi-no-Mikoto is the *kami* of origins and people should worship this *kami*. Another example is (2) that Shinto acts as the fundamental force of all things, as seen in *Yuiitsu Shintō Myōbō Yōshū*:

> If no Shinto exists in the heavens, the three lights (sun, moon, stars) do not exist, and the four seasons do not exist. If no Shinto exists on earth, the five elements do not exist, and all things cease to exist. If no Shinto exists in man, no life exists, and no law exists.[31]

Here Shinto means the power-force of *kami*, rather than the way of *kami*.

It is understood from such passages of YOSHIDA Kanetomo's that Shinto acts as a basic, fundamental force of all things, from nature to all that affects human life. YOSHIDA Kanetomo's Shinto can be summarized as follows: Shinto is the "way" of the Japanese, and it concretely means to worship Kuni-no-Tokotachi-no-Mikoto. YOSHIDA Kanetomo considers Kuni-no-Tokotachi-no-Mikoto one with the myriad *kami* and since the *kami* are the origin of the universe, one could say that a life worshipping the *kami* is the essence of Shinto. It is quite difficult to understand this conception of *kami* being the origin of the universe and of every phenomenon.

Suika Shinto was established and preached by YAMAZAKI Ansai (1618-1682). He originally practiced Buddhism and became a monk. During his early years, he converted to Confucianism and became a renowned Neo-Confucian scholar of that time. His major contribution to Shinto occurs during his forties, but he expressed his strong interest in Shinto soon after his conversion to Neo-Confucianism. It is probably correct to assume that Neo-Confucianism played a major role in the formulation of YAMAZAKI Ansai's Shinto theology. YAMAZAKI Ansai's answers to the question "What is Shinto?" can be found in his books, *Jindaikan-fūyoshū* and *Suikashago*, "The Way is the way of the Sun Goddess, and the teachings are what Sarutahiko *kami* leads us to."[32]

"The way of the Sun Goddess" is obviously referring us to Amaterasu-O-Mikami. Then the next question is "How should the way of Amaterasu be interpreted?" Let us refer to YAMAZAKI Ansai's other texts to answer this question. Amaterasu ordered Ninigi-no-Mikoto, Amaterasu's grandson, the imperial grandson, to descend and rule the realm, the Japanese islands. Following this heavenly edict, the emperor, who is the imperial descendent, came to rule Japan. YAMAZAKI Ansai claims in his book, *Yamatōshogaku*, that this represents the fundamentals of Shinto. In this sense we can interpret YAMAZAKI Ansai's views of the essence of Shinto as the way the emperor rules the nation under the order of Amaterasu.

In the case of the Kokugaku Shinto school, I would like to mention the definition provided by the renowned MOTOORI Norinaga, who brought Kokugaku Shinto to completion. MOTOORI Norinaga is a scholar who compiled *Kojikiden*, which provides a complete interpretation of the *Kojiki*. MOTOORI Norinaga's definition of Shinto is based on excerpts of the first volume of the *Kojiki*:

> Speaking in all reverence, this Way was begun by gods Izanagi no Okami and Izanagi no Okami in accordance with the august creative spirit of Takamimusubi no kami, and then transmitted by the sun goddess Amaterasu Omikami, namely, it is the Way which was established in this fashion by the imperial ancestral deities and passed on to later generations, and that is called the 'Way of the kami,' or Shinto.[33]

The basic idea here is that the "way," which Amaterasu received and maintained, is Shinto. But this is rather vague. If we look at other passages we can interpret them to mean that Shinto is the way of the emperor's rule over Japan where he, as the imperial descendent, rules with the heart of Amaterasu. It is known that MOTOORI Norinaga attacked Suika Shinto fiercely, but the interpretation of the essence of Shinto, offered by both, is quite similar.

Kokutai Shinto, which flourished from the Meiji period until the end of World War II, also attempted to provide a definition of Shinto. Numerous Shinto scholars appeared at this time, but particularly interesting is KOUNO Seizo (1883-1963, at one time of Kokugakuin University), who contributed to the writing of *Kokutai no Hongi*[34] published by the government in the Showa era. He also wrote numerous articles on Shinto, Kokugaku,[35] and public morality. He states in the introduction of his book, *Shintō no Kenkyū*,

> Shinto is the "Way of Kami". The Way of Kami is the basic principle of life since the times of the ancestors of the Japanese race. The Japanese race considered the act of glorifying, enhancing, and worshipping the heavenly virtues of Amaterasu Okami the principle of life, and the principle of the Japanese nation.[36]

In other words, Shinto is the principle of life for the Japanese people. Put in more concrete terms, it is for the subjects to serve the emperor, who is the descendent of the heavenly *kami*. This could be considered a modern application of YAMAZAKI Ansai's and MOTOORI Norinaga's definitions.

3. *The Life of the Japanese and the Role of Shintō*

This brief overview of some basic trends of Shinto philosophy in the Chusei (1192-1543), Kinsei (1593-1859), and Kindai eras (1859-1945) indicate how theories are based mainly on ancient Shinto texts, and, at the same time, the slight differences among them. The meaning and content of Shinto in Ise and Yoshida Shinto is an emphasis in serving and worshipping the *kami*. In contrast, Kinsei and Kindai Shinto emphasize Amaterasu-O-mikami and state that the emperor's rule of the nation is Shinto. The various theories are based on social and religious circumstances of each period and one must respect each for one has a lot to learn from them. But with the development of archeology, history, anthropology and studies of ancient texts, it came to be seen that these theories on Shinto, although based on ancient texts, are not necessarily based on the basic Japanese *kami* worshipping tradition. One notes such views in the works of YANAGIDA Kunio, the most famous folklorist, *Shintō Shiken*, "Views on Shinto," and TSUDA Sokichi, a great scholar of Japanese and Asian history, *Nihon no Shintō*, "Japanese Shinto."

"What is Shinto?" My basic view is as follows: archaeology has demonstrated that fundamental, archaic elements of Shinto have been formulated for 2,500 years. The crux of the Shinto phenomena is reverence for the *kami* and the performance of *matsuri* rites. I believe that the essence of Shinto will become apparent by analyzing the role of these in the daily lives of the Japanese people.

Ever since the Japanese established themselves on the Japanese archipelago, it is archaeologically proven that they offered prayers to a spiritual existence. For example, the Hibita Shrine and Afuri Shrine in Kanagawa Prefecture are known to be ancient shrines, and religious relics and sites have been excavated from the compounds of both. Standing stones used as seats for the *kami* to descend and pottery believed to be used for religious practices have been excavated. They are believed to be from the Early or Middle Jamon Period, which means 6,000-8,000 years ago.[37] These may not be used as proof of Shinto phenomena, but at least the origins of shrines can be understood to be as old. When one analyzes the contents of food offerings made to the kami during ceremonies, one can say that crops, especially rice crops, were considered important. Taking into consideration the relationship between crops and Shinto, the birth of Shinto can be dated to the Yayoi Period (300 B.C.-300 A.D.) when rice agriculture became widespread in Japan.[38] It is also noted by anthropologists that this period witnessed the formulation of Japanese views and thought processes.

In order to make apparent the role of Shinto in the lives of Japanese from the Yayoi period to the present, I would like to categorize shrines into two ideal types:

(1) *Ubusana*-type shrines, also called *ujigami* type. They are worshipped by the whole village as a single unit and activities are basically communal. They are shrines where the name of the worshipped *kami* is unknown.

(2) *Kanjo*-type shrines, also called worshipping types where prayers and wor-

ship by individuals dominate. The syncretization of Shinto and Buddhism appears strongly as a defining character and the names of the *kami* are known. Examples include Inari, Hachiman, and Tenmangu.

The function of *ubusuna* type shrines is to pray for the preservation of the village (*mura*), and the most important rites were the spring and autumn festivals: called *kinen-sai*, which involves prayer to the *kami* for a successful harvest, and *niiname-sai*, which is a ceremony for thanksgiving for a successful harvest. Agriculture was the basic lifestyle of the Japanese from the Yayoi period to recent times, and considering the fact that crops were the basic sustenance of the Japanese, it was crucial for the villagers to have a good harvest. This in turn could suggest that the *kami* worshipped in these *ubusuna* shrines were relied upon as a source which supported the fundamental lives of the Japanese.

Kanjo-type shrines are a more recent phenomenon (tenth century), and worshippers from other localities would come to visit them also. The origins of such shrines vary from shrine to shrine; thus the purpose of the shrines cannot be generalized. But the major role of such shrines can be characterized by the personal prayers offered: for longevity, safety of the family, curing disease, doing away with evil omens, prospering in business, and prosperity for descendants. Outsiders basically do not worship at *ubusuna*-type shrines, and personal prayers are not offered. Thus the offering of personal prayers could be considered a characteristic of *kanjo*-type shrines. The sense of trust towards *kami* worshipped in such shrines, as seen in the role of *kanjo*-style shrines, signifies a resolution of anxiety in the daily lives of the people. In other words, this signifies that a sense of trust that the *kami* have the power to eradicate anxiety in human lives existed among the Japanese people.

Today, spring and autumn festivals performed basically by *ubusuna*-type shrines still continue. With a large decrease in the population engaged in agriculture, and with a high dependability on imported goods, the significance of offering prayers for a successful harvest has decreased. Nevertheless, with emphasis on the significance of praying and thanking the gods for peace and prosperity of the village or town, and the Japanese community as a whole, the traditional role of Shinto is still maintained. Furthermore, the role of *kanjo*-type shrines has not changed even today. Prayers for good health, prosperity and such are still performed frequently. And what is more, with anxiety newly created and increasing in modern times, new festivals and prayers are created to meet such needs. Examples would include traffic safety prayers, prayers offered for success in entrance examinations, and prayers offered to ward off evil omens which descend at particular moments of life (*yaku-yoke*). These are extremely popular in shrines throughout the nation.

4. *Conclusion*

I would like to explain my personal interpretation of the definition and meaning of Shinto. Taking into account what I have said previously about the shrine and the *matsuri* tradition, as well as the various theories of the Shinto scholars and accounts in ancient texts, Shinto is a way of life based on trust and faith in the Japanese *kami*. Here, trust and faith indicate unconscious belief and conscious belief respectively. Such a definition is not particularly unique. Thus it becomes necessary to explain the characteristic of Japanese *kami*.

First of all, Japanese *kami* can be understood as "a force supporting fundamental human life." Such interpretations can be seen in ancient sources, such as *Kojiki* or *Nihongi*. The same can be seen in the concept of *kami* expounded by YOSHIDA Kanetomo and MOTOORI Norinaga. For example, MOTOORI Norinaga, like YOSHIDA Kanetomo, stresses that

> Every phenomena in this world, from the changes of the seasons, the falling of the rain, the blowing of the winds, and every good and evil occurrences which befall upon the people and nation is the will of *kami*.[39]

They go as far as to say every natural phenomenon is the *kami*'s doings. MOTOORI Norinaga's faith in Shinto makes a strong impression.

Second, although the Japanese *kami* possess the above characteristics, they are not the absolute creators segregated from humans. The *kami* and humans have the characteristic potential of being one. This can be seen in the history of shrine worship. For example, clan-*kami*, *ujigami* (who are the ancestors of the clan, or *uji*) and human spirits, although this is a recent phenomenon, could be worshipped as *kami*. Examples include SUGAWARA Michizane (845-903), TOYOTOMI Hideyoshi (1536-1598), TOKUGAWA Ieyasu (1542-1610), HOSHINA Masayuki (1611-1672) and NOGI Maresuke (1849-1912). Most recent examples include heros of the war-dead worshipped in Yasukuni Shrine in Tokyo. God and human beings in Christianity are differentiated as the creator and created, but Shinto texts mention that the *kami* "continued to reproduce," showing no distinction between *kami* and human beings.

Third, although the Japanese *kami* were "a force supporting the fundamental life of humans," the *kami* paradoxically do not use this heavenly power according to their own will. In other words, the *kami* and humankind are interdependent. The writings which illustrate this are *Goseibai Shikinoku* ("Formulary for the Adjudication of Suits") and *Yamatohime no Mikoto Seiki*, which is thought to have been compiled in the middle Kamakura period. A passage from it reads,

> The Great Nation of Japan is *Shinkoku* (the nation of *kami*). With the protection of the

kami, national safety is attained, and with the nation's honorable reverence, the spiritual powers of the kami increase.[40]

In other words, the prosperity of the nation rests in the protection by the *kami*, but simultaneously, their power can be displayed only when human beings continue to worship them. Such mode of thought brings birth to a concept which commends our efforts. Thus the Japanese did not think that their problems would be solved if they continued to pray to the *kami*. Rather, there is evidence which scorned attitudes where one's proper efforts were neglected and substituted by merely praying to the *kami*. Therefore, success in society was judged as the result of our efforts and protection of the *kami*.

By viewing Japanese *kami* with such characteristics in mind, it can be understood that the *kami* worshipped by the Japanese, although conceived as the fundamental source of the universe, are related in a complementary manner with humankind where future development depends on an interaction of the good will of the *kami* and humankind's undying efforts.

VI
The Concept of *Kami*
Kenji Ueda

One of the most difficult tasks one might undertake in a study of Shinto is to attempt to define the concept of kami. Guiding our thinking to a notion of givenness which inspires awe, Professor Ueda weaves an interpetive tapestry of pluralism among deities and of particularity among Japanese in mythology, in history, and in cross-cultural understanding.

I think it is best to begin an analysis of the subject, the concept of *kami*, with such a presupposition: if one wants to know the essential nature of something unfamiliar, it is best to examine the way, or process of how, that something happened to come into existence. In the oldest text of Shinto, the *Kojiki*, on ancient matters, compiled in 712 A. D., is written,

> At the beginning when the heaven and the earth were divided into heaven and earth, the three *kami* revealed themselves in the heaven, whose names were the head of central heaven, the high life producing spirit, and the divine life producing spirit.[41]

What do you feel and think, I wonder, when you read this kind of expression? Probably you may feel that something more is necessary for the true understanding of the meaning of that sentence.

It becomes clearer if you compare this sentence with the Old Testament creation story: in the beginning, God created the Heavens and the Earth. It mentioned clearly the original cause as God, who created the universe. In Shinto mythology, there is no mention about such a pre-existing being as the creator. Therefore, it should be clear that Shinto mythology is not a kind of creation story. In spite of this fact, it was a surprise to me that until I myself pointed out the matter, there was no scholar in the history of Japanese mythological studies who realized this fact. Even today, there are many who still say these Japanese myths are creation stories. Be this as it may, let us continue.

I understand the beginning part of the *Kojiki* in such a way that ancient Japanese at that time, when this mythology began to be narrated, had unconsciously a presupposition that there was something already existing before it began to be divided into heaven and earth. This something was simply given, without condition. By using the word *given*, I do not wish to imply a presupposition that there was some pre-existing being, which created or made that something, that made it to exist.

Perhaps I should say the ancient Japanese simply presupposed the existence of something from the beginning, without positing a notion of a creator or creators. This difference comes from a categorical difference in the frame of thinking that existed between West and East, and by *East*, I mean in this case China, Korea and Japan. I know the idea in the West of God as the creator or original cause of all existence came from Judaism, and some might say it represents an oriental frame of thinking, but certainly it does not represent an East Asian one. I might add that I think Indian culture does not belong to this East Asian frame of thinking.

The problem then will be: what characteristics does the Japanese way of thinking have?

I think we should start, as the mythology started, with a state that is simply given without focusing on a so-called problem of how it might have been before that something came into existence. The narrative says that *kami* reveal themselves from that something. If you link this way of thinking with the basic religious way of thinking, that the object of religious faith, god or *kami*, cannot be grasped in its totality by the believers, and cannot be described by ordinary words of daily usage, even though it can be felt by some mystics through their religious experiences, then you may reach the understanding, I believe, that ancient Japanese had such a faith in which *kami* was conceived as the life-producing power innately or potentially held in that same material existence.

As a matter of fact, before and even after we Japanese learned the concept of nature from Taoism, for the first time in the Edo period, and also from the Western world, after the Meiji Restoration, Japanese in general continue to feel something spiritual in material existence, which sustains and affects the life of human beings. For example, Shinto priests are asked to purify modern machines with a prayer that those machines work well and do not harm the workmen who will use them. Even Japanese Buddhist monks are also asked to perform memorial services for the spiritual peace of the man-made dolls that have already finished their functions in this world.

When Western scholars explain Shinto they often use a technical phrase, *nature worship*, in order to make Westerners, who are basically oriented to the Judeo-Christian tradition, able to understand the characteristics of the subject. But this type of interpretation is not correct to Shintoist eyes. For the Japanese, nature is not a bundle of matter and material which is under the control of natural law, but a totality of each individual spiritual being and therefore, in the Japanese mind, there is no such psychological process existing to personify nature or deify nature.

There are three classes of spirits. (1) The first class of spiritual being is called *tama* in Japanese. Included in this class are *kami*. It is this kind of spirit, *tama*, which can be enshrined and worshipped in public, if it shows strong affection for, or exert power upon, people living in a particular area, or the nation as a whole. In the case of human beings, most of them are worshipped by their own descendants even though they cannot be enshrined officially.

(2) The second class of spiritual being is called *mono*. In this class, every living animal belongs. This kind of spiritual being can sometimes benefit or harm human be-

ings. Therefore, even in such a modern institution as a hospital, in Japan, doctors and nurses are having religious services for those animals sacrificed for medical research. Even in the case of human beings, however, if one's spirit, after death, harms somebody or society in general, in some unauthentic way of events, one's spirit is very often also called *mono*.

(3) The third class of spirit is called *mi*. This covers organic and even inorganic existence: plants and stones, man made tools, machines.[42] These existences are thought to be procreated by *kami* or by human beings and they have their own spirits. Therefore, if we misuse them, from the point of view of traditionally minded Japanese, we feel awful. Every part of the human body is also thought to have such a *mi* spirit, under the control of *tama*. Therefore, even many contemporary Japanese hesitate to have their own internal organs transplanted to someone, some unknown person other than their own relatives. Taking into consideration all the aspects of Shinto faith in spirits, however, we have to admit the fact, as you may have noticed already, that the identities of all three classes of spirits are not clear as to their precise origin. Sometimes they are very fluid in relation to each other. This is because, I believe, in Shinto, from the beginning, when it was recognized as a religion by the Japanese themselves in their relationship with Buddhism, which was brought from Korea, there was such a stage of faith, which united manaism, animism, and deity according to Western terminology, which already existed. Therefore, for example, Mount Fuji, which is nothing but a totality of *mono* and *mi*, had been worshipped as *kami* in different ways at the same time; such as the mountain itself, as a body of the *kami* (*konohana-sakuyahime*), and as the dwelling place of that same *kami*. Before attempting to provide a definition of the word *kami*, I would like to mention one other point.

According to Shinto mythology, there are two types of *kami* appearances. The first one has already been mentioned, the case of the first three *kami*. Our mythology starts with these three *kami* and in continuation mentions two more *kami* as the second generation. In total, five *kami* are called the special heavenly *kami*. Then, the myth tells us the names of the *kami* from the third generation to the ninth. This ninth generation consists of a couple of *kami* whose names are Izanagi and Izanami. These two *kami* moved from heaven to the island called Onogoro-jima and became husband and wife. They gave birth to the islands of Japan which included the original Japanese people. After this stage, mythology begins to tell of a second type of *kami* appearance, namely, the female *kami* Izanami who gave birth to many kinds of *kami* of nature, even though she became ill when she gave birth to the fire *kami* Kagutsuchi, and left this world to the world of *yomi*, the other land. After this some of the *kami* of the first type appeared again. The important fact I would like to point out here is that in both cases, when the myths narrate the *kami* appearance, there were always preceding existences and all the names of *kami* are composed of the word which shows their functions. In a special case like the *kami* Okuninushi, the great Land Possessor *kami*, as a matter of fact, carries five different names. Concerning all the points I have made here, I think I can now attempt to define the word *kami*, following in the footsteps of the most famous scholar, MOTOORI Norinaga, who established the so-called National Learning School (Kokugaku) in the Edo Period.

Kami is a spiritual being, including those who appeared in mythology, those who are enshrined and worshipped in individual shrines all over Japan, including human beings and also birds, animals, even mountains, rivers, trees and grasses--whatever shows unusual virtue and makes one feel *awe-full*.

It is, however, necessary to stress again the following points, in order to avoid possible misunderstanding. First, although Shinto is a polytheistic religion it is not pantheistic because all things are not *kami*, even though they are all spiritual beings. Second, Shinto does not begin to think of the presence of *kami* without having any pre-existing material existence. Therefore, when we are going to have a religious ceremony, we always set the body of *kami* before us. This body can be a mountain sometimes, or a symbolic object in which the *kami* is thought to be dwelling, or staying a while, at least, in response to the special invitation ceremonies.

There is an important theological aspect of Shinto, a brief discussion of which might contribute to a better understanding of its fluid complexity. I refer to this as the principle of pluralism. As we have noted, Shinto is a polytheistic religion. In other words, there are countless numbers of *kami* in the Shinto faith, and if you study Shinto mythology, you will quickly find that there is no absolute *kami* who is omniscient and omnipotent. For example, even Izanagi and Izanami, the parent *kami* of Japan, whom I have already mentioned, committed a serious mistake when they began to give birth to the first island of Japan. When they found that it was a mistake, they went up to the heavens and asked the heavenly *kami* what to do next. The heavenly *kami* did not give any direct answer. Instead, they said "You must follow the result of divination." In the case of Amaterasu, who is held in the midst of the highest and most noble *kami* in the Shinto pantheon, and the ancestral *kami* of the imperial household, she felt awful when she saw the behavior of her younger brother Susanoo in heaven, and she hid herself in a cave.

If I take mythological stories into my account, in order to clarify the Shinto way of thinking, and for the avoidance of unnecessary confusion, I like to use the word *truth* here, instead of *god* or *kami*. In the Shinto way of thinking, there is no absolute truth. There is no absolute *kami*. Therefore, there is no absolute justice or goodness. As a matter of fact, in the Shinto faith, even Amaterasu, the supreme *kami*, is believed to have an unpredictable spirit. If it becomes active, it will give unthinkable amounts of damage all over the nation. Therefore, there is a separate shrine where the unpredictable spirit of Amaterasu is enshrined in order to pacify it, behind the main building of the inner shrine of Ise Grand Shrine.

We may sometimes feel how difficult it is to understand religions or cultures other than our own. In my experience, when I attended various meetings for peace and happiness in the world it was always a disappointment because the delegates who came from monotheistic bodies always assumed as a matter of course that everyone should pray for the mercy of one God.

In order to clarify characteristics of this principle of pluralism in Shinto, I would like to mention the many different types of *kami*. For example Kuebiko who knows everything about this world, cannot do anything by himself; he cannot even walk one step. There is also the case of SUGAWARA Michizane (845-903), who was an aristocrat in the Heian period and died in despair because of a false charge. After his death the people of Kyoto believed that his *tama* became a *kami* of thunder because many leaders of the aristocracy at that time were hurt by retaliatory thunder he brought. Then, people enshrined his *tama* at the Kitano shrine in Kyoto in order to pacify it. After his *tama* was enshrined he became a *kami* of learning because he was also the leading scholar of his time. Even today, many students who want to pass the entrance exams of any high school or university come to visit this shrine and to pay tribute.

These examples indicate a kind of living principle in Shinto suggesting a way of thinking which is capable of feeling holiness or seeing divine nature in each individual's spiritual being, even though it might not be perfect. This Shinto principle of pure or simple pluralism, however, could not be maintained very long in our history. From the time of Shomu (724-749), the 45th emperor, it became a custom that the emperor himself confess his personal faith in Mahayana Buddhism, and by the end of the Nara period, around 766-67 A.D., Buddhist temples began to be built in the sanctuaries of Shinto shrines or some place nearby. Ceremonies or rituals of traditional shrines came to be taken care of by so called shrine monks. Therefore, since the Heian period, from 781 A.D., Buddhist monks began to explain the *kami* of Shinto as embodiments of Buddhas. This tendency existed until the Meiji Restoration (1868). As a result, even Shinto priests were affected by originally an Indian way of interpreting the existential world, that is, there is an absolute truth of eternal being, and this absolute truth reveals itself in all the different styles of existences. In Mahayana Buddhism it is said that the eternal Buddha reveals himself in all the Buddhas and Bodhisattvas, in different ways. This principle I call the "one equals many principle."

Because of the influence of this principle, Shintoists became Buddhist, in a sense, in the middle ages in Japan. For example, in the case of the Ise Shinto school, which was established by a priest's family of the outer shrine of the Ise Grand Shrine, it identified the *kami* Toyuke, who is enshrined in that particular shrine, with Siva, a Hindu deity. This tendency can even be observed in the case of MOTOORI Norinaga (1730-1801), who is considered to be the best scholar in the history of the National Learning School (Kokugaku) in the Edo Period, and who criticized Buddhism and Confucianism very severely. He argued that all *kami* evolve from a creative power of the life producing spirit, whose name is Musubi, the first *kami*. Other *kami* are given the spirit of this *kami*, like the Indian notion of *avatārs* . Even today, there are many Shinto priests who follow this understanding of Musubi, life-producing *kami*.

In the case of HIRATA Atsutane (1776-1843), the other most prominent Shinto scholar in the Edo period, who affected very much those disciples who participated in the political revolution of Meiji, he identified the central *kami* of heaven in the Shinto faith with Yahweh in Judaism, God in Christianity, Allah in Islam, and the Emperor of Heaven in Confucianism. Of course, the reason why this kind of amalgamation could happen is because Mahayana Buddhism, which entered Japan, was based on the principle of the inseparability of the one and the many, and also, at the same time, was based on the principle that truth must be universal. According to my understanding, however, there must be principles of pluralism *and* particularism in order to call that faith Shinto. As a matter of fact, Shinto mythology started its narration with the story about the beginning of the universe but after mentioning the ninth generation of *kami*, it changed the subject and talked about nothing but Japan as a nation; namely, it became particularistic.

In spite of this fact, after learning the principle of universalism through Confucianism and Buddhism, Japanese intellectuals began to understand their own traditional mythology with the eyes of universalism. This is the cause of the amalgamation tendencies. It became obvious in every aspect of Japanese culture. This tendency of course can be evaluated as good from some points of view, but to my eyes, the bad side of it brought about the tragedy of the Pacific War. Because, I think, the expression which was used in the *Nihongi*, the ancient *Chronicle of Japan*, namely to make the world the home of one family, the hope of the first emperor of Japan, was used in a universalistic sense in wartime for the purpose of making Asian countries fight against Western countries as invaders, in spite of the fact that the expression was originally meant to make Japan one unified country. I have been trying, however, to develop Shinto theology in its authentic, original style.

You see, the time when Tenno, the emperor, began to be called a living *kami* was the time when Japan established a country which was politically centralized, and could make all the people and clans belong to the Tenno system. Before that time, Japan consisted of many different clans which held lands and people by themselves. In 646 A.D., these clans supported the Tenno, or imperial, system. No one but Tenno was called a living *kami*. From that time on, Tenno was seen as a living *kami* and at the same time a human being.

The time when a person was enshrined as *kami* for the first time was in 947, when SUGAWARA Michizane, whom I have mentioned, was enshrined.

However, until the end of the sixteenth century there was no one enshrined and worshipped except SUGAWARA Michizane. Around the beginning of the Edo period, TOYOTOMI Hideyoshi (1536-1598) and TOKUGAWA Ieyasu (1542-1616) were both warriors and governed Japan with military forces. They were enshrined after death as the second and third cases representing persons becoming enshrined. TOYOTOMI Hideyoshi was enshrined in 1599 and TOKUGAWA Ieyasu, in 1626.

It was after the Meiji Restoration, in 1868, that the government started to establish shrines for those historical persons who contributed to the nation as a whole. Even after 1945, there was a group of persons who wanted to establish a shrine for YUKAWA Hideki, who was the first Nobel Prize recipient of the Japanese, although they did not succeed.

There are, of course, no such Japanese today, I believe, except some enlightened Shintoists, who called the present Tenno a *kami*. This is because the edict issued by the last Tenno Showa on January, 1, 1946, was named by a journalist at that time the "Edict For the Declaration of Human Being." Of course, in that edict there was no expression like "he is not a *kami*" or "he believes he is only a human being," but those who wanted to sever the deep relationship which had been in existence throughout the history of Japan, between Tenno and Shinto, thought it was time to make Japanese believe that the reason why Japan was not only defeated in the war but also started such an evil war came from such an unreasonable faith: that Japan is a *kami* land and Tenno is a *kami*.

As I have suggested, the meaning of *kami* is completely different from the concept of God in Christianity. But, when Protestant missionaries came to Japan at the beginning of the Meiji era, they translated the Gospels into Japanese and used the Japanese word *kami* as the translation word of *God*. From that time on, Japanese tended to confuse the concept *kami* with the concept *God*. This tendency was due in part to attempts of the Meiji government to develop a Western style country with people educated in Western ways. At that time, to learn meant to study Western culture and to become educated was to become Western-like.

As you can imagine, the result was that Japanese began to think of everything in a Western way, even in tastes of religion--they began to think of *kami* as if it was God. Serious confusions and mixtures had occurred. Therefore, when the leaders said that Tenno is *kami*, Japan is the *kami* land, in school or in public, in wartime, it came to mean to the public that Tenno was absolute, the Almighty Being, and Japan was a country which had an appointed task: to lead other countries. Unfortunately, during the war, there was no one who could officially or openly point out this wrong usage of the word *kami*.

If we take this historical fact into our consideration, we can say the person who called the edict of 1946 the declaration of Tenno as a human being was correct in a sense. But we must not forget the fact that the person himself did not conceptualize the matter this way nor did he have bad intentions. He was misunderstood because he was seen through the mental filters of the American Occupation Forces as using the notion of being a *god* as a tool to justify his hidden political purposes. Based on the original concept of *kami*, it is needless to say that Tenno is *kami* even today. If we recall the first sentence of the Japanese constitution, it says that Tenno is the symbol of the Japanese nation and the unity of the Japanese people. There is no one among the Japanese, other than Tenno himself, who could be put in such a position. If we recall again the definition of the word *kami*, given by MOTOORI Norinaga, one continues to call Tenno a *kami*.

Among Shinto priests today, there are many who want to establish a shrine for the last Tenno Showa, but considering the possibility of contributing to all kinds of misunderstanding to contemporary Japanese in general, and to the people all over the world, and the possibility that such a proposal might become the target of attack by the ultra-leftist groups, they tentatively converted their wish to establish a foundation for the purpose of adoring the imperial virtue of the Tenno Showa.

I hope you have come to understand better the concept of kami in Shinto, or have I put you in such a confusion that there is no way out?

VII
Foundations of Mt. Hiei
Hisao Inagaki

Professor Hlawatsch gave us a glimpse of Mt. Hiei, the mountain to the northeast of Kyoto, symbol of protection, at times source of anxiety for the populace below, site of ancient temples, place of magnificent vistas, aperture for the introduction from China of the Buddhist tradition which significantly shaped the worldview of Japanese. Professor Inagaki turns our attention to this mountain bridge of religious and cultural transmission, this center of creative assimilation of Buddhist ideas and catalytic source for developments within the Buddhist cumulative tradition in Japan.

When Saicho (766-822) founded Mt. Hiei, it was in the Heian period, and the capitol was here in Kyoto, having been moved from Nara to Nagaoka, in 784, and from Nagaoka to Kyoto, in 794.

Saicho was born at the foot of Mt. Hiei around 766. Tradition says that he was of Chinese descent. He went up Mt. Hiei at the age of nineteen, and he resolved not to descend the mountain to the capitol city for twelve years. He built a small hut wherein he enshrined a Buddha image carved by his own hands. At that time, there were very few people living on Mt. Hiei, but now, of course, it is quite different. It is modernized, even secularized. Now many people can visit there very easily. When Saicho was there it was a closed mountain, a difficult terrain with many dangers. Saicho loved to stay there and he did for twelve years. When you go there you, too, will be tempted to stay longer than just one day.

In those days, China was the country of great literature and religion, and considerable spiritual influence came to Japan from China. So the eminent monks were invited to Japan during the Nara period. In the Heian period Japanese monks went to China, although it was not very easy to get there. First, one had to get imperial permission, board a ship and launch a very dangerous voyage, one taken at the risk of life.

So, Saicho went to China in 804, and stayed there for one year returning with the traditions of four strands of the Buddhist tradition.

The first was (1) the Tendai strand; the second was (2) the Endonkai, stressing the Mahayana Tendai precepts; the third was (3) the Zen strand and the fourth was (4) esoteric Buddhism. These four strands of Buddhism were transmitted by Saicho to Japan. Primarily, Saicho himself was a Tendai monk and is looked upon as the founder of the Japanese Tendai school.

(1) Tendai was founded in China and was based on the *Lotus Sūtra*, one of the most important Mahayana *sūtras*. Master T'ien-t'ai systematized the Tendai teaching, based on this *Lotus Sūtra* and Nagarjuna's theory of the Middle Way or Path

(*madhyamika*).[43]

Master T'ien-t'ai was a great person. He gave lectures on the *Lotus Sūtra* which were later compiled into three major works. He was also an expert on meditation. The Mahayana has a variety of meditation practices ranging from a Zen type of meditation, a Tendai type of meditation, Pure Land meditation, and also esoteric meditation. In a work called the *Mahāyāna Śamatha and Vipaśyanā* are noted the Mahayana *samādhis*. In that work, master T'ien-t'ai systematized all the current meditative methods. That was a very formidable, massive work, and he included varieties of meditation, not only mentioning the methods of meditation, but also cautioning us about the dangers of falling into the wrong type of meditation.

Those four *samādhis* are especially important because they are the different types of the major meditative methods which are classified in accordance with the postures of meditation: sitting posture, standing posture and so on.

The first is constant sitting *samādhi*, or meditation. You sit in meditation for as long as 90 days--three months. Of course you are allowed to eat and to sleep a little. But, for three months, you are supposed to be sitting as much as possible.

Second is the constant walking *samādhi*. That is especially important in the Tendai teaching, and also in Pure Land Buddhism because that is the preferred way of the meditation, walking around the Buddha statue, again for 90 days--three months, while chanting, reciting the Buddha Amida's name, *namo Amitābha*, repeatedly. Also, you are to keep thinking on the Buddha all that time, so you mentally concentrate on the Buddha and with the mouth you verbally concentrate on that name. So if you do that, based on the certain *sūtra* which is called *Pratyutpanna Samādhi Sūtra*, then you will be able to see Amida's Pure Land and also visualize Amida himself. The third *samādhi* is a half sitting, half walking meditation practice. The fourth one refers to unspecified postures of meditation. These four *ssamādhis* became a very important part in the Tendai meditation, especially the second one, walking *samādhi*.

The teaching or doctrine of Tendai is very complex and sophisticated. It recognizes the reality of all existence by presenting three aspects of this reality: voidness, temporariness, and the middle path, which are dimensions of what is called the triple truth. When this view of reality is combined with actual meditation you can become enlightened to that reality.

(2) In the Buddhist tradition there are precepts which a monk is to fulfill. In the Theravada tradition there are 227 precepts for a monk. According to the Chinese-Japanese tradition, the Hinayana has 250 precepts for one who wants to live as a monk. In the Mahayana, the precepts are based on the *Brahma-jāla Sūtra*. Here you see one distinction between the Theravada and Hinayana precepts on the one hand and the Mahayana precepts, on the other. To make a long story short, according to the Mahayana point of view the Theravada, or Hinayana, precepts are for your own sake; to abide by these precepts in order to calm down your mind and to attain wisdom for your own spiritual

deliverance. The Mahayana precepts are more for other people, to benefit other people, to assist one in doing good for other people. The Tendai adopted this Mahayana sense of precepts, which is called *endonkai* (*en* means perfect, and *don* means abrupt, quick, and *kai* means precepts). By abiding by these precepts, you attain the perfect enlightenment very quickly.

The idea of Mahayana precepts was attributed to the disciples of T'ien-t'ai and it is this tradition that existed in China, and that Saicho brought to Japan. The precepts were very important for Saicho. Saicho abandoned the ordinary Buddhist precepts which he received at Todaiji in Nara. There is a special platform where you have to take or receive the precepts from a master. In those days there were three places in Japan where one could receive the Buddhist precepts. One of them is in Nara. If you go there you will see the *kaidan*, the place where the precepts are conferred.

Saicho himself went to Nara and received the precepts, but he was not satisfied. He wanted to spread the Mahayana understanding of precepts on Mt. Hiei. He needed the permission from the imperial court. But because of the objections of the Buddhists in Nara, his dream was not realized while he was alive. It was only a few days after his death that the permission was granted to erect a platform for Mahayana precepts. With its erection, the *endokai* was established in Japan.

(3) Third is Zen. Although you are probably familiar with Zen, I want to note that Zen has many forms. After World War II, for example, Dr. D. T. Suzuki popularized the Zen teaching in the West. Some people call that "Suzuki Zen." Also many young people are attracted to a kind of Zen, and this variety has been called "beat Zen." There are types of Zen and they are now available throughout the world.

In those days, some orthodox traditions of Zen were found in China. Originally, according to tradition, Bodhidharma brought Zen to China from India. He was himself Indian, a prince of a royal family. He abandoned the secular world and became a Buddhist monk. He received the transmission of Zen and became the twenty-eighth patriarch of the Zen tradition, and is considered the first patriarch of Chinese Zen. In China, many disciples followed Bodhidharma's Zen teaching. In time many schools and sub-schools of Zen developed.

Saicho received two forms of the Zen tradition. While he was still in Japan, he received the tradition of one of them, called Northern Zen (*hokushūzen*), founded by Shen-hsiu. Rinzai and Soto Zen, the more popular forms of Zen in Japan today, both belong to the Southern Zen. Saicho received this Zen tradition from Gyohyo, who was himself the successor of this Zen teaching from Tao-hsüan, a disciple of Shen-hsiu.

The second tradition of Zen Saicho received in China. This form is called "ox head zen" (*gozuzen*). Although this school was developed in China by Fa-jung, it did not tend to flourish. Saicho also received this Zen tradition from Hsiao-jan and transmitted it to Japan.

Two great figures in the transmission of Zen to Japan were Eisai (1141-1215) and Dogen (1200-1253) who later transmitted from China Rinzai and Soto Zen, respectively.

(4) The fourth one, the esotericism, was very popular in China when Saicho was there. By esotericism, I mean the very elaborate liturgical utilization of ritual trappings and profuse symbolism. By the 7th or 8th century in India, esoteric Buddhism, called *Vajrayāna*, arose. So, it is said that Buddhism developed from the Hinayana to Mahayana, and from Mahayana to Vajrayana. So, in terms of *yāna*, "vehicle, means of soteriological conveyance," one has Hinayana, Mahayana, and Vajrayana.

The main emphasis of esotericism is to find contact with the Absolute, the Deity or God or Buddha, which is symbolized in the pure forms communicated by means of a *mandala*. So you concentrate on the *mandala*, and you chant *dhāranīs* and you think of the deity or the Buddha, eventually visualizing the absolute. There are many deities, Buddhas, and Bodhisattvas depicted in the *mandala*. You may not know which Buddha or which Bodhisattva is close to you, so you might use a method to determine this whereby, under the guidance of a master, you throw a flower or something on the *mandala* and the deity on which that flower drops is your deity. This way you can find your Buddha or deity. You choose one of those deities and you concentrate on him and say his *dhāranī* and you form the special symbolic hand gestures (*mudrās*). By these means you become one with that deity and eventually you attain the absolute. So, the whole universe is symbolized, is depicted in symbolic form. In modern science, the universe is given in scientific terms. But, the esoteric approach is that the whole universe is symbolized as the Buddha, called Dainichi (Sanskrit: Mahavairocana). This Buddha is the center of the universe and is the universal Buddha. He represents the whole universe. To become one with the Mahavairocana is the final objective. This can even be achieved while you are alive, in this life. So, the final objective of esoteric Buddhism is to come into unity with the ultimate Buddha.

This is the very sophisticated teaching with elaborate rituals. One of the most popular rituals involves burning firewood. Not only are the doctrines complicated, but the actual rituals are so complicated that one has to learn them from a master over the course of many years.

Among many in Japan, it is believed that through praying to your Buddha or Bodhisattva or deity, your problems will be solved. If someone is sick, then you can pray for recovery from that sickness and for that purpose esoteric Buddhism is very effective. Centuries ago, in India, a lot of Hindu elements were absorbed to formulate esoteric Buddhism there. Then, Indian esoteric Buddhism was brought to China in the eighth century and it gained great popularity.

Actually, when Saicho went to China, he sailed with Kukai, who played such an important role in the transmission of esoteric Buddhism to Japan.

Saicho stayed in China for one year, while Kukai stayed there for two. Kukai became more conversant with esoteric Buddhism. Saicho learned from Hsun-hsiao the details of esoteric Buddhism and brought the tradition to Japan. The Emperor Kammu, Saicho's patron, fell ill at the time and was very anxious to receive the benefit from esoteric Buddhism. Saicho performed esoteric rituals for recovery from illness and it worked.

Saicho was the first to conduct the esoteric ritual, the performance of ordination to many people, to many monks. The esoteric confirming ordination, which involves the sprinkling of water on your head (Skt., *abhiṣeka*), took place in Kyoto at the Takaozanji, a place which is very well known today as a medicinal retreat. Later, Kukai, when he returned to Japan, lived in Takao and became the abbot there and was also given a temple in Nara. Later he founded the temple complex at Mt. Koya, Koyasan.

It was natural for Saicho to bring back the tradition of esoteric Buddhism because it was so popular in China, where it also enjoyed imperial patronage.

These are the four traditions of Buddhism which Saicho brought to Japan. The first, Tendai, and the last, esotericism, are more important in understanding Saicho's contribution than the others: Mahayana precepts and Zen. He was a Tendai Master and at the same time he was a master of esoteric Buddhism. For Saicho, the esotericism is as good as Tendai. His disciple, Ennin, and his successor Enchin, learned still more about esoteric Buddhism in China and brought back more of that, thinking esoteric Buddhism was superior to the Tendai teaching. So, there was an "esotericization" (if there is such a word). Just as Indian Buddhism became "esotericized" in the seventh and eighth centuries, the Tendai teaching became "esotericized" to a great extent after Saicho.

Ennin was a great disciple of Saicho's. Ennin's diary is a very important document, which was translated by Reischauer. Since Saicho stayed on Mt. Hiei for twelve years, he stipulated that serious students also must stay on Mt. Hiei for twelve years. Ennin followed Saicho's teaching and stayed on Mt. Hiei for 30 years practicing the four *samādhis*. Then he went to China in 838, where he stayed for nine years learning much of esoteric Buddhism, returning home in 847. He also went to Mt. T'ien-t'ai, right across from the Japanese island of Kyushu, on the *Yangtze River* in China. This was the center of the Tendai school. Since Saicho went there to learn Tendai, he wanted to set up a center of study and practice in Japan on a mountain. Mt. Hiei provided a similar mountain setting.[44]

Ennin also learned the practice of chanting the name of Amida Buddha (Chinese, *nien-fo*; Japanese, *nembutsu*) on Mt. Wu-t'ai from master Fa-chao. It shows that Fa-chao initiated the Pure Land way of *nembutsu*. He is believed to be the successor of Shan-tao, who systematized the Pure Land teaching in China in the T'ang Dynasty. Fa-chao practiced the *nembutsu-samādhi* so much that he is said to have attained the visualization-*samādhi*.

It is not easy to discuss the practices of meditation in such a short time because there are so many and they each involve developing complex perspectives.

The Pure Land meditation, for example, consists of meditating on the Buddha. By performing the prescribed method of meditation, you can actually visualize Amida and the Pure Land. Sitting meditation is also imperative. Reciting the name is equally effective in attaining the state of *samādhi* concentration. If you attain that you will see, visualize, and realize the Pure Land. Fa-chao attained this *samādhi*. He also initiated a special way of chanting the *nembutsu* in five cadences, five tones, which Ennin learned in China and brought back to Japan. Ennin incorporated Fa-chao's name chanting in a constant walking *samādhi*. The constant walking *samādhi* is the practice of the *nembutsu* while walking around the Buddha's image. Ennin also brought back the tradition of esoteric Buddhism because Saicho, who stayed in China only for one year, wanted Ennin to stay longer to learn more about esoteric Buddhism. Ennin stayed in China for nine years learning esoteric Buddhism. After he returned home, he ordained more than one thousand people in the esoteric way.

His successor in significance was Enchin, who followed Gishin, a disciple of Saicho. Gishin went to China with Saicho. Because travel to China was dangerous, Saicho, being very careful, wanted someone to bring back the Buddhist tradition to Japan should he meet his death en route. So he brought Gishin, his disciple, to China. Gishin also received the traditions which Saicho received. Although Enchin was Gishin's disciple, he became the successor of the tradition on Mt. Hiei.

Enchin received the Mahayana precepts on Mt. Hiei in 833 and he stayed there for twelve years. After that, he went to another sacred mountain, Mt. Omine, in another prefecture, and there must have been inspired. A new development in practice took place on this mountain, a form and practice that has come to be called "mountain Buddhism." It appears that this was begun by a man named En-no-ozunu. Mountain Buddhism, a very special form of Buddhism, has shamanistic elements, not unlike Shinto. Enchin, in the year 853, went to China, remaining there for five years and received the traditions of esoteric Buddhism and T'ien-t'ai.

Soo (831-916), our next leading figure to consider, started the practice of *kaihōgyō*, which is the practice of visiting peaks, namely a pilgrimage to peaks on Mt. Hiei. It is a tremendous task. Perhaps you have heard about something like this. There is the one thousand day practice on Mt. Hiei. You do not do the one thousand day practice consecutively in a short period, but you are allowed ten or fifteen years to complete the one thousand day practice. Customarily, the practice covers seven years. The first one hundred days of practice you do in the first year. You walk about every day at the rate of about thirty kilometers a day. You walk up and down the mountain, visiting specific places, chanting *sūtras* and *dhāraṇīs* and worshipping. The second 100 days are performed in the second year. One does the thirty kilometers walk each day. The third one hundred day practice takes place in the third year. The fourth and fifth one hundred day practice are done in the fourth year, a kind of two hundred day practice. It gets very hard to complete the fourth and fifth hundred day practice. The sixth and seventh one hundred day practice should be performed during the fifth year. What is more, after completing the seventh one hundred day practice you are not supposed to eat anything for nine days. You are not even supposed to drink water. This is the most difficult part. One can live for many days just on water. One may live, perhaps, for several days without sleeping. For nine days, however, you deny all human needs. Actually some people have successfully completed this practice--no water, no food, no sleep. You are also not supposed to sit or lie down. This is completed in the fifth year. In the sixth year, the eighth one hundred day practice should be performed. Every day, you walk sixty kilometers, the distance is now doubled. The ninth and tenth one hundred day practice is performed in the seventh year. You walk much longer and walk up and down Mt. Hiei. You come down to Kyoto and go back, this is part of the practice.

The sages on Mt. Hiei actually performed that practice. About twenty or thirty years ago, one of them came to give a lecture a few days after he completed the one thousand day practice. He was so weak he had to be supported by people. He told me that this actually extends the limits of human beings, physically and mentally. He was able to perform even beyond that because of the power which was given to him by Buddha. Also, while performing the one thousand day practice, he constantly remembered the deity Fudo, of whom there are many images and paintings throughout Japan, especially on Mt. Hiei. Fudo is supposed to be a messenger/incarnation of Mahavairocana (Japanese, Dainichi, "great illumination").

Soo had this inspiring experience of Fudo, and because of this Fudo worship became very popular. Fudo holds a sword in the right hand and in the left hand he holds a rope. The sword is to cut or sever evil passion and the rope is to catch or ensnare an evil person or passion. Fudo looks so fierce because he is protecting us. The one thing which I remember in the talk by the monk who finished the one thousand day practice was that he said he actually visualized Fudo, and that after practicing a week or so he began to realize the presence of Fudo. So, with the guidance and protection of Fudo you can complete the one thousand day practice and do what ordinary people cannot do with ordinary human power.

Then came Jomyo, or Jokan (843-927), who instituted the constant walking practice and established the constant walking practice hall (jōgyōzanmaidō), which was particularly designed for the monks to perform the constant walking samādhi, walking around a statue of Amida Buddha for 90 days while calling upon his name and maintaining mindfulness of him. He also started what has come to be called by the local people of Kyoto the mountain nembutsu (the mountain here means Mt. Hiei).

A number of outstanding figures visited Mt. Hiei and received inspiration while on the mountain. One of them, named Koya (903-972), was on Mt. Hiei for some time. He received inspiration and he went down to walk around in the city of Kyoto carrying the image of Amida on his back. He urged people to say the nembutsu. He did not actually go through the streets dancing, as is often thought, but the way he recited the *nembutsu* and recited the hymns was in the tune and rhythm of *odori* dancing. So his practice was called the *odori* (dancing) *nembutsu*. Koya moved about, he did not stay on the mountain for very long.

The next significant figure was Ryogen (912-985) who was very important because he wrote a Pure Land work called *Gokuraku-kuhon-ōjōgi*. According to one of the three Pure Land *Sūtra*s, which is called the *Contemplation Sūtra*, the Pure Land aspirants are divided into nine categories. Ryogen's work on the nine grades became very important in the development of Pure Land Buddhism on Mt. Hiei. He is said to have had three thousand disciples. There were four special disciples, one of whom was Genshin (942-1017), the author of *Ōjōyōshū* which is a collection of the important passages pertaining to the matter of birth in the Pure Land. This is an encyclopedic work drawing from many *sūtra*s and commentaries from India and China. When he completed this work he sent a copy to China. The monks there were very surprised, and rated Genshin as the "little Sakyamuni" in Japan.

He remained on Mt. Hiei and started the Eshin School of Tendai, which is based on the "original state of enlightenment" (*hongaku*) teaching, meaning that everybody is originally enlightened, even the most ordinary person. You do not actually attain enlightenment but you are from the beginning enlightened and you only need to become aware of this. This is an alternative view to what has been called "entering upon enlightenment" (*shikaku*), in the sense of working your way up to enlightenment from the beginner up to the master stage.

Although Genshin is remembered as starting the Eshin School of Tendai, from the point of view of the *Ōjōyōshū* compilation with its focus on birth in the Pure Land he is looked upon as the 6th patriarch by Shinran, who founded Jodo-Shinshu.

Ryonin (1072-1134) was a Tendai monk very much interested in chanting. He systematized Tendai chanting and left Mt. Hiei to live in nearby Ohara. He built a temple there where he concentrated on the Tendai *nembutsu* chanting.

Ryonin concentrated on the *nembutsu* practice and he is looked upon as the founder of Yuzunembutsu Sect. *Yūzū* means "fusing and penetrating," interpenetration. Ryonin received inspiration from Amida, saying that one person's practice is all people's practice. So, if one person says the *nembutsu* all people say the *nembutsu*. Further, the practice of all people penetrates one person's practice. One person's *nembutsu* can be increased by the joining of other people. He instituted the chanting *nembutsu*; he himself chanted 60,000 times a day. Also, the "one million times *nembutsu*" was originated by him. So the *nembutsu* was chanted one million times in Kyoto. Although the temple of the Yuzunembutsu Sect is now in Osaka, the actual practice of chanting for many times was originated by Ryonin at Ohara.

The Yuzunembutsu Sect did not enjoy the great popularity that Jodo-shu, or Jodo-Shinshu did, but Honen's chanting was similar to that of the Yuzunembutsu.

Eiku (d. 1179) was a disciple of Ryonin, a master both of Tendai Mahayana precepts as well as the practice of chanting the nembutsu. He was a teacher of Honen.

Honen (1133-1212), the founder of the Jodo Sect, went to Mt. Hiei at the age of fifteen and studied under various scholars. At twenty-four he left the mountain and visited distinguished scholars in Nara and Kyoto. Later he went up Mt. Hiei again to seek the way to salvation. It is said that he read through the entire *tripiṭaka* five times yet without finding inspiration. At the age of forty-three, as he read Shan-tao's commentary on the *Contemplation Sūtra*, he came across a passage which taught continuous recitation of the *nembutsu* and found in it the way to salvation. He instantly realized Amida's saving power and took refuge in him. He left the mountain to live in Kyoto and began to propagate the *nembutsu* teaching among people of all walks of life. In 1198, at the request of the Lord Chancellor FUJIWARA Kanezane, he wrote *Senjaku-hongan-nembutsushū*, presenting the essentials of the *nembutsu* teaching and declaring the independence of the *nembutsu* school. While Honen was on Mt. Hiei, he received from Eiku the tradition of the Mahayana precepts. So, Honen is said to have given the Mahayana to his disciples. His teaching is characterized by exclusive recitation of the *nembutsu, namu amida butsu*, "Homage to Amida Buddha." He discarded as futile all other methods of Buddhist practice, such as meditation and even Bodhi-mind, the aspiration for enlightenment. The reason for this is that the *nembutsu* originates from and is supported by Amida's original vow.

Honen had many disciples. One of the leading disciples, Bencho (1162-1238), later known as Chinzei Shonin, first went up Mt. Hiei in 1183 and studied Tendai under Shoshin. He returned to his native place in Kyushu in 1190, and seven years later went to Kyoto and became Honen's disciple. Bencho's school of Jodo-shu came to be known as Chinzei. Today Chion-in in Kyoto is its general head temple, and the famous Zojoji in Tokyo is one of the major head temples.

A more important disciple of Honen was Shinran (1173-1262), the founder of Jodo-Shinshu, popularly known as Shin. Bereft of his parents when very young, he entered the priesthood at the age of nine and then went to Mt. Hiei. He studied and practiced the Tendai method of salvation until he was twenty-nine. Unable to find a solution to his spiritual problems, he left the mountain and attempted a one hundred day confinement at Rokkaku-do in Kyoto, which was built by Prince Shotoku. At dawn on the ninety-fifth day, he received an inspiration from Kannon, the main object of worship at the temple. Then he went to see Honen and became his disciple. While following the master's teaching of *nembutsu*, he developed and systematized the theory of salvation by Amida's power. The head temples of the two main schools of this denomination, Nishi Honganji and Higashi Honganji, have under their jurisdiction millions of followers.

If we turn our eyes to Zen, both Eisai (1141-1215) and Dogen (1200-1253) spent important years of their lives on Mt. Hiei. Ordained at the age of fourteen, Eisai first studied and practiced the Tendai teaching. In 1168, he went to Sung China and brought back Tendai scriptures, but after visiting China again, from 1187 to 1191, he transmitted Rinzai Zen to Japan. He built the first Zen temple in Kyushu, and the then shogunate government built Kenninji in Kyoto and appointed Eisai as the first chief abbot. Under pressure from Tendai monks, however, Kenninji was made a center of three schools: Tendai, esoteric Buddhism and Zen.

Dogen entered Mt. Hiei at the age of thirteen to become a novice. Later he went to see Eisai at Kenninji to become his disciple. In 1223, after Eisai's death, Dogen went to China with Myozen, Eisai's successor. Dogen attained *satori* under the guidance of Ju-ching, and returned to Japan in 1227. After living in Kyoto for more than ten years, he retired deep into the mountains of Echizen, north-east of Kyoto, and built Eiheiji, which became the center of Soto Zen.

During the Kamakura period (1185-1333), several new schools were founded, and they were to leave great influences on the spiritual life of the Japanese. What is worthy of special notice is the fact that the founders of those schools stayed on Mt. Hiei when young, and derived much inspiration from the Tendai and esoteric teachings studied and practiced on the mountain. Some of them carried part of the traditions into their new systems, and others revolted against the traditional teachings or the tendency to secularization and degeneration. The person who took the most radical attitude is Nichiren (1222-1282).

Nichiren entered the priesthood at the age of twelve, and received ordination at eighteen. After studying various teachings, including Tendai on Mt. Hiei, he came to a conclusion that none of the traditional teachings was applicable to the last Dharma-age. He thus declared the foundation of a new school based on the *Lotus Sūtra*, and vehemently criticized all the other teachings.

Recitation of the *nembutsu* which had been transmitted on Mt. Hiei in various forms found another form of its expression in Shinzei (1443-1495). When young, he went up to Mt. Hiei and stayed there for more than twenty years, studying exhaustively both Tendai and esoteric Buddhism. In 1483 he retired to Seiryuji at Kurodani on Mt. Hiei and began to concentrate on the Pure Land practice of reciting the *nembutsu*. In 1486 he rehabilitated Saikyoji at the foot of the mountain, and made it the center of both precepts and *nembutsu*. This temple became the head temple of the Shinzei school of the Tendai Sect.

A major event in the history of Mt. Hiei took place in 1571. ODA Nobunaga sent an army to burn down the temples and halls at the top and base of Mt. Hiei. Thousands of monks and laymen were killed. Earlier, the power of monk soldiers, needed to protect temple properties on Mt. Hiei, had become very strong and their outrageous acts had often caused troubles in Kyoto. When the anti-Nobunaga allies were formed and Enryakuji on Mt. Hiei and Honganji in Kyoto joined them, ODA Nobunaga resolved to destroy both. The mountain, however, was not completely ruined. Tendai monks tried very hard to restore the temples, and TOYOTOMI Hideyoshi, as part of his grand rebuilding program, gave permission for the restoration of the temples on Mt. Hiei. However, over the centuries many of the fine buildings were destroyed by fire or by vicious acts. Yet when you go to Mt. Hiei you will see many fine buildings and beautiful statues. Mt. Hiei remains important in the consciousness of Buddhists in Japan. Even as recently as 1966, less than three decades ago, the 1,200th anniversary of Saicho's birth was celebrated.

VIII
On the *Lotus Sūtra*
Michio T. Shinozaki

Without doubt the *Lotus Sūtra* is one of the most important written documents in the history of East Asia and of our world. Professor Inagaki mentioned this important text in the context of the transmission of Tendai Buddhist orientations from China to Japan at Mt. Hiei and in the creative work of Nichiren. The school that formed around Nichiren's interpretation of his own life and of the *Lotus Sūtra* (Nichiren-shu) and the dynamic movements that have coalesced in the wake of this heritage have been marked by a commitment to social involvement. Professor Shinozaki, Dean of the Seminary of Rissho Kosei-kai, an impressive organization that was formed under the leadership of Nikkyo Niwano (1906-1999), that is committed to social justice and world peace and is based on the *Lotus Sūtra*, lets us see how the teachings, of this great text simultaneously provide for motivation in the particularity of the Bodhisattva way and openness in a religiously plural world.

In this chapter, I would like to discuss *The Sūtra of the Lotus Flower of the Wonderful Law (Myōhō-renge-kyō)* or, in short, the *Lotus Sūtra*. I approach the *Lotus Sūtra* not primarily as a common academic subject, but as a source of living faith. So, what I have to say might be different in some ways from the opinions expressed by Japanese Buddhist scholars. Generally speaking, the *Lotus Sūtra* is the most popular and influential *sūtra* in the Japanese Buddhist tradition.

Japanese civilization, we may say, began with the introduction of the philosophy of the *Lotus Sūtra*. Since the time of Prince Shotoku, who wrote the first Japanese commentary on it and produced the country's first law code, a seventeen article constitution, the ideas of the Lotus *Sūtra* have been kept alive in the country's religion and culture. Most of the so-called Japanese New Religions have sprung from this tradition of the *Lotus Sūtra*. Japanese religious practices based on the *Lotus Sūtra* show amazing diversity and include synthesized forms influenced by other Buddhist *sūtras* and other religions as well. We wonder why these practices are so varied and how they could all be based on the *Lotus Sūtra*. They can be analyzed according to their form, their transformation, and their relationship to the *Lotus Sūtra*, a rich tradition. They can also be analyzed by examining the religious practice that the *Lotus Sūtra* advocates.

In this chapter, I would like to explain briefly the content and essence of the *Lotus Sūtra*. Let me refer you to a book written by President Nikkyo Niwano, of Rissho Kosei-kai, *Buddhism For Today*.[45] I will be drawing from this work in formulating what I have to say.

We at Rissho Kosei-kai call our one scripture the threefold *Lotus Sūtra*. It consists of three divisions:

(1) The *Sūtra* of Innumerable Meaning (*Muryōgi-kyō*)

(2) The *Sūtra* of the Lotus Flower of the Wonderful Law (*Hoke-kyō*)

(3) The *Sūtra* of the Meditation on the Bodhisattva Universal-Virtue (*Kanfugen-gyō*)

First I will attempt to explain the *Sūtra* of Innumerable Meaning, considered the opening *sūtra* of the *Lotus Sūtra*. It consists of three chapters. There are three important messages in this first of the threefold *sūtra*s of the *Lotus Sūtra*. The first is the truth that the Buddha had not yet had the occasion to reveal the innermost truth of Dharma. The second truth is that all that the Buddhas have expounded is only one message originating from one Dharma, namely the real state of all things, the reality of all existence. All the teachings, or *dharmas*, originate from one Dharma, the reality of all existence. The innumerable meanings arise from one Dharma. The third is that Buddha preached various teachings in accordance with the level of comprehension on the part of his audiences. We call this the Buddha's way of preaching with skill in means in an appropriate manner, in Sanskrit, *upāya*, utilizing appropriate means. The Buddha's realization of Dharma is one, yet the Buddha preached its message to the particularities of his listeners and observed that his listeners have innumerable natures, capacities and desires.

So, the Buddha preached this one Dharma by expounding appropriate teachings for his audience by utilizing appropriate means or ways. These various teachings represent the various conditions in cultures and expressions of languages. In this way, these teachings are ever contemporary. The core message of the *sūtra* is that the innumerable meanings or *dharmas* originate from one Dharma. Following from this, the *Lotus Sūtra* takes this philosophical message and expands it in an understandable way.

The *Lotus Sūtra*, which the Japanese and Chinese people have used, is Kumarajiva's translation into Chinese. The absolute truth expounded in the *Lotus Sūtra* is the wonderful law, *saddharma*. The wonderful Dharma represents the real state of all things. The lotus flower, appearing in the title, represents the ideal image of the Bodhisattva. The complete *Lotus Sūtra* consists of twenty-eight chapters.

The T'ien-t'ai (Jap.: Tendai) master, Chih-i, who was an early formative figure of the T'ien-t'ai school in China, divided the *sūtra* into two parts. He defined the first fourteen chapters as "the realm of trace, or appearance," a "subordinate or temporary doctrine," and the latter half, beginning with Chapter XV, as the "realm of origin," or "of fundamental doctrine."

He also observed that the first half, the realm of the trace, centered on Chapter II: tactfulness or skillfulness or utilization of appropriate means, *upāya*, explained in the wonderful law as the one vehicle for all beings. The second half, centers on Chapter XVI, in which the eternal Buddha is revealed. These concepts, the wonderful law as the one vehicle, and the eternal life of Sakyamuni Buddha are the central features of the *Lotus Sūtra*.

In addition to these two concepts, one more important idea is the way of the Bodhisattva. Thus, the *Lotus Sūtra* communicates three profound ideas. There are, of course, many ideas in the text, but primary focus is usually made on these, especially at Rissho Kosei-kai.[46]

(1) Buddha---life

(2) Dharma---truth

(3) Bodhisattva way---practice

In short, the central idea of the *Lotus Sūtra* is this--the issue of unity held in diversity by means of three basic concepts: the life, the truth and the practice; the Buddha, the Dharma and the Bodhisattva way. To explain this, let us consider the parable of a burning house.

Once upon a time, there was a great elder in a certain kingdom. He possessed boundless wealth and lived in a spacious house. This huge house had only one gate and many people dwelling in it. The condition of this house was terrible and dangerous. Fire suddenly started when the elder was out, and the house was enveloped in flames. When he returned to the house, his children were absorbed in play. They had no fear and no desire to escape from the burning house. The elder pondered--"this house has only one gate, and it is narrow. My children do not know that they must go out of the gate." He tried to lure the children with kind words, yet they did not listen to him because they were joyfully attached to their games. The elder reflected--"If I cannot get them to leave at once, they will certainly be burned. I know that my children like toys, they are always attracted by such things." He shouted to the children "Your favorite playthings--goat carts, deer carts and bullock carts--are now outside the gate for you to play with. All of you come quickly out of the burning house and play with these attractive toys." As soon as they heard this, they eagerly began pushing and racing against each other and came scrambling out of the burning house. The children then asked their father to give them the goat cart, the deer cart and the bullock cart, but the elder gave each of them equally a great white bullock cart.[47] This, in brief, is the story of the burning house.

Needless to say, the elder as father corresponds to the Buddha. The decayed house represents the dangerous and miserable state of this world. Each of the three attractive carts indicates the enlightenment of the "hearers" (*śrāvakas*), which we consider the "hero type," the solitary Buddhas (*pratyekabuddhas*), which we refer to as the more "philosophical type," and Bodhisattvas, which I will try to comment on more fully later.

The three different *vehicles* symbolize the pluralistic state of human beings. Vehicle is a term used for the way across the river to the land of enlightenment. Sometimes the metaphor of a raft or boat is used.

Traditionally, the former part of the *Lotus Sūtra* is understood as presenting the "Teaching of Opening Up the Three Vehicles and Revealing One." Historically speaking, there are many different ways of interpreting this teaching in the history of the T'ien-t'ai school of Chinese Buddhism. I will not discuss this in detail. I think that the three vehicles signify the diversity of this world. Everyone has a different nature and different desires; we are all different. The important issue is how we understand the one vehicle as it points to one Dharma.

As I mentioned earlier, the central message in the *Sūtra* of Innumerable Meaning is that "all the teachings, or all *dharmas*, originate from one Dharma, the reality of all existence." This central message is also expressed in the formulation of "Opening Up the Three Vehicles and Revealing One." The Three Vehicles point to all *dharmas*, and One Vehicle signifies the One Vehicle.

The notion of "opening up" has many dimensions relating to how we understand. Opening up signifies not negating but letting go. Also, the notion of revealing is important, relating, as it does, to *upāya* and truth, or wisdom.

In the *Lotus Sūtra*, the three vehicles of *upāya*, or skillful means, are the truth and the truth is *upāya*. This is the central issue for us in the *Lotus Sūtra*. In order to explicate the "Teaching of Opening Up the Three Vehicles and Revealing One" I want to apply John Hick's typology of understanding other religions. Such an application is justifiable because the three vehicles signify the relative and various ways of seeking the truth in this actual world. However, the One Vehicle signifies the absolute equality (sameness) going beyond the relative differences. The following chart may be helpful for an ongoing discussion.[48]

First, exclusivism cannot belong to the "Teaching of Opening Up the Three Vehicles and Revealing One." The "three" signifies other religions. The "One" signifies only my religion (faith). The one is absolutized and monopolized as the absolute truth, denying the possibility of the truth in other religions. It means "denying (or closing)" the three vehicles and "absolutizing" One.

Second, in the case of inclusivism, "opening up" the three vehicles means admitting the possibility of the lesser truth in other religions. But, seeing the One Vehicle as my own religion ultimately absolutizes it.

Third, in the case of pluralism, the three vehicles signifies my religion and other faiths. The One Vehicle signifies not my own religion, but the ultimate reality, which emerges in the "radical openness." The One Vehicle cannot be relativized, but emerges unexpectedly.

Paradigms	The Truth of the Middle Way	
	The Truth of Temporary Three Vehicles	The Truth of Emptiness The One Buddha Vehicle
exclusivism	Other religions are false. (not opening up the three vehicles, but negating them)	Only my faith (religion) is absolute.
inclusivism	Various religions hold the relative truth. (Opening up the three vehicles)	My faith (religion) (My particular and specific religion is absolutized (Not revealing the One, but concretizing it in the absolute form)
pluralism (the ultimatereality-centrism)	Various religions including my own religion are relative and hold the relative truth. (Opening up the three vehicles)	In the radical openness the ultimate reality spontaneously and unexpectedly emerges (is revealed).
	the realization of the Middle Way	

Rissho Kosei-kai, under the guidance of President Niwano, emphasizes the notion of harmony, which is the truth of the middle or the middle way. Rissho Kosei-kai takes the middle way in the sense of *wa*, which is "the state that is not in dispute."

Let me explain this in the context of religious cooperation. Rissho Kosei-kai has been working for interreligious cooperation, partially because of President Niwano's way of understanding the *Lotus Sūtra*. This doctrine of "Opening Up the Three Vehicles and Revealing One" provides one of the basic foundations for this work. The three different carts may symbolize different religions. Each of the three vehicles pursues its own way to salvation. Each vehicle emerges out of its own culture and historical background in which people have been attracted and attached to their own carts. In the cases of exclusivism and inclusivism the problem in the three vehicles lies in the exclusiveness in salvation. This is the idea that "my own cart is the ultimate and absolute one," and others are false or of lesser value. In other words, the people in the three vehicles have not yet awakened to the one Buddha vehicle. The problem with the one Buddha vehicle is how we understand it.

The one Buddha vehicle means all people can become Buddha according to the *Lotus Sūtra*. Everyone has the potential to be a Buddha. This is the central message. It signifies inclusiveness and openness to difference or diversity. The important point is to awaken to the one Buddha vehicle. If the one Buddha vehicle is understood as the one absolute religion, such as Buddhism or Christianity, etc., then this doctrine becomes the justification for the unification of all religions. It should be understood as radical openness.

Radical openness works through the principle of working together and living together and enhancing one another in the reality of diversity. The truth of dependent origination is working within the realm of this radical openness. The *Lotus Sūtra* responds to the issue of unity in diversity in terms of Buddhas, teachings (*dharmas*) and the practice. By the time the *Lotus Sūtra* emerged, there were so many Buddhas: future Buddhas, present Buddhas, past Buddhas--many Buddhas had appeared. How could we try to understand these various Buddhas in a more comprehensive and integrated way? So, the *Lotus Sūtra* took this up. Then in Chapter XVI the eternal Buddha, like the life of the universe, serves as the symbol of integrating among different Buddhas appearing in the past, present and future.

Further, the Buddha taught, after he became enlightened around the age of thirty, for almost fifty years. So, many teachings appeared. Again, the *Lotus Sūtra* takes this up. There is one truth; in all the teachings (*dharmas*) there is the wonderful Truth (Dharma), which is the Dharma as the ultimate reality.

Moreover, there are many practices, such as the Bodhisattva's practice of six perfections (*pāramitās*).[49] But, the *Lotus Sūtra* takes the inclusive way in that the earlier and various forms of practices in the Buddhist tradition are affirmed as a way of enlightenment.

Rissho Kosei-kai emphasizes the Bodhisattva way in the broad sense that the *Lotus Sūtra* describes. The importance of the Bodhisattva way of practice is expounded in the *Lotus Sūtra* in Chapter II. It says that the Buddha teaches only Bodhisattvas. A Bodhisattva is a person who made a vow to attain Buddhahood together with all people. In other words, Bodhisattvas are those who seek their own salvation through saving others. These Bodhisattvas know the significance of being with others and living together with others. From a Bodhisattva's point of view real enlightenment is "I become enlightened--all other beings become enlightened; I am saved--all others are saved." Thus, my own salvation or enlightenment comes simultaneously with that of all others. The Bodhisattva way, as we understand it, is any practice which enhances oneself through the practice of helping and saving others. The Bodhisattva, therefore, makes a vow to achieve Buddhahood and seeks to benefit others.

The Lotus Sūtra begins by saying that all sentient beings are Buddha's children and that they can be like him. Bodhisattvas carry this message into this suffering world. One's own true enlightenment is inseparable from the enlightenment of others. It is not enough for individuals to seek enlightenment for themselves, since the *Lotus Sūtra* says that the Buddha appeared in this world to cause all living beings to apprehend the truth. If we take these two statements seriously, we understand that the Buddha wanted all living beings to be Bodhisattvas, to apprehend the truth and attain enlightenment without exception.

That fundamental truth is expressed in the maxim "Only one Buddha vehicle." This means that only through the gate of Bodhisattva practice can living beings become Buddhas. The *Lotus Sūtra* talks about so many stories of the Bodhisattva. I cannot mention all of them.

The tradition in Japan that follows the teaching of Nichiren, the Nichiren-shu, emphasizes four Bodhisattvas. In our Great Sacred Hall, located at the headquarters of Rissho Kosei-kai, there is a beautiful image of the eternal Buddha surrounded by these four great Bodhisattvas.

This image in the Great Sacred Hall is based on the story in Chapter XV of the *Lotus Sūtra*.[50] The chapter opens with numerous Bodhisattvas, who have come from other worlds, asking the Buddha to allow them to preach this *sūtra*. He refuses because there would be no need to do this. When the Buddha had spoken, the world trembled and shook, and from its midst there issued innumerable Bodhisattvas. All these Bodhisattvas, their golden hued bodies bearing the same sacred signs as the Buddha, had been dwelling in the infinite space below the world.[51] These Bodhisattvas who had emerged from the earth have ably learned the Bodhisattva way and are untainted with worldly things, as is the lotus flower in the water. This image has symbolized the ideal way of life for the Bodhisattva. They should live in the secular world but not belong to it. The title of the *Lotus Sūtra* refers to this symbol for the Bodhisattva, which is the lotus flower. The lotus flower takes root in the mud and is nourished by it, and yet blooms with pure and beautiful petals unsoiled by the mud. Among the host of Bodhisattvas are four leading teachers known as Eminent Conduct (Visistacaritra), Boundless Conduct (Anantacaritra), Pure Conduct (Visiddhacaritra) and Steadfast Conduct (Supratisthacaritra). These Bodhisattvas came out of the earth. Steadfast Conduct vows, "However innumerable living beings are, I vow to save them." Pure Conduct vows, "However inexhaustible the passions are, I vow to extinguish them." Boundless Conduct vows, "However limitless the Buddha's teachings are, I vow to study them." Eminent Conduct vows "However infinite the Buddha's truth is, I vow to attain it."[52]

In the *Lotus Sūtra*, the eternal life of the Buddha is revealed by relating it to the Bodhisattva way. The historical Buddha, the historical appearance of the Buddha in human form in India, reveals the activity of the Bodhisattva because after he attained enlightenment, he preached to all the people and tried to save them. So, the activity of the historical Buddha is that of a Bodhisattva. Not only the historical Buddha, but also the eternal Buddha continues to follow the Bodhisattva way. This is what we believe.

In Chapter XVI, the chapter that reveals the eternal Buddha, the *Lotus Sūtra* says, in the closing remark,

Ever making this My thought:
"How shall I cause all the living
To enter the Way Supreme
And speedily accomplish their Buddhahood?"[53]

Here the Buddha's deep compassion is expressed in the Bodhisattva way. The eternity of the Buddha is not everlasting quietness. The eternity or the eternal life of the Buddha is revealed in the concrete and absolute activity of the Bodhisattva way because the eternal Buddha keeps in mind all sentient beings and watches over all the living and leads all the living beings toward achieving Buddhahood.[54] The threefold *Lotus Sūtra* also says that whenever the Bodhisattva way is actualized, the Buddha appears, abides there and expounds the Dharma.

The Bodhisattvas who sprung out of the earth symbolize those who have had much suffering and hardship during their lives, yet possess real power to help and benefit other people. These Bodhisattvas are those who bring people to the realization of the Buddha's compassion. So, in Chapter XVI of the *Lotus Sūtra*, there are many Bodhisattvas in the audience, but Buddha rejected their offer of disseminating the Buddha's teaching. Then, many Bodhisattvas came up out of the earth. So, the Buddha asked *them* to disseminate this teaching to this world. The important point is that only people from this world who share the same plight are appointed to help others in this world. Thus we, at Rissho Kosei-kai, take that passage quite seriously.

Another important Bodhisattva image is Bodhisattva Never-Despise. We interpret this Bodhisattva, with the virtue of nonviolence, as having great relevance for the modern situation. Chapter XX relates Sakyamuni Buddha's previous life. In a time of the distant past, there was a Bodhisattva named "Never-Despise." Whenever he met someone, he would revere their Buddha nature, saying "I do not despise you for you will become a Buddha." By the end of his life he had attained enlightenment through the single practice of revering the Buddha nature in others, even in the face of serious persecution.[55] Reverence for the Buddha nature in others means the recognition and acceptance of the Buddha nature in all people and helping them to cultivate and enhance it. So, one of the fundamental elements of the Bodhisattva way in the *Lotus Sūtra* is the practice of revealing and revering the Buddha nature innate in others. This is the *Lotus Sūtra*'s fundamental message that all sentient beings have the Buddha nature, innately. The first step in the religious practice of the *Lotus Sūtra* is to recognize the Buddha nature in oneself and then to nurture and cultivate it throughout one's whole life. In the process one spontaneously becomes aware that others equally possess this Buddha nature.

Thus, I think that in the *Lotus Sūtra* the various practices of the Bodhisattvas are opened up (or approved) and integrated into (or revealed into) the activities of the Eternal Buddha, namely, the Buddha's compassion of saving all people.

In summary, I have discussed so far the three important concepts such as Buddha, the Dharma and the Bodhisatttva way from the perspective of the Teaching of Opening Up the Three Vehicles and Revealing One. As a concluding remark, the *Lotus Sūtra* teaches the integration (or unity) in diversity, and the way to achieve the integration is expressed in this "Teaching." It is so in a way that all people are to be awakened to their own various possibilities and attain the integrated One, through the practice of mutual enhancement and by seeking the ultimate truth without absolutizing the particular truth in this actual world.

IX
On Zen
Keido Fukushima Roshi

Some Americans might be surprised to learn that the Zen heritage in Japan represents, from the point of view of institutional development, only one strand of the complex and variegated Buddhist tradition that has blossomed among the Japanese. At the same time, Zen is by far and away the most popular expression of Buddhist religious sensibilities in North America. The beauty of the monasteries, the impressive regimen of the disciples, and the careful guidance of the meditation masters are alluring. No less attractive is the affirmation, gently set before us by Fukushima Roshi, abbot of Tofukuji, that when the ego is placed aside, abandoned, one discovers creativity ever afresh and compassion abounding.

It is a pleasure to receive you at Tofukuji, to offer you biscuits and Japanese tea, to get to know you, to let you have a brief period of meditation, to let you know a little about me and to speak with you a little on Zen. I first heard of Chapel House at Colgate University many years ago. My Zen master, Zenkei Shibayama, was there teaching about Zen and conducting *zazen* sessions. His lectures were published as *Zen Comments on the Mumonkan.*[56]

I first went to the United States in 1969. At that time, I stayed there for only three months. My second visit was in 1973 when I stayed for one year. In both cases, I was at Claremont College in California. Because of that, there is now a very special arrangement between Pomona College and Claremont in California and this monastery at Tofukuji, one in which students, primarily those studying philosophy and religion at Pomona, are allowed to come to Tofukuji to experience Zen, and they can stay for as long as they wish. In the past 10 years or so, some fifty people, both students and teachers, have come here. Those who stay for short periods of time may last only 1 week. In terms of Zen monastic tradition, usually women are not allowed into Zen training monasteries. However, in this particular monastery, I allow both American men and women to come and participate. Among the fifty or so people who have come from Pomona, two of them were young women who were able to sit through a very severe week of *zazen* training.

For a while, I was not able to go to America myself. However, since 1989, I have been able to go once a year. These days, I have been able also to visit the University of Kansas, Xavier University in Cincinnati, and Hendrix College in Arkansas. The reason I decided to go to the United States at least once a year and talk a little about Zen is that in the 1960's there was a so-called "Zen boom" in America. However, this boom settled down somewhat, and in the 1970's those who were really *serious* about Zen began to practice more. One example of this would be, then, the sessions that were given at

Chapel House at Colgate by Shibayama. I thought that Americans were taking a rather positive direction in their understanding of Zen. Because those who have come to visit here also had a proper understanding, I was rather at ease about the whole situation.

However, upon my visit three years ago, during which time I heard a number of different stories, I realized that Zen in America is not always correct in its teachings. That is, there is a certain tendency for Americans to think that any kind of meditation is Zen.

Zen is one sect of Buddhism in general, which was founded in China by the Indian Bodhidharma, as you know. There is a tendency sometimes to call Tibetan Buddhist forms of meditation Zen, too. This is because it is derived from Indian Buddhism where there was a form of meditation. However, in this day and age, when we use the term *Zen Buddhism*, we refer to the founding of the sect in China by Bodhidharma and the subsequent development of that sect here in Japan. Korean Buddhism has also gone to the United States. Much of that movement is called Korean Zen Buddhism; however, it differs rather greatly from Japanese Zen Buddhism. Therefore, I have been attempting to explain in Japan and in the United States what traditional Zen Buddhism really is.

Since time is limited, I would like to talk briefly on what Zen is about.

We may say Zen is a religion of *mu*, or nothing. We may say that Zen is original *satori* enlightenment. We also may say that it is a religion in which one gains *satori* enlightenment of this *mu*. What is it, then, for us to gain this understanding of *mu*? Zen is a religion that teaches us to become this *mu* and to live by becoming this *mu*. What is it, then, to become *mu*? Basically, it is a condition in which one eliminates the ego and develops an egolessness in oneself. But, for you and me it is very difficult to attain this state of no ego. Therefore, in Japan, monks will come to a monastery and engage in training that is hard fully to imagine in order to gain this state of selflessness. If you do not undergo this kind of training, you truly cannot attain the state of *mu* or nothingness because it is so very difficult to eliminate the ego. Thus the *satori* enlightenment means this realizing within yourself the becoming of this "no ego." We call this, in Zen, the self of *mu*. It is also referred to by the phrase *mushin* which you might translate as "no mind," as did the Japanese scholar D. T. Suzuki. But this translation is not exactly an appropriate translation.

Suzuki realized, of course, that the phrase "no mind" does not truly and fully incorporate all the meanings of *mushin*. He also realized that in order for Americans and Europeans to get a general understanding of what *mushin* incorporates, he tried to translate it as "no mind," or sometimes as "empty mind." As you can see, from the translation "empty mind," in this state one attains a mind of emptiness. Because the mind is empty, one is able freely to respond to anything and everything. Because the mind is empty, one is able freely to take in everything. Therefore, we can say that this state of *mushin* is also the state of having a very *free mind*. Because one is constantly going through a condition of adapting and accepting things as they really are, this state is a very fresh condition. We can say that the *mushin* of Zen is a very *fresh mind*. Because one is constantly adapting or interacting with things around one, this state is also a very creative process. We can also say that the *mushin* of Zen is a very *creative mind.*

Thus, Zen is a religion that tries to teach us that by becoming *mu*, or nothing, and by developing the state of *mushin*, one is able to live a free, fresh and creative way of life. In the tradition of Zen, this sense of fresh and creative living, the sense of freedom, is greatly emphasized. This freedom of Zen is not a state in which you just decide things by and only for yourself. Rather, it is a freedom in which, because one has a truly empty mind, one is able freely to adapt to anything and everything. When you are able to eliminate your own ego, you are able to eliminate the concept of opposition towards all other people. There is a condition in which, because you are eliminating your own ego, you are able to give life to all others around you. Therefore, this condition in which you try to give life and aid to all other people is a condition in which you love all others.

Religion, and this means also all religions, no matter which one you discuss, must ultimately come to a position of having complete compassion. So, in Zen, and in Buddhism in general, by eliminating your own ego you are able to have compassion (*jihi*) towards all other people. We can say, then, that those who have reached this level have truly completed their own Zen *satori* enlightenment. Zen in its completed form is a religion that tries to save all other beings.

Let me now attempt to discuss Zen from a slightly different perspective. As I mentioned before, in order to attain the state of no ego, one must engage in training that is hard fully to imagine, not only for beginning Zen monks, but for most people.

For example, say you wish to study very hard at a time when the egotistical self says "Wait, let's go out and have a good time." When this occurs, the desire to study cools down somewhat. We can see that the ego can exert quite a lot of influence. If we were to think that we could consciously eliminate our own egos, we, in Zen, would call this a state of grand illusions. When we live our daily life, there are many times in which the "subconscious ego" will come out and show itself. This subconscious ego that comes out does so like embers embedded in a fire; it is the part that is left behind that you cannot quite remove. Passions and illusions that can be removed through conscious activity can be done by conscious activity, but it is very difficult to remove those illusions that are subconscious. In order to remove these subconscious passions and illusions, it is necessary to undergo rigorous and disciplined training. The daily life here in the monastery is rather severe.

In the daily schedule, there is *zazen* in the morning and evening. However, for Zen monks, this is not enough time. Thus, if we are to take a yearly average of the time sat in *zazen* every day it would come out to about six hours. In order to increase the amount of *zazen*, there are seven special *zazen* weeks every year. In these special seven day periods, *zazen* starts at 3 a.m. and continues until 10:30 p.m. in one hour units. In the daily schedule, monks will go out on begging rounds in the morning and engage in manual labor in the afternoon; however, during these special training weeks, none of that takes place. Of these seven special weeks, the one that occurs in the first week of December is by far the most severe. For those seven days, no one is able to lie down. In other words, one tries to sit *zazen* by ignoring the need for sleep. As you can see, this is something that is quite unimaginable. Even as a Zen master, I cannot help but feel that this is a rather crazy thing to do. There are many cases where monks have been able to remove the subconscious ego while engaging in this one special training period.

I had two masters under whom I studied. One of them was Roshi Shibayama who visited Colgate University. He was able to remove these remaining parts of his ego in this one special training period during his third year at the monastery. We can call this, then, the very start of having the *satori* enlightenment experience. My other master also had this kind of experience during the one special training period. I myself had this experience during my third year while sitting this one special week in December. In other words, historically there is a great amount of evidence that verifies the true value of this one special week. For those who are able to gain this unusual experience of *satori* enlightenment, they have then entered into a process in which they continually deepen that experience.

For Japanese monks, at least ten years training under one's master in the monastery is necessary. This is not called the complete development of *satori* enlightenment. That is to say, after the monks leave the monastery they must enter into another period in which they engage in training after *satori* enlightenment, which they do by themselves. This is a very important factor. We can say that during this period of training after initial monastic training, the monks will try to complete the true religious self. If one is not able to complete this part of the training, then one does not develop the true complete *satori* enlightenment. For Japanese monks, after graduating from college, they would then go to a monastery and study for at least ten years. Then they would engage in another ten year period, at least, of this training after the monastery. If this is not done, the true *satori* enlightenment is not fully developed. Therefore, after a period of at least twenty years, the Zen Master is fully developed. There are also cases when it took thirty or more years to do this.

Even after becoming a Zen Master, one's training does not end. The Zen Master must continue in his efforts to deepen his *satori* enlightenment even until the time of death. My reason for trying to tell all of you how *satori* enlightenment is developed through this monastic system is because in America there is a tendency to view Zen training in rather simplistic terms. There are many people who think that if they go and sit at a Zen center for a little while they will be able to have satori enlightenment. It is nonsense for those people to think that they are able to become a Zen Master after only five or six years of training. I hope, therefore, that Americans will come to understand that the Zen way of training is a very long and severe path.

I understand that you will have some lectures on Jodo-Shinshu. We can say that the two great representatives of Japanese Buddhism are Zen Buddhism and the Jodo-

Shinshu form of Buddhism. In the Jodo-Shinshu sect, they emphasize greatly the term *shinjin*. Basically it is a term that describes true faith in the Buddha called Amitābha or Amida. There is absolute faith in Amida Buddha's ability to save humankind. However, in order truly to have faith in Amida Buddha in this way, one must not have an ego to begin with. Therefore, the basic religious experience is exactly that which Zen has, too.

I have tried to give you a glimpse of what Zen is about. In the Jodo forms, they chant Amida Buddha's name in order to create an absolute existence of this Buddha. In terms of their doctrinal structure, there are a number of similarities with Christian ideas. In the end results, however, Buddhism, even Jodo-Shu and Jodo-Shinshu, are different from Christianity. That is, in Christianity we never say that one becomes God himself. In Buddhism, one trains and makes an effort in order to become the Buddha itself.

Nevertheless, I think that if one were to line up Christianity, the Jodo forms of Buddhism, and Zen, and compare them all, it would be easier for Christians to understand what Buddhism is truly about. I once gave a public lecture at a Jesuit school. After the lecture, one senior father asked me what was the difference between Christianity and Buddhism. One main difference, of course, is that in Buddhism one becomes the Buddha itself. This is somewhat different from Christianity. The father understood the point. He went on to say that he understood how the doctrinal forms were different, but he asked whether through one's own personal religious experience there were any similarities between the two religions. I said that I personally believe there is a very close, similar personal religious experience within the two traditions. I told the father I thought it was in this matter of "no ego." The father understood the point very well.

A Catholic priest associated with Sophia University in Tokyo mentioned, upon hearing about this notion of "no ego," that when this state is attained, you are able to realize God within you. So, for a Zen priest, this enables me to understand Christianity much better. As the British historian Arnold Toynbee said some years ago, the twenty-first century will be the age of dialogue between Eastern and Western religions. While waiting for the beginning of the next century, this kind of dialogue has already started. Surely this dialogue should be encouraged.

X
The Relation of Buddhist Thought to *Zazen*
Gudo Nishijima Roshi

The efflorescence of Zen in Japan is so consistently tied to the magnificent heritage received from China that one might fail to notice the memory of India, as it were, that is still alive in the tradition today. Gudo Nishijima Roshi indicates the continuing relationship between the intellectual articulation of the life situation passed on in the old doctrinal formulations and the existential immediacy of *zazen* in that both are designed to enable us to see clearly reality that is not "out there" or "off in the future," but right here and right now.

In this chapter, I would like first to discuss what I consider to be the fundamental principle of Buddhism and then to attempt to explain the relation of that fundamental principle with the practice of *zazen*.

If I want to express Buddhism succinctly, I usually say it is *belief in reality*. The English words belief in reality sound a little strange because we are always living in reality. Therefore, there is no doubt about reality. So, why should one use *belief* in the phrase *belief in reality*? It sounds strange.

Actually, however, in our day-to-day life, after waking up in the morning, we begin to think about many problems. Almost throughout our day, we are always thinking about something. But, at the same time, we have other times when we receive external stimuli: we enjoy times to eat delicious meals, to watch television, to see movies, to listen to music, and so forth. In such times, our minds are occupied by external stimuli. Therefore we can say that we are living in the world of external stimuli.

In our day-to-day life we are usually living those two kinds of situation: intellectual thinking, and sensual perception. In such a life, it is rather difficult for us to find that we are really living in reality. Gautama Buddha discovered this fact and he taught us to find that we are living just in reality. This is the fundamental teaching of Buddhism.

To explain such a theory in Buddhism, I would like to mention three objects of worship: Buddha, Dharma, and Sangha.

Buddha means, first, Gautama Buddha, who was the establisher of Buddhism. But there are many people who believe in Buddhism, who practiced *zazen* and attained the same state as Gautama, and who realized reality. Those people are also called Buddhas. Further, *Buddha* means a person who can follow the rule of the universe. Therefore, people who behave morally in their day-to-day life can also be called Buddhas. According to Buddhist theory, all human beings have the possibility of becoming Buddhas. So in the ultimate sense, all human beings can be called Buddhas. *Buddha* has those four meanings. Such Buddha is the object of worship in Buddhism.

The second object of worship in Buddhism is Dharma. *Dharma* first means Gautama Buddha's teachings, but Gautama Buddha's teachings are the realization of reality. Therefore, Dharma or reality includes the meaning of this world, this external world, or the universe. In Buddhism, *Dharma* means both the rule of the universe and at the same time the external world, the physical world or nature itself. Further, *Dharma* refers to morals themselves. We Buddhists want to follow the rule of the universe. To follow the rule of the universe is called morals. So, moral behavior in our day-to-day life is also called *Dharma*. And in the ultimate sense, we believe in something which cannot be described with words. Such a thing is also called *Dharma*. When I translate *Dharma* into English, I usually use the word *reality*.

The third object of worship in Buddhism is the Sangha. *Sangha* means the orders which are pursuing Gautama Buddha's teachings. And the orders are constructed of four kinds of people: monks, nuns, Buddhist laymen, and Buddhist laywomen. In a more practical sense, all people who are pursuing Buddhism in their day-to-day lives can be called Buddhists and they can be called *Sangha*. In the ultimate sense, all people have the possibility of becoming Buddhas. Therefore we can call all human societies *Sangha*. We can call all people in the world *Sangha*.

These three, *Buddha*, *Dharma*, and *Sangha*, are the objects of worship in Buddhism. In this situation *Buddha* suggests the people who attained the Buddhist truth that is belief in reality, *Dharma* is reality itself, and *Sangha* is the people who pursue Gautama Buddha's teachings that is reality itself, and so Gautama Buddha's teachings are concentrated into Dharma or reality. Therefore, when we think about what Buddhism is, it is necessary for us to grasp what Dharma is, or what reality is.

Thinking about the meaning of Dharma or reality, we can find the fundamental Buddhist theory in the Buddhism of ancient India.

There are four philosophies (Skt.: *catvāryāryasatyāni* -- *catvārya*-four, *ārya*-sacred, *satyāni*-philosophies or theories) in Buddhism. They are, in Sanskrit, (1) *duhkha-satya*, (2) *samudaya-satya*, (3) *nirodha-satya*, and (4) *mārga-satya*.

Duhkha means "suffering," and *duhkha-satya* means "philosophy of suffering." *Samudaya* means "aggregates," and, similarly, *samudaya-satya* means "philosophy of aggregates." *Nirodha* means "denial," so *nirodha-satya*, means "philosophy of denial." With *mārga* meaning "way," *mārga-satya*, means "philosophy of the way." These four philosophies are the fundamental theory in Buddhism. I would like therefore briefly to explain the meaning of each philosophy and why Gautama Buddha insisted on these four philosophies.

The philosophy of suffering has bearing on idealistic philosophy. We human beings think about many philosophical problems. We use concepts and ideas to propose ideals in philosophy. But ideals can never be realized in this world. In this world it is rather difficult for us to get perfect situations or attain completely perfect states. Therefore, when we think about this world on the basis of idealistic philosophy, we usually feel suffering. The philosophy of suffering is an ancient expression presupposing an idealistic philosophy in Buddhism.

The second philosophy is the philosophy of aggregates, referring to molecules. Even in ancient India there was an idea that this world is constructed of very small particles like molecules or atoms. Relying upon such an idea ancient Indian people also had the idea of the world which is constructed by physical molecules. So, the philosophy of aggregates refers to an objective philosophy of matter.

In ancient India, brahmanism was a very powerful tradition. Brahminism was an idealistic philosophy. They thought that this world was created by God, so every person has the same character or spirit as God. If we individuals identify ourselves with the spirit in the world, we can be happy. Therefore, we can think that brahminism belongs to such a kind of spiritual religion. Also at the time of Gautama Buddha there was materialistic philosophy, or skepticism. So, during his life-time there were conflicts between idealistic philosophy and materialistic philosophy.

Gautama Buddha wanted to solve the conflict between two such fundamental philosophies: idealism and materialism. After many efforts he at last arrived at his conclusion, that he was living in reality. After recognizing that he was living in reality he established his philosophy on the basis of reality. This is the philosophy which is called Buddhism. The philosophy of denial suggests denial of both idealistic philosophy and materialistic philosophy.

Among the four philosophies, the third philosophy, the philosophy of denial, indicates Buddhist philosophy. Buddhist philosophy is a denial of idealism *and* a denial of materialism. Gautama Buddha found a new philosophy which was different from idealism or materialism.

But when you think about this problem, it is difficult for us to believe, in the sphere of our intellectual thinking, of the existence of a philosophy other than idealism and materialism. When we think about philosophical problems we can find the existence of idealism easily, we can find the existence of materialistic philosophy easily, sometimes we can find a mixture of idealism and materialism. But, it is difficult, if not impossible, to find a philosophy which is different from idealism and from materialism and from a mixture of both. However, Gautama Buddha insisted on the existence of a philosophy which is different from idealism and materialism. So, we should think carefully about the meaning of the philosophy of denial.

When we think about the philosophy of denial and the functioning of our intellectual thinking, it is impossible for us to *affirm* the existence of such a philosophy in an intellectual sense. So, when we think about Buddhism, we have to think about an area of human awareness which is different from an intellectual dimension. This is a very important point.

Many people think of Buddhist philosophy as an aspect of intellectual thinking. But, we should consider Buddhism as belonging to an area other than intellectual thinking. Then, we have another problem, whether we can conceive of an area of awareness which is different from intellectual thinking. This is also a very important point in the explanation of Buddhism. Gautama Buddha insisted on a philosophy other than idealism, materialism, and a mixture of both. So, perhaps we are thinking--where does such a strange philosophy exist? Gautama Buddha believed in the existence of reality. Therefore, reality is his fundamental basis of thought. By practicing *zazen*, he recognized reality, and relying upon such reality, he *established Buddhism.*

So, we should think that Buddhism belongs to another area of awareness than intellectual thinking. It is very ironic because without relying upon our intellectual ability, we can never think anything. Therefore, on the basis of such an idea we have to doubt whether Buddhism exists or not.

On this problem, I remember the presence of dialectic in Western thought, in 18th and 19th centuries, with the famous, and powerful thinkers, Hegel and Marx. Hegel and Marx utilized the method of dialectic in their thinking.

When we rely upon this dialectical method of thinking, that is, dialectic, we can get a small sense of the possibility of the existence of a Buddhist philosophy. So, we should think that idealism, materialism, and Buddhism are in the relation of a dialectic. In a dialectic we utilize the construction of thesis, antithesis and synthesis, and in the case of Buddhism, idealism is the thesis, materialism, the antithesis, and Buddhism, perhaps, is the synthesis. When we rely upon the thinking method of a dialectic we can find a remote possibility of the existence of Buddhism. Gautama Buddha also relied to some extent on such a method.

Therefore, Gautama Buddha's thoughts have three philosophies: philosophy of suffering, philosophy of aggregates, and philosophy of denial. And the three of these philosophies can be thought within the area of our intellectual thinking. But objects of the third philosophy do not belong to the intellectual area. In our day-to-day life we are *living* in *reality.* Therefore we need a philosophy of reality. Such a kind of philosophy of reality is called Buddhism. Buddhist philosophy is different from logical theories of propositional sentences. It is a kind of description of our life. It is a kind of description of this world. It is a kind of description of the universe. We have those three kinds of philosophies in Buddhism.

Gautama Buddha sought to progress even further. He thought those three kinds of philosophies are merely philosophies, just theories. We have to realize that we are living in reality. Gautama Buddha recommended to us the practice of *zazen* in order to find reality. So, we can think that *zazen* leads to a realization of reality. Actually speaking, when we are sitting in *zazen*, we can realize ourselves because in *zazen* we do not think anything intentionally. We do not feel anything intentionally. We are just sitting.

At that time we can recognize ourselves, as we sit on a cushion. In such a situation we can find ourselves. When we find ourselves, we can find the universe which surrounds us. So, *zazen* has the character of the realization of the universe. We usually live in very small worlds. For example, in families; for example, districts; for example, states; for example, on the earth; for example, in the solar system. But, we live in a much wider area. We are living in the universe. By practicing *zazen* we can recognize the real situation that we are living in the universe. At the same time, we are diligent in keeping our spine vertically straight in *zazen*. Such effort teaches us what action is. So, *zazen* is a kind of realization of action itself.

And when we are sitting in *zazen*, quietly, we *are realizing reality*. This is Gautama Buddha's realization when he practiced *zazen*. So, we imitate him. We practice *zazen*, imitating Gautama Buddha. Then we can realize the same state as Gautama Buddha did. That is the meaning of *zazen*.

So, we can think that Buddhism is belief in reality, and to explain the importance of reality Gautama Buddha used the theory of the four philosophies, which also have bearing on the philosophy of subjectivism, philosophy of objectivism, philosophy of action, and the last one, reality itself. Buddhist philosophy has such a comprehensive structure. We can think that at the center of Buddhism is the realization of reality itself. To practice *zazen* is just the realization of reality. Such, very briefly, is the relation between Buddhism and *zazen*.

XI
The Significance of the *Nembutsu*
Shojun Bando

We turn now to the most popular form of Buddhist piety in Japan to consider the perspective of the Pure Land school, particularly that of the "True Pure Land Sect" (*Jōdo-Shinshū*). It is probably impossible to understand what Pure Land Buddhists have called *nembutsu*, to understand that which stands under the universe. Our hope, it seems, is to be enabled to recognize it when spontaneously at the same instant wisdom and compassion arise and one finds oneself transformed, never again to be the same. Professor Shojun Bando leads us now into a consideraton of the profound notion of *nembutsu*, more than a concept, more than a religious symbol, more than a sacrament: the utter simplicity in spontaneous simultaneity of the salvific arising of wisdom and compassion.

Quite some time ago, around 1960 or so, I wrote a brief article on the significance of the *nembutsu*. I believe it was based on a talk I gave in Cambridge for the Buddhist Association in England. At that time, I was a student and I was requested by the members of the Cambridge Buddhist Association to talk on something about Japanese Buddhism. So, I chose that subject. For many years I have not seen it, so I have completely forgotten what I had written. I should like to say something about my thoughts, my recent thoughts, that is, on this practice.

It is probably true that the *nembutsu* derives from the Indian tradition of the *mantra* or *dhāraṇī*, of which there are many kinds. The most well known is *OM* which is called the sacred sound in Hinduism. I do not know how far we can go back to discover its origin, but we understand that its sound has been transmitted from ancient times, from the unknown past to the present.

In many Mahayana *sūtras*, there are also passages dealing with these *dhāraṇīs* and *mantras*. For example, Chapter XVI of the *Lotus Sūtra* is devoted to them. One of my friends once remarked, most profoundly, that their origin must have been spontaneous and not created by human beings. He was referring to another setting, to the Christian practice known as *glossolalia*, mentioned in the Bible. This is said to be spontaneous, when one is inspired by the Holy Spirit, as at Pentecost. On such occasions, one utters some inexplicable words. According to my friend, the origin of *dhāraṇī* must have been something like that, where it was originally spontaneous, not created or thought by humans. As these are words or sounds coming from an inspired person, those who hear them become affected or inspired themselves. Let me now attempt to analyze this.

The subject is *nembutsu* and its significance. *Nembutsu*, as I have said before, can be traced back to the Indian tradition of *dhāraṇī* or *mantra*. According to the Indian Buddhist tradition, *dhāraṇīs* are sounds whose meanings are not readily understandable.

They are natural sounds, not created by human beings, but spontaneously appearing from somewhere, like in the case of *OM*, as we have noted previously.

The word *dhāraṇī* comes directly from the root *dhṛ*, which means "to hold, preserve, keep something." We believe that each *dhāraṇī* represents a rich religious experience, possessing a great amount of teaching, which one has in the mind. We listen to the teaching but soon after, we forget what we have heard, though, in fact it continues to survive, deep in our consciousness. On unexpected occasions, it comes to the surface and we realize--"Oh, it was not lost after all!"--it has been kept somewhere deep inside us. *Dhāraṇī* serves as such a tool, to hold and revive a certain moment in which all our past experiences are kept as a memory deep in our consciousness. We understand *dhāraṇī* in this way. The *nembutsu* is such a form of this.

Likewise, the *mantra* is very often equated on the same level as *dhāraṇī* and we can find many in the Mahayana Buddhist *sūtras*. For example, there is a well known *sūtra*, the *Heart Sūtra* (of the Sanskrit *prajñāpāramitā* literature) which has at the end a *mantra* that goes *gate gate pāragāte pārasaṃgāte bodhi svāhā!* Most people cannot understand what it means because it is recited in the original Sanskrit.

Generally speaking, Chinese scholars did not translate these *dhāraṇīs* and *mantras* into their own language, but kept them in the original due to the sacredness of their sounds, which could never be replaced otherwise.

The word *mantra* comes from the Sanskrit root *man*, meaning "to think, remember, recall" and *tra*, which means "tool." If one recites a *mantra*, it reminds one of a past memory, it revives one's past experiences, which have long been thought lost. In this respect it means "a tool to remember," a tool to recall, revive or reconfirm such a past memory in the present moment, just as if we experience it for the first time. *Dhāraṇī* and *mantras* have such functions, which usually take the form of words or sounds.

In Japanese Buddhism, the so-called *nembutsu* has many forms. *Butsu* basically means "Buddha," but sometimes it embraces also the idea of the Bodhisattva, which term is derived from *bodhi*, meaning "enlightenment," and *sattva*, "person."

Ordinarily, a Bodhisattva is regarded as a "way-seeker," someone who seeks enlightenment, but at the same time a Bodhisattva is one who is being inspired by *bodhi*, or *satori*. If we define *Bodhisattva* as merely "a way-seeker," or a person who is seeking enlightenment, whose state is ever here all the time in this world, though, as yet unknown to us, then there is some distance between the seeker and enlightenment. The seeker feels that he is not there yet, though someday it will be achieved. So, there is distance, say, between myself and enlightenment. If we regard a Bodhisattva as "a person who is being inspired by the truth," then there is no distance at all between oneself and the truth.

In early Buddhism, the term *Bodhisattva* was used to refer to the former lives of Sakyamuni who, as you know, attained enlightenment in this life. According to Theravada, or the southern tradition, only Gautama Buddha attained enlightenment or became a Buddha while in this world. What about all the other people, such as his disciples and those who followed him? They were not thought to be qualified to attain complete enlightenment. The highest that they could possibly hope to reach was *arahatship*, which is a combination of Sanskrit and English, meaning "the state of a saint," "a perfect man," *arhat*. In early Buddhism, therefore, all sentient beings could only reach this stage, unlike Sakyamuni who was able to attain Buddhahood, or complete enlightenment.

The question naturally arose, why Sakyamuni alone was able to do this. People in later times explained that Gautama Buddha was the exception because only he had accumulated a great amount of virtue or merit (Sanskrit: *puṇya*) in his previous lives. As you know, in the Buddhist tradition, there is a concept of *saṃsāra*, "transmigration," where one form is reborn into another in the next life, and this is repeated endlessly. Gautama Buddha had many births before he was born as a human. Therefore in his former lives he had performed great amounts of self-sacrifice in order to save others and hence could attain enlightenment.

So, the term *Bodhisattva* was originally applied to the former existences of Gautama Buddha, which later came to be used by the Mahayana Buddhists to mean "way-seekers."

In Mahayana, or the northern tradition, all sentient beings are believed to contain seeds for Buddhahood, and hence are all potentially Buddhas. So, in the stages prior to Buddhahood, people are called *Bodhisattvas*, that is people who are seeking *bodhi*, or enlightenment.

Unlike the Theravada tradition, in which the historical Sakyamuni Buddha is the object of worship, the Mahayana tradition worships many other Buddhas, such as metaphysical ones, and Bodhisattvas.

Mahayana

Buddhas and Bodhisattvas Representing
The Unity of Wisdom and Compassion

Buddhas	Bodhisattvas
Dainichi "great sun"	Daiseishi "wisdom"
Amida "infinite light and life"	Kannon "compassion"
Yakushi "master of medicine"	Fugen "practicer of loving kindness"

The Buddha Dainichi is associated with the great sun. The sun has light and warmth. Light and warmth are one in compassion. The Buddha Amida is also the unity of wisdom and compassion. Yakushi is the master of medicine, who is also the personification of the virtue of compassion.

In the word *nembutsu*, *nen* means "to think, thinking on," and *butsu* means "Buddha." The *nembutsu* practice is the thinking that Bodhisattvas do, which in other words means "to remember the Buddha," "think of the Buddha." In this way, we remember that in this world there are precious virtues of wisdom and compassion, without which we can never grow as human beings. However, thanks to these virtues we can maintain and nurture our true humanity so that our existence can be something other than just animal instinct. The problem here is that as wisdom and compassion have neither form nor color, we cannot easily think of them. So, for this reason we personify them into forms of Buddhas and Bodhisattvas so that it is easier for us to think of these virtues in such ways.

Have you ever seen statues of Kannon? Do they not remind you of warmth and compassion? It is easier to associate, to think of the virtues of wisdom and compassion through concrete images. That is why all of these personalities were created. However, please do not forget that the original wisdom and compassion are not made or created by humankind, but their origin was spontaneous, as it were, just springing up.

For example, consider a family whose members are very happy and healthy. Suddenly one person falls ill and then all the others, however healthy they might be, are, in their minds, greatly concerned and not completely happy until that person has totally recovered. So, what do the other members do at that time? They naturally pray for an early recovery of the person. That prayer arises spontaneously. This is the expression of love and compassion, which is not created, not made, but arises spontaneously, without human design. Now what causes this to appear? A situation like an illness may be the cause for compassion. In Buddhism, it is taught that all things arise through the relationship of cause and condition. So, love appears through causes and conditions. We cannot speak of only one cause or one condition, but of many, many conditions, some of which may be conscious. One thing arises, one thing appears through many causes and conditions, which happens spontaneously.

How about wisdom? Do you think wisdom is created by us? I do not think so. When we say "Ah, I see!" or something like that, something about which we are enlightened appears. That experience is the opening of our minds to truth, to previously unknown truth. For the first time we become conscious of something. This is the working of wisdom, which is a function of our minds and awakens us to truth. This is true wisdom.

So, wisdom and love are not created by us but appear spontaneously and therefore are free from human design. Wisdom and compassion are very strange as they have no special color, or form and their appearance is not limited to one occasion but recur many, many times to human beings. How many times, you might ask? Endless, countless, infinite times they occur.

This word infinity is called, in Sanskrit, *amita*. *A* means "no," and *mita* means "limited." *Amita* means "infinite," "infinity," "not measurable." What of love and wisdom then? They are limitless. This is the origin of the Buddha Amida, who is not the historical Buddha, but the personification of infinite love, compassion and wisdom, whose essence is not made by us, but spontaneously arises without our thinking, whenever right conditions exist. Enlightenment encourages us like this. Love and wisdom, which function constantly through prayers, through our association with friends, teachers, relatives, where we receive an infinite amount of love and wisdom, nurture us. Please remember once again, these are not imagined or created by us as they are beyond our thinking, imagining or effort to produce.

In Japan, there was a well known Catholic writer, Shusaku Endo, who remarked some years ago that Christians listen to the teachings of Jesus who existed historically, whereas there is a type of Buddhism in Japan, which is based on the personality of Buddha Amida. This Buddha is not a historical figure, merely a product of human imagination. Endo asks how one can believe in something which is a product of human imagination. When I heard this question, I was quite amused in some respects because if he mentions Jesus Christ, a historical person, then I think Sakyamuni should be used as a comparison and not Amida. If he wishes to talk about Amida, then God could well be equated.

Concerning his statement about Amida Buddha being a product of human imagination. Is it really so? As I noted just now, the essence of Amida is infinite compassion and wisdom which are not the products of our imagination but of reality, which affects us every day.

For example, as I suggested earlier, a person who is seriously ill is encouraged by his friend's words of comfort containing love. Thanks to that love, that person endures the suffering. Students receive wisdom from teachers all the time. What is the evidence that this wisdom is received? If we look at the response, we can see this in such exclamations as "Ah, I see!" or "Now I realize!" Every time one says this, one has received wisdom which is unseen by one's physical eyes, though it is evident that one has received it. Likewise, how about love? Though it has no definite form or color, we can never doubt its existence. What then is the evidence of having received it? This is shown when we say "Thank you." Therefore, love expresses itself through activities, such as giving pleasure, comfort and joy to others and easing people's suffering. Though having no existence or material substance of its own, it is seen through its function. Wisdom is the same: no material substance, only having a working process. Wisdom enlightens people. Wisdom awakens people to the truth which they have hitherto not known, and its activity is precisely that--awakening people. The function of love and wisdom is very subtle. Love warms and comforts and acts to extricate beings from pain, give peace of mind, whereas wisdom awakens and enlightens us from the state of ignorance to that of awareness.

Let me stress again that the essence of Amida cannot be created by us as it is beyond our own efforts to do so. Yet, whenever conditions gather to produce love, it just appears and embraces people. Wisdom is the same. So we may say that the essence of Amida is prior to our efforts. Would you say--*a priori*? So, contrary to what Shosaku Endo said, Amida exists prior to our effort, free from human interference.

When you travel in Japan, sometimes you will see images of Dainichi (Skt.: Mahavairocana), an object of worship in the Buddhist Shingon school. The word *Dai* or *Mahā* means "great" and *nichi* "the sun." The sun has warmth and light. Warmth signifies love and light symbolizes wisdom. He is called *Mahā* because, unlike the sun in our experience, he can be seen by our spiritual eyes at all times. Amida is the central object of worship in the Pure Land tradition. Yakushi is the Buddha of medicine and is compared to a doctor who administers medicine to a sick patient. His image is enshrined in the main hall of Enryakuji on Mt. Hiei. In Mahayana Buddhism, other than the historical Sakyamuni Buddha, these Buddhas have appeared and remain objects of worship in various schools.

There are many such schools in Japanese Buddhism. In some, the object of meditation or worship is not only the Buddha but also Dharma--the teaching, the truth. We are now having these lectures as guests at the facilities of the Rissho Kosei-kai. In this school, the object of devotion is the truth contained in the *Lotus Sūtra* and hence it is recited here. In the case of *nembutsu*, the *namu amida butsu* is recited. It is reduced to *nāmādā*, or even to *nā*, which can be recited even faster and can be carried out by anyone at any time, even by children. Some years ago, I visited Mt. Athos in Greece, where a type of prayer called the "Jesus Prayer" is practiced and is recited in Greek, *kyrie eleison*, "Oh Lord, have mercy." If it is recited quickly enough it becomes *kleisō*. Anyone can recite this and when repeated many times, it becomes identified with breathing. When this is done, the prayer becomes natural and hence breathing and prayer are identical. When you reach this state you are not conscious of saying it. This is like the *nembutsu* in the Japanese Pure Land tradition. Its recitation is identified in the consciousness of believers as not something special. It is completely identical with breathing. Ordinarily, in daily life, breathing itself is recitation of the *nembutsu*, though on ceremonial occasions, it is done formally.

For example, devotees listen to the teaching, reciting the *nembutsu*, in their hearts, not necessarily saying it out loud, merely reciting it with their breathing, repeating it many times. When we listen to teachings for the first time, we are struck and moved, though after a time, we forget what we have heard. However, unexpectedly, if one recites the *nembutsu* casually, the teaching is recalled. It appears freshly in our minds, and this teaches us anew. This experience is repeated again and again, with equal freshness. It is not weakened after a while, but remains the same, vivid experience. How many times can we recollect it? Each time, it strikes us the same as if for the first time. So, in this case, the *nembutsu* serves as a tool for remembering past experiences. It has the same power as the first time. The power can be recalled. On such occasions the *nembutsu* has much significance. This function can be compared beneficially with the Jesus Prayer.

Such significance I see in the practice of the *nembutsu*. Do you know the Japanese instrument for calculating--the abacus? When you use it, you have first of all, to reduce all the beads to zero, otherwise you cannot start. In the same way, our consciousness is ordinarily disturbed by what we see, by what we hear. When we must think seriously of something, our minds must be calm and quiet, else we cannot understand the meaning of even one sentence. For us, Pure Land Buddhists, those who recite the *nembutsu*, *mantra* or *dhāraṇīs*, recitation serves to clear our minds, and hence reduces all our various thoughts to zero. It makes way for us to open up, to start something anew, dispelling all our miscellaneous thoughts and emptying our minds. This kind of function helps to calm and prepare our minds for the state of study. Therefore *nembutsu* is often called *nembutsu samādhi*. In a *samādhi*, the mind is completely pure and still. When it attains such a state, we are able to see all things as they really are, unfettered by preoccupation or preconceptions. Reality is clear. Objects appear as they truly are.

If our minds are disturbed, all things appear only partially, revealing themselves incompletely. The act of really seeing can be experienced only when our minds are in the state of *samādhi*. The *nembutsu* practice makes it possible for us to get to this point and therefore is a tool which brings our mind to this state easily.

Also, in the state of *samādhi*, wisdom functions. What do we usually do when we try to remember something? I think most of us shut our eyes. Why? In order to avoid stimuli from outside. *Nembutsu* has such a function because by reciting it, it is possible for us to get to this state easily, where transcendent wisdom functions very quickly. One can obtain many unexpected insights when the mind is in such a state.

Wisdom and *samādhi* are inseparable. Only when the mind is in the state of *samādhi*, wisdom appears as from nowhere and not at any other time. So, if one wants to receive transcendent wisdom, the mind should be calm. This is the teaching of Zen Buddhism. Some years ago, a well known Soto Zen master, Kodo Sawaki Roshi, said a person sitting in meditation is not an ordinary human, he is a Buddha, a Buddha doing a Buddha's work. So, as you see *samādhi* and wisdom are inseparable. In Zen, it is taught that if you want to attain wisdom, do not try to get hold of it, just cast away your desire to grasp, just sit in meditation. Place your mind in *samādhi*. Without seeking with the mind, wisdom comes to you. It is the same with the recitation of *nembutsu*.

What might be these insights? Inspiration, unexpected thoughts, enlightened thoughts come to you in the state of *samādhi*. As I have stated before, recitation of the *nembutsu* provides this state. I should like to explain enlightening insight in terms of unhappiness and happiness. For example, when one falls into a very unhappy state and just rejects it, the unhappy condition will not change much even though one has rejected it. However, if you accept it for what it really is, then it may give you unexpected insights leading to happiness. For example, recently at a hospital, a doctor told me that I was suffering from glaucoma in both eyes. I was not conscious of it until I was told about it. If I might express my feelings with only a little exaggeration, every morning I feel that I am thankful for my present state because I have been given eyesight for this day. So, since I was told that I had glaucoma, every day I have renewed my joy that I can see. In this respect, insight means the unity of unhappiness and happiness.

There is a story of a lady living at the time of Gautama, who lost her only child and as she was suffering very much, she went to see the Buddha, who said to her, "I will teach you how to overcome your sorrow. Go around this village and bring back a poppy seed from a family where no one has died." All day long she went around but could not find a family who had not experienced the death of someone. Towards the evening, on her way back to the Buddha, her mind became very calm and clear and her grief disappeared. She had realized that she was not alone in suffering such loss, although the fact that she had lost her only child remained unchanged. Such awareness brought a new spiritual point of view to her, an unexpected insight.

When Shinran was staying in an area north of Tokyo, a mountain ascetic (*yamabushi*) called Bennen, who had many followers, was jealous and wanted to kill him. One day he discovered Shinran was staying nearby and so went to him shouting, demanding to see him. Shinran appeared. Looking at his calm countenance, Bennen was struck with surprise and he became Shinran's disciple. At that moment, Shinran did not try to convert him, it was Bennen who changed. So, that experience was something like the transforming experience of Saul, recorded in the New Testament.

What brought about such transformation? Where Christians call it the Holy Spirit, Buddhists call it the Other Power. The fact remains that the person undergoes a complete transformation and it remains so until death. Saul hated Jesus at first, but underwent a transformation and became Jesus' disciple. Likewise, Bennen hated Shinran but yet, he became his disciple. He was then named Myōhōbō by Shinran and became a noteworthy Buddhist personality. This changed personality remained so until his death.

In both cases, these two people may be called men of faith. Usually, we think that *we* have faith, but I think it is faith that holds us. *We do not hold faith, faith holds us.* It is bigger than us. We are sustained by faith. The insights bring us a change in values, which in turn comes from insights derived from wisdom.

When the persimmon fruit is not ripe, it is very bitter. Yet if one puts it in the sun, it becomes very sweet. In this case, the bitterness is compared to evil passions.

In the early formulations of the Buddhist tradition, evil passions are regarded as something to be discarded, whereas in Mahayana Buddhism all of these harmful qualities came to be valued as something essential for attaining enlightenment. So, the former is a form of Buddhism which renounces and the Mahayana can be characterized as the form which transforms, not regarding evil defilements (Skt.: *kleṣa*, Pali: *kilesa*) as something to be rejected. They are precious, valuable building materials. With Pure Land Buddhists, the practice of *nembutsu* automatically brings a transformation of *kleśas*. Supposing you have a baby crying for a toy and you try to stop the crying, that baby will still continue. Therefore, instead of trying to persuade the baby to stop, if we can make some interesting sounds, this will work. The baby's seeking hand will stop searching. I think the nembutsu is like this, making some interesting sounds. If we try consciously to destroy the evil defilements (Skt.: *kleśas*), they will grow bigger, but if we stop fighting against them by relying on some useful device, then they will cease. The *nembutsu* practice functions in this way.

In the history of Buddhism, many devices for controlling the *kleśas* have been offered: such as in Zen Buddhism, Tantric Buddhism, Pure Land Buddhism. The practice of *nembutsu* is just one of them, functioning just like that sound for the baby. We do not try to destroy the desire, or *kleśa*, it disappears of its own accord. It is the way of *naturalness*; therefore it is the way of Other Power.

There is a distinction between self-power and Other Power. In Pure Land Buddhism, Amida Buddha's power is called Other Power. Though I think we are made of self-power, the Other Power is something that sustains this self-power. From the beginning there was no self-power distinct from Other Power. The entirety of self-power is Other Power. This is my conviction. From the beginning, there is nothing called self-power. It is called so because of the Other Power behind it, sustaining it. Only Other Power exists.

Though we tend to call our own ability as "my own," the entirety of my own power is given to me. We are not moving our heart by ourselves, something beyond us is making this function. So I feel that there is no-self power, only Other Power. Whatever we perform is due to the Other Power. So it is with *nembutsu*.

XII
Shinran's View of True Religion--
From Amida Worship to the True and Real Religion
Nobuo Nomura

Turning our attention to the religious quest of Shinran, Professor Nobuo Nomura introduces us to other key notions in the teaching of the True Pure Land Sect. Introducing the
three major texts of this important Buddhist sect, and letting us see the importance of the
great vows and of their interrelationship, Professor Nomura, in a comparativist context,
provides an example of how a tradition hands down provisional means that provide a
basic orientation in one's existential setting and the way responses to and through those
means by persons of faith and discipline, while perhaps personally beneficial, are, nevertheless, not in themselves salvific. Human agency does not bring with it salvation, nor do
provisional means initiated by men and women. In the final analysis, salvation is initiated afresh solely by "Other Power," by Amida Buddha.

In thinking about the foundation of Jodo-Shinshu, I want to begin by considering, in some detail, the first few pages of an article written by Keiji Nishitani, who saw
himself as transferring Eastern culture to the Western world by utilizing Western philosophical terminology. This article, entitled "What is Religion," translated into English by
Jan Van Bragt, is well known to American scholars in religious studies; some say the
translation is much better than the original. Excerpts from this article might help us to
understand what the structure of religion is before we move to Shinran's basic idea of
religion. This article is very convenient in helping us to understand Shinran's thought.
Nishitani asks,

> "What is religion?" we ask ourselves, or, looking at it the other way around, "What is the
> purpose of religion for us? Why do we need it?" Though the question about the need for
> religion may be a familiar one, it already contains a problem. In one sense, for the person
> who poses the question, religion does not seem to be something he needs. The fact that
> he asks the question at all amounts to an admission that religion has not yet become a
> necessity for him. In another sense, however, it is surely in the nature of religion to be
> necessary for just such a person. Wherever questioning individuals like this are to be
> found, the need for religion is there as well. In short, the relationship we have to religion
> is a contradictory one: those for whom religion is *not* a necessity are, for that reason, the
> very ones for whom religion *is* a necessity. There is no other thing of which the same can
> be said.[57]

The issue of religion always contains a paradoxical or contradictory problem. He says
there is no other thing in our experience about which this can be said. He raises two
aspects of human activity: one is the so-called human cultural activity, the other is food.

Nishitani goes on,

> When asked, "Why do we need learning and the arts?" we might try to explain in reply that such things are necessary for the advancement of mankind, for human happiness, for the cultivation of the individual, and so forth. Yet even if we can say why we need such things, this does not imply that we cannot get along without them. Somehow life would still go on. Learning and the arts may be indispensable to living well, but they are not indispensable to living. In that sense, they can be considered a kind of luxury.
>
> Food, on the other hand, is essential to life. Nobody would turn to somebody else and ask him why he eats. Well, maybe an angel or some other celestial being who has no need to eat might ask such questions, but men do not. Religion, to judge from current conditions in which many people are in fact getting along without it, is clearly not the kind of necessity that food is. Yet this does not mean that it is merely something we need to live *well*. Religion has to do with life itself. Whether the life we are living will end up in extinction or in the attainment of eternal life is a matter of the utmost importance for life itself.[58]

The final sentence here, as Nishitani deals with it later, signifies that our attitude toward life and death is the key issue that sets our conceptual understanding of our daily life based upon our ignorance apart from the realization of the true and real. He continues,

> Herein lies the distinctive feature of religion that sets it apart of the mere life of "nature" and from culture . . . . Religion must not be considered from the viewpoint of its *utility* any more than life should.[59]

In our ordinary mode of being, people think that individuals are at the center looking out onto the world for the sake of utility or efficacy which might be drawn out of things and matters outside the individuals:

external world <----- (eye) ▶ I

In religion, the question must be asked, for what purpose do I exist; one looks upon the "I".

(eye) ◀ -----> I

In our ordinary mode of being, the "*I*" sees everything outside self. "*I*" forgets what "*I*" is, or what being is. There is a premise that one exists and one's existence is taken for granted. Nishitani raises two points. He begins,

Two points should be noted from what has just been said. First, religion is at all times the individual affair of each individual. This sets it apart from things like culture, which, while related to the individual, do not need to concern each individual. Accordingly, we cannot understand what religion is from the outside. The religious quest alone is the key to understanding it; there is no other way. This is the most important point to be made regarding the essence of religion.[60]

When you want to attain the correct answer of what religion is, you cannot get the correct answer. When you keep yourself in the safety zone and ask what religion is, you cannot get the correct answer. If you move one step outside your safety zone and ask existentially what religion is for yourself, then you can get the answer to the question.

Nishitani raises the second point:

from the standpoint of the essence of religion, it is a mistake to ask "What is the purpose of religion for us?" and one that clearly betrays an attitude of trying to understand religion apart from the religious quest. It is a question that must be broken through by another question coming from within the person who asks it. There is no other road that can lead to an understanding of what religion is and what purpose it serves. The counter question that achieves this breakthrough is one that asks, "For what purpose do I myself exist?" Of everything else we can ask its purpose for us, but not of religion.[61]

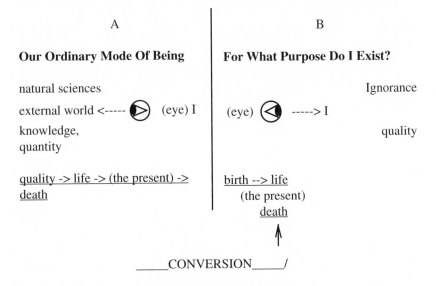

The positions are *A* and *B*. In *A*, people think that "I exist" as an unexamined premise, and that everything else is what has a meaning for *I*. For example, natural science is where people are trying to find out a kind of first principle, asking for the utility of the principle. In technology, people try to take advantage of this and make a device, like a computer or a car, for convenience. In position *B*, people must ask the question, for what purpose do I exist? This is a very crucial point.

In position *A,* life, of course, is very important. In *B,* the question of ignorance and the matter of quality are very important. Nishitani writes, further,

> But religion upsets the posture from which we think of ourselves as *telos* and center of all things. Instead, religion poses as a starting point the question: "For what purpose do I exist?"
>
> We become aware of religion as a need, as a must for life, only at the level of life at which everything else loses its necessity and its utility. Why do we exist at all? Is not our very existence and human life ultimately meaningless? Or, if there is a meaning or significance to it all, where do we find it? When we come to doubt the meaning of our existence in this way, when we have become a question to ourselves, the religious quest awakens within us. These questions and the quest they give rise to show up when the mode of looking at and thinking about everything in terms of how it relates to *us* is broken through, where the mode of living that puts us at the center of everything is overturned. [62]

If you come to ask, "For what purpose do I exist?" you overturn position *A* into position *B.*

Nishitani observes,

> In fact, that abyss is always just underfoot. In the case of death, we do not face something that awaits us in some distant future, but something that we bring into the world with us at the moment we are born. [63]

Position *A* holds that death and life are separate, and that death will come to us in the future, we are headed towards death. Position *B* holds that life and death are one thing, something we face at the same time every day:

> Our life runs up against death at all times. Our life stands poised at the brink of the abyss of nihility to which it may turn at any moment. Our existence is an existence at one with nonexistence, swinging back and forth over nihility, ceaselessly passing away and ceaselessly regaining its existence. This is what is called the "incessant becoming" of existence. [64]

This is a very Buddhist way of thinking. In our ordinary mode of being we are to think that life continues up to death, but I think this would be merely an expectation or an illusion. Reality shows us that life and death are opposite sides of one sheet of paper. Life and death are different and yet they are one.

At this point, Nishitani introduces the term, "conversion," which means "to transform."

In the forward progress of everyday life, the ground beneath our feet always falls behind as we move steadily ahead; we overlook it. Taking a step back to shed light on what is underfoot of the self--"stepping back to come to the self," as another ancient Zen phrase has it--marks a conversion in life itself. This fundamental conversion in life is occasioned by the opening up of the horizon of nihility at the ground of life. It is nothing less than a conversion from the self-centered (or man-center) mode of being, which always asks what use things have for us (or for man), to an attitude that asks for what *purpose* we ourselves (or man) exist. Only when we stand at this turning point does the question, "What is religion?" really become our own.[65]

Here Nishitani emphasizes transforming, or converting. This term does not simply mean moving from A to B. Once you forsake position A, then you can get a new one (B), but this knowledge or experiences you have gained in your life will be given a new meaning when you shed light on them: this refers to "returning" from B to A. This is why Nishitani uses the word conversion and not "move". It must be transforming from A to B. Then knowledge and experiences will be given a new life in a new way.

Shinran, as we have seen, first studied Buddhism at Mt. Hiei, the stronghold of the Tendai school. He then came down and studied in Honen's school. Before he came to Honen, he understood religion as so-called Amida worship, which followed position A. In so-called Amida worship, people abhorred this world and expected to be born in the Pure Land in the future. Shinran did not think this way. He converted to B as the real religion. But position A still remained in him as the negative medium. Shinran, having become transformed into B, the so-called Amida worship (position A) now takes on new life, and is seen to be the working of Amida's skill in means (Skt. *upāya*). We might discern this movement by considering Shinran's view of the three Pure Land *sūtras*.

There are three *sūtras* which are very important for Shinran's soteriology, as well as Jodo Shinshu and the Pure Land Tradition in general. One is the *Larger Sūtra*, the second is the *Contemplation Sūtra*, and the third is the *Smaller Sūtra*, which is called the *Amida Sūtra*.

(1) The *Larger Sūtra* begins with the reason for and situation in which Sakyamuni Buddha expounded the *sūtra*. Right after this introductory part, the main body of the text describes, first of all, a process through which the protagonist of this mythical story becomes a Buddha and, at the same time, establishes his own Buddha land. Secondly, another process is described in which sentient beings are born in the Pure Land. In the ending, Sakyamuni states, in effect, that all people should listen to this teaching and that he would keep this *sūtra* alive even when many other teachings disappear from this world.

What is important in this *sūtra* is the main body of the text, especially the first part of it: a protagonist, who met and listened to Lokesvararaja Buddha (the last of 53 previous Buddhas), appears before a king, in the secular world, abdicates royalty, and becomes a *śramaṇa*, or practicer, and calls himself Dharmakara. He resolves to save all sentient beings from suffering and asks Lokesvararaja Buddha to show him beautiful scenery in various Buddha lands. He plans to build an ideal land based upon the scenery in many Buddha lands that he has seen, in order to enable people in suffering to be born there. He keeps thinking on and considering it for a very long time, and finally establishes forty-eight vows. In order to fulfill the vows he sets out to perform practices for eons. Finally he builds his own Pure Land far beyond the west from our world and becomes a Buddha. Dharmakara calls himself Amida Buddha, and his land is called Sukhavati or "Utmost Bliss," although the Pure Land traditions, both in China and Japan, have been often referring to it as "the Pure Land."

(2) The *Contemplation Sūtra* has a much more dramatic introductory part than the other two. When Sakyamuni was preaching on a mountain (Grdhrakuta), a tragedy was going on in Rajagrha, the capital of the kingdom Magadha. A prince of the kingdom, called Ajatasatru, strongly influenced by Devadatta, a cousin of Sakyamuni, raised a *coup d'état* and confined his father to prison, expecting him to die of starvation. Finding out his mother Vaidehi was giving him food, the prince imprisoned her as well.

Vaidehi was stricken with grief and sorrow. Facing Mt. Grdhrakuta from afar, she bowed her head to the Buddha and prayed for him to preach Dharma to relieve her misery. When she was about to raise her head she found Sakyamuni sitting on a lotus flower in front of her, together with his disciples and heavenly beings. Then she asked the Buddha to teach in detail about a place for her to be born where there were neither sorrows nor afflictions. The Buddha, on hearing this, sent forth a light from between his eyebrows. Therein appeared all the pure and exquisite lands of the Buddhas in the universe. She chose from among many the land of Utmost Bliss, the land of Amida Buddha, and entreated him to describe how to get there.

In the main body of the *sūtra*, in this context, Sakyamuni responds to Vaidehi's request, and illustrates the method to be born in the Pure Land. First, he describes the method called meditative practices, in which practicers concentrate their mind and contemplate on various aspects of the Pure Land, Amida Buddha, and Amida's attendants. Secondly, Sakyamuni describes non-meditative methods in which practicers should perform various good deeds including worldly moral acts. In addition, he states that especially those in the lowest ranks of the lowest grade should say the name of Amida and that, in consequence, Amida will come to welcome them all when they are about to die.

In the epilogue, in contrast to the main body of the text, emphasis is put solely on saying the name of Amida, and one who says the name is compared to the most excellent lotus (*puṇḍarīka*) among men and women.

(3) The *Smaller Sūtra*, the most popular one, prevails in the *nembutsu* community, and is often chanted in daily services. This *sūtra*, after the description of the place of, and audience for, Sakyamuni's exposition, first illustrates what the Pure Land is like and what the sacred beings in the Pure Land are like. Secondly, it clarifies how one is to be born there: people should hear what is preached about Amida and keep the name of the Buddha in their minds for even one through seven days and nights. When they come to

die, the *sūtra* affirms, Amida with the sacred attendants will appear before them, and they will depart this life with their minds undisturbed. Thirdly, the *sūtra* enumerates all Buddhas in the six directions and states that they praise Sakyamuni and that they confirm that what he expounds is true.

In the epilogue, Sakyamuni says that all Buddhas in other lands praise his exposition of this teaching which is difficult for ordinary people in this defiled and corrupted world to accept. On hearing this, the audience, including Sariputra, a chief disciple, becomes joyful in mind and leaves.

These are outlines of the three *sūtras*. The central *sūtra* is the first one, the *Larger Sūtra*. The second one is the *Contemplation Sūtra*, which explains the methods to be born in the Pure Land. The *Smaller Sūtra*, the *Amida Sūtra*, explains what the Pure Land is like and what the sacred beings there are like.

Shinran's Insight into the Three Pure Land Sūtras

When we turn to Shinran's *magnum opus, Kyogyoshinsho*, we can clearly see how he accepts the three *sūtras*. He refers to a twofold structure in the three *sūtras* by speaking of "explicit and implicit teachings." As far as the *Larger Sūtra* is concerned, however, he sees it as having the only explicit teaching and says, "To reveal the true teaching; It is the *Larger Sūtra* of Immeasurable Life."[66] He takes it as the central *sūtra* of the three. Moreover, Shinran regards the forty-eight vows as the crucial and most important part of the *Larger Sūtra* . He continues:

> The central purport of this sutra is that Amida, by establishing his incomparable Vows, has opened wide the dharma-storehouse, and full of compassion for small, foolish beings, he selects and bestows his treasure of virtues . . . . Thus, to teach the Tathagata's Primal Vow is the true intent of the *sūtra*....[67]

Of the forty-eight vows, the eighteenth vow is called Primal Vow, and it is central because it represents the true intent of Dharmakara Bodhisattva. Shinran, as well as many other Pure Land thinkers, considers the forty-eight vows to be the one and only vow, the eighteenth vow. To the contrary, the *Contemplation Sūtra* and the *Smaller Sūtra* he takes as having the double structure. He articulates with this regard to the *Contemplation Sūtra*:

> When I consider the *Sutra of Contemplation on the Buddha of Immeasurable Life*, taking into account the interpretation of the commentator [Shan-tao], I find there is an explicit meaning and an implicit, hidden, inner meaning.[68]

He continues:

"Explicit" refers to presenting the meditative and non-meditative good acts and setting forth the three levels of practicers and the three minds . . . .[69]

The *Contemplation Sūtra* divides humans into three levels, and each level consists of three ranks according to their capacity to perform religious practices. They aspire to be born in the Pure Land having as condition performing either meditative or non-meditative practices according to their levels and grades. Shinran dwells continuously on the "implicit" meaning of the *sūtra*.

"Implicit" refers to disclosing the Tathagata's universal Vow and revealing the mind that is single, to which [practicers of the three minds] are led through [Amida's] benefiting others. Through the opportunity brought about by the grave evil acts of Devadatta and Ajatasatru, Sakyamuni, with a smile, disclosed his inner intent. Through the condition brought about by the right intention in Vaidehi's selection, Amida's Primal Vow of Great Compassion was clarified. This is the hidden, implicit meaning of the sutra.[70]

Shinran thus, on the one hand, understands that the *Contemplation Sūtra* in its explicit meaning has revealed the meditative and non-meditative practices as the condition for practicers to be born in the Pure Land. The explicit meaning has the significance of demonstrating the provisional means or salvific technique. He, on the other hand, considers it to stand on the same position as the *Larger Sūtra*, the true and the real teaching, especially when he sees its epilogue, where saying the name of Amida, i.e., the *nembutsu*, is emphasized.

In the same vein, the *Smaller Sūtra* is understood to have a double structure. Shinran states,

By taking the *Contemplation Sūtra* as a model, we know that the [*Smaller*] *Sūtra* also possesses an explicit meaning and an implicit, hidden, inner meaning.
Concerning its "explicit" meaning...the sutra teaches "[Saying the Name] is the act of many roots of good, many virtues, and many merits," and a commentary states, "The nine grades of beings should all direct [the merit of the *nembutsu*] and attain the stage of non-retrogression." . . . This is the explicit meaning of the sutra: it is the provisional means within the "true" gate.[71]

This explicit meaning of the *sūtra*, according to Shinran, is that the *nembutsu* here is a self-striving act in order to get merit to attain the stage of non-retrogression. Hence Shinran regards it as a provisional means to lead practicers to the true and real teaching. The reason for this can be seen in the following passage. He continues:

In its implicit meaning, the sutra discloses the true and real dharma that is difficult to accept. It reveals the inconceivable ocean of the Vow, seeking to bring beings to take refuge in the ocean of unhindered great Shinjin . . . . The commentary states: "Solely through the greatness of Amida's universal Vow, Foolish beings, when they become mindful of it, are immediately brought to attain birth."[72]

This passage is based upon the epilogue of the *sūtra* where Sakyamuni teaches that this *sūtra* is "difficult to accept." The birth in the Pure Land can be attained solely by entrusting oneself to Amida's Universal Vow, but foolish beings are entangled with their own self-striving efforts to achieve it, and they cannot throw them away. The *sūtra*, therefore, states that it is difficult to accept the true and the real meaning of this *sūtra*.

Thus far we have seen the double structure of the *Contemplation Sūtra* and the *Smaller Sūtra*. We now examine how Shinran relates the two to the *Larger Sūtra*. In his *Kyōgyōshinshō*, Shinran writes about the true and real in the first five volumes, and about the provisional means in the sixth, the last volume. It is in the last volume that he discusses the *Contemplation Sūtra* and the *Smaller Sūtra*. In so doing, he applies the nineteenth and the twentieth vows to them respectively.

The Nineteenth Vow:

If, when I attain Buddhahood, the sentient beings of the ten quarters--awakening the mind of enlightenment and performing meritorious acts--aspire with sincere mind and desire to be born in my land, and I do not, surrounded by a host of sages, appear before them at the moment of death, may I not attain the supreme enlightenment.[73]

The Twentieth Vow:

If, when I attain Buddhahood, the sentient beings of the ten quarters who, on hearing my Name, place their thoughts on my land, cultivate the root of all virtues (i.e., endeavor in the nembutsu), and direct their merits with sincere mind desiring to be born in my land, should not ultimately attain it, may I not attain the supreme enlightenment.[74]

In other words, he thinks that the two *sūtra*s clarify the contents of the nineteenth and twentieth vows in the *Larger Sūtra*. Thus we come to be aware that the discussion on how Shinran accepts the three Pure Land *Sūtra*s may turn into one on the relationship between the religious stances represented by the three vows: the nineteenth, twentieth, and eighteenth vows. He writes about his religious experiences by revealing the significance of the three religious attitudes of the Vows:

Thus I, Gotoku Shinran, disciple of Sakyamuni, through reverently accepting the exposition of [Vasubandhu], author of the *Treatise*, and depending on the guidance of Master Shan-tao, departed everlastingly from the temporary gate of the myriad practices and various good acts and left forever the birth attained beneath the twin sala trees. Turning about, I entered the "true" gate of the root of good and the root of virtue, and wholeheartedly awakened the mind leading to the birth that is non-comprehensible. [The inverted commas around *true* are mine because in this case it does not mean the really true or the true and real.][75]

It is quite plausible for one to turn from performing the myriad practices and the various good acts, that is, the stance of the nineteenth vow, into the "true" gate of the twentieth vow where one performs the single good act of saying the name of Amida, i.e., the *nembutsu*, regarded as one's means by virtue of which one aspires to be born in the Pure Land depending upon one's self-striving or self-power.

Shinran's spiritual journey, however, does not stop in the twentieth vow--it moves on:

> Nevertheless, I have now decisively departed from the "true" gate of provisional means and, [my self-power] overturned, have entered the ocean of the selected Vow. Having swiftly become free of the mind leading to the birth that is non-comprehensible, I am assured of attaining the birth that is inconceivable. How truly profound in intent is the Vow that beings ultimately attain birth![76]

The Vow that beings ultimately attain birth, in the last part of this passage, is the other appellation of the twentieth vow. Shinran says, here standing on the eighteenth vow, that he has entered the ocean of the selected vow through the twentieth vow, the "true" gate of provisional means. But we should not take the provisional means as his own means to get to the true and real of the eighteenth vow. Rather, this passage alludes to the provisional means for Amida Buddha to let people move on to the true and real. We should note that the self-power is not the necessary step placed right before entering the eighteenth vow.

Here lies the crucial significance Shinran singles out about utterance of the *nembutsu*, because the *nembutsu*, based upon the self-power, by itself, will not become the true and the real *nembutsu* based upon the Other Power, and, at the same time, the *nembutsu* based upon the Other Power presupposes the provisional *nembutsu* of self-power.

This leads us to further discussion on the issue between the provisional means and the truth. In order to make the discussion more general, first we look at the position taken by Mircea Eliade, and then move to Shinran and Paul Tillich.

The Profundity of Provisional Means

The important function of religious symbolism, according to Eliade, is its capacity to express paradoxical situations or certain structures of ultimate reality. This aspect is closely related to the existential value of religious symbolism. A type of symbolism, like that of the Symplegades or clashing cliffs, well represents the paradoxical passage from one mode of being to another, from a profane to a sacred mode of existence.

In the same vein, we must note that symbols often have a capacity of expressing the contradictory aspects of ultimate reality, that is, the "*coincidentia oppositorum*" in the nature of God, which shows itself simultaneously "actual and potential." An important point concerning the "*coincidentia oppositorum*," for Eliade, is that although it has been used in a systematic fashion since the beginning of philosophical speculation, the symbols that dimly revealed it were not the results of critical reflection, but of an existential tension.

Eliade discusses the *coincidentia oppositorum*--coming together of the sacred and the profane--in another way in terms of mediums through which the sacred manifests itself. He, instead of using the term *mediums*, coins the term *hierophany*, which may be some object close at hand or a symbol. The paradoxical coming together of the sacred and the profane is what every hierophany reveals. Whatever a hierophany may be, i.e., whether it is a stone, a tree, or an appearance of Yahweh, his emphasis is put on the point that the sacred "can be manifested at all," and that "it can become limited and relative."[77] That is to say, a hierophany plays the role of a medium for that which is paradoxical and beyond our understanding. Furthermore, this paradoxical situation within the hierophany as a religious symbol has a single direction: from the sacred to the profane. Thus, idolatry occurs when humans give a religious value to a material thing. In other words, idolatry is directed from the profane to the sacred. For humans, therefore, the paradox of the coming-together of the sacred and the profane has been expressed in concrete things, i.e., idols. All hierophanies, Eliade concludes, "are simply prefigurations of the miracle of incarnation, and every hierophany is an abortive attempt to reveal the mystery of the coming-together of God and man."[78]

Thus, the religious symbolism reveals that "There is a mode of being inaccessible to immediate experience, and one cannot attain to this mode of being except through renouncing the naive belief in the inexpungeability of matter."[79] According to Eliade, one can avoid idolatry through the paradoxical situation symbolized by hierophanies only when one realizes that one is capable of detaching oneself from immediate reality with one's imagination and intelligence.

Eliade, as a historian of religion, provides us with the existential structure of the divine revelation of the sacred through mediums or hierophanies. In addition, he suggests to us that humans can overcome idolatry by their imagination and intelligence. On this basis, he criticizes theologians claiming that "the theologian is doing no more than translate into more explicit formulae what is implied in the paradox of the idol (and of all other hierophanies too): the *sacred* manifesting itself in something profane."[80] But, in my opinion, this is not the case. Shinran, for example, clarifies the existential and paradoxical situation within revelatory mediums. What is more, he gives us a solution different from the complex structure of Eliade's logic.

Let us now look first at Shinran's argument on the relationship between a revelatory medium and an idol, then consider Paul Tillich's articulation of the soteriological structure in Jesus Christ.

Among many interpretations of the notion of provisional means (Skt.: *upāya*) in Buddhist history, Shinran's interpretation, as it appears in his *nembutsu* teachings, is similar to Eliade's hierophany, and it is most suggestive for understanding the relationship between ultimate reality and idols. *Nembutsu* utterance is a traditional Buddhist practice where devotees utter the name of Amida Buddha in order to escape from this defiled world and to be born in the Pure Land, the realm of Amida Buddha. This is what I call "so-called Amida worship," as in position *A* noted previously. But Shinran's characteristic interpretation of the religious symbol of *nembutsu* is to attribute it completely to Amida Buddha's practice. In other words, he insists that it is impossible for humans to be born in the Pure Land by means of uttering it. Humans are so perverted that they have no ability or possibility to be born there by themselves. Shinran, however, admits the important significance of human utterance of the *nembutsu* when he calls it the provisional means of salvific technique. Utterance of the *nembutsu* is the medium for Amida Buddha to reveal himself in order to save all sentient beings.

In addition, as we have seen in the discussion on the twentieth vow, Shinran analyzes the inextricable attachment to the *nembutsu* as the means to be born in the Pure Land. Human utterance of the *nembutsu*, without an exception, is human effort. Although it is futile for humans to consummate their volition for birth in the Pure Land by the *nembutsu* as their own means, they cannot but keep uttering it. Thus, the *nembutsu* utterance turns into an end in itself. When the *nembutsu* uttered by humans as the provisional means for Amida Buddha is taken as a divine end, we call the *nembutsu* utterance "idolatry."

Here it cannot be emphasized enough that, in Shinran's position, provisional means and idols are all one and the same in the religious symbol of the *nembutsu*. It is impossible for humans to discern whether the very sound, *Namo-amida-butsu*, "I take refuge in Amida Buddha," uttered by humans, is a provisional means or an idol. That is to say, it objectively is neutral for a third party. However, to those uttering the *nembutsu*, it is always an idol. Yet, the *nembutsu*, at the same time, is a salvific technique for Amida. In actuality, Amida Buddha reveals himself to humans through idols as provisional means. It is impossible, however, for humans to transform their idols into the provisional means. Only Amida Buddha can make idols as revelatory mediums. In this sense, humans can make idols come close to the revelatory mediums endlessly, but idols cannot reach them.

The revelation of the truth is necessarily mediated. It is quite possible, in my opinion, that idols cannot be the truth but that they can be absorbed by the revelatory mediums. The reason for this is that the truth, from the Mahayana perspective, presupposes something finite through which the truth reveals itself. Idols and the mediums are identical in that both of them are in the finite order. However, we must pay careful attention to the fact that the mediums, which can be either idols or provisional means, on the contrary, do not necessarily presuppose the truth. It is interesting to see in Tillich a similar structure of revelatory mediums and idols in this sense.

> Every revelation is mediated by one or several of the mediums of revelation. None of these mediums possesses revelatory power in itself; but under the condition of [human] existence these mediums claim to have it. This claim makes them idols.[81]

What Tillich calls mediums refers to the locus of revelation, that is, provisional means, and the mediums become idols when they are elevated to "the dignity of the revelation itself."[82] The similarity between Shinran and Tillich lies in that both of them deal with idols always along with revelatory mediums or provisional means, not with God or Amida. Eliade also says that "idolatry and its condemnation are . . . attitudes that come quite naturally to a mind faced with the phenomenon of the hierophany."[83]

Although Tillich presents the idea of idols in relation to mediums of revelation in general, he discusses Jesus the Christ as the final revelation: "the decisive, fulfilling, unsurpassable revelation."[84] Let us see, next, how Tillich distinguishes Jesus as the Christ from idols.

According to Tillich, every revelation is conditioned by the mediums in and through which it appears, but the mediums, as they are, cannot be holy unless they negate themselves in pointing to the divine. In the same vein, for Jesus of Nazareth to be the bearer of the final revelation, he must have the power to negate himself without losing himself. For Tillich the distinction between Jesus Christ and the idols is consummated through the death of Jesus on the cross as the negation of his own finite condition. In other words, since his disciples tried to make him an object of idolatry,[85] Jesus of Nazareth became the Christ by conquering his finitude on the cross. But there is a pitfall for Tillich because Jesus Christ who was himself crucified two thousand years ago may become a new idol for Tillich himself.

We come to know that Jesus Christ and the *nembutsu* are very similar to each other in that they can both function as provisional means and idols. Unlike Jesus Christ, however, the *nembutsu* which is not an item of historical existence, like Jesus, cannot negate itself. But this task of negation in pointing to the divine or ultimate reality must be achieved in the *nembutsu* as well in some way. As we have seen, the *nembutsu* is always an idol for humans insofar as they are attached to it as the means for birth in the Pure Land. This attachment is rooted in the human wish to be born there. In Shinran, what those who utter the *nembutsu* need to do, in order to eliminate their volition to be born there, is to hear in the *nembutsu* Amida Buddha summoning them to come to the Pure Land. In so doing, they are to empty the "I" in the *nembutsu* utterance ("I take refuge in Amida Buddha"), only then the *nembutsu* becomes the provisional means of Amida exclusively.

The "negation," therefore, is being performed not by the *nembutsu* but by humans in striving to eliminate their self-centered volition aiming at their own interests. In the same way, for Jesus Christ who was crucified on the cross to be a real Christ for Tillich in the twentieth century, Jesus the Christ must be incessantly crucified in Tillich himself.

Conclusion

We come to know from our considerations that the tension between provisional means (Skt.: *upāya*) or hierophany, on the one hand, and idols, on the other, have three moments. (1) Provisional means or hierophany and idols are essentially one neutral thing symbolized by such things as the *nembutsu*, Jesus of Nazareth, and everything in the world. (2) Idols can approach provisional means or hierophany but they cannot reach it. Yet, a provisional means or hierophany is always an idol for humans. (3) Through negation idols are turned into provisional means or hierophany.

As a historian of religion, Eliade suggests to us that we should know there is a way to attain the mode of being inaccessible to immediate experience. That is to say, it is only "through renouncing the naive belief in the inexpungeability of matter." In other words, it is possible to pass through the idolatry to the sacred only when one realizes that one is capable of detaching oneself from immediate reality with one's imagination and intelligence. But, as we have seen, Shinran would deny Eliade's "methodology" because what Shinran means by volition and attachment is, in my opinion, strongly related to the calculation of humans based on their intelligence and reason. For Shinran, it is in the elimination of human calculation that humans become transcendent.

We have seen a couple of stances concerning religious symbols in relation to revelatory mediums and idols. Mediums, which are also called "hierophany" or "provisional means," are always in imminent danger of falling into idols because of person's self-centered volition aiming at their own interests. Humans, if they try to approach the truth in the direction from the profane, become idolatrous. In my opinion, this tendency is inextricable, as Eliade suggests, to avoid idolatry by human imagination or intelligence. It is only in the process of negation that idols are turned into the true and real revelatory mediums. Shinran and Tillich have a similar understanding of the relationship between revelatory mediums and idols. Thus, religious symbols such as the *nembutsu* and Jesus of Nazareth, which have the function of negation in themselves, give humans incessant self-reflection. In other words, religious symbols which contain inexpungeable antagonism towards idols give us the true existential tension between humans and symbols.

The religious stance explicitly described in the *Smaller Sūtra* might be so-called Amida worship (position *A*, which is characterized as self-centered), in which practicers abhor this world as defiled and corrupted, and they aspire for the ideal place of Amida's Pure Land as preferable to this world. In this belief, they make use of the *nembutsu* as their own means to get into the ideal realm of Amida. Shinran finds this position holding the significant role as the negative condition for realizing the true and real expressed in the eighteenth vow (position *B*), that is the true intent of the *Larger Sūtra*. In other words, the true salvation is consummated only by the absolute Other, Amida, and not by a person's self-centered, trivial and naive efforts.

Positions *A* and *B* are very similar to each other in their phenomena, but they are different, and yet they are not separated. Position *B* lies in the process of negating position *A*. So-called Amida worship must be negated as far as it is human-centered, but if it were not for this, the Pure Land tradition characterized by the *nembutsu* would disappear from this actual world. The true and real must not be considered to be set apart from this actual world. Position *B* sees *A* as a necessary mode of religion as a negative medium and then position *A* would be given a new meaning that devotees who are necessarily entangled with so-called Amida worship are always forced to reflect and criticize themselves by Other Power through the *nembutsu* they hear in this world.

XIII

The Dialectic of "*Shinjin*"
Michio Tokunaga

The subtle teachings of the Pure Land Buddhist heritage, and more particularly of the True Pure Land Sect (Jodo-Shinshu), are disclosed only after one moves beyond a kind of first blush level of interpretation, that takes terms as concepts and seeks for straight-forward referents, to a level of apprehending a dynamic interplay of profound religious symbols. There is a delicate dialectic in the matter of *shinjin*, the blessed event in the lives of Jodo-Shinshu men and women, a kind of hoped for spontaneity. One hopes for the arising of *shinjin*, strives for it, knowing all the while that *shinjin* arises with the absolute negating of one's self-power. Professor Michio Tokunaga leads us through some of the related intricate issues that hinge on one's fundamental knowledge of oneself, on the one hand, and the source of one's salvation, on the other.

Shin Buddhism is the largest Buddhist organization in Japan. First of all, one should note that the *shin* appearing in Shin Buddhism is very often misunderstood because there are three important words (or *kanji* characters) that sound alike but which have different meanings. Webster's Third New International Dictionary lists *shin* as:

> *shin*: Jap. lit., belief, faith: a major Japanese Buddhist sect growing out of Jodo that emphasizes salvation by faith alone, has a married clergy, and holds to the exclusive worship of Amida Buddha--called also Shin-shu[86]

The *shin* of Shin Buddhism is usually regarded as "faith" or "belief" because in Japanese this *shin* appears in the important term *shinjin*. *Shin* of Shin Buddhism has been taken to be the *shin* of *shinjin*, but this is quite wrong. *Shin* of Shin Buddhism is not *shin* of *shinjin*, which is, in English, very close to faith. There is another sense in which the term *shin* is confused, made more complicated, because people think that the *shin* of Shin Buddhism is the *shin* appearing in Shinran, the founder of Shin Buddhism. So the *shin* of Shin Buddhism appears neither in *shinjin* nor Shinran.

Shin in the case of Shin Buddhism means "true," which directly indicates the teaching revealed by Honen, who was Shinran's master of the Pure Land tradition of Buddhism. Shinran believed that Honen's presentation of the Pure Land teaching is most true among a diversity of teachings. The term "Shin Buddhism" (Jap.: *Shin-shū*), however, is not one created by Shinran, but was first used by a Chinese T'ang dynasty Pure Land master, Fa-chao (766-822) in a passage, "Attaining birth in the Pure Land through saying the *nembutsu* is the true purport of Buddhism." Using the term *Shin-shū*, Shinran clarified that the ultimate truth of the Pure Land tradition was represented by Honen's *nembutsu* teaching.

Rennyo, the eighth Abbot of Hongwanji, defines *shin* as "Other Pure Land schools admit various sundry practices [other than *nembutsu*], but our master rejected those sundry practices, because of which we can attain birth in the true Pure Land constructed by Amida. For this reason, *shin* was specifically added to the ordinary term 'Pure Land school'."[87]

First, I would like to say a few words locating Shin Buddhism in the long history of the Buddhist tradition. D. T. Suzuki, a well known Zen thinker who was instrumental in introducing Zen to the West, has said,

> The Japanese may not have offered very many original ideas to world thought or world culture, but in Shin we find a major contribution the Japanese can make to the outside world and all the other Buddhist schools.[88]
>
> Of all the development Mahayana Buddhism has achieved in the Far East, the most remarkable one is the Shin teaching of the Pure Land School. It is remarkable chiefly because geographically its birth place is Japan and historically it is the latest evolution of Pure Land Mahayana, and therefore the highest point it has reached.[89]

Although Suzuki was a Zen thinker and Zen writer, he was much interested, especially in his later years, in Shin Buddhism. His last work is a translation of Shinran's *magnum opus* called *Kyōgyōshinshō*, the most important book among the extant writings of Shinran. Unlike other Zen priests, Suzuki was a great sympathizer of Shin Buddhism. In this quotation from Suzuki's book, there are two important terms: "Mahayana Buddhism" and "Pure Land School". Both of them are necessary for understanding Shin Buddhism. Let us look briefly at these two important terms.

About three centuries after the death of Sakyamuni Buddha, there appeared a movement called Mahayana, a Sanskrit term meaning "Great Vehicle," which held that everybody was able to attain the same enlightenment that Sakyamuni did. While, at the same time, criticizing the teaching then regarded as orthodox and traditional, the Mahayanists tried to go back to the essence of Sakyamuni's enlightenment. This meant that everybody can attain enlightenment; everyone can be awakened to the same ultimate reality as Sakyamuni was; namely, everybody can become a Buddha--an enlightened one. This Mahayana movement attracted people and grew into a dominant theme of Buddhism in India. Based on Sanskrit texts, compiled and delivered to northern India, the Mahayana moved first to Central Asia, later to China, Tibet, Mongolia, Korea and Japan. There are many Buddhist schools in Japan, and they are all within the Mahayana tradition.

Pure Land Buddhism appeared around the first century of the Christian era. Those who pushed forward the Mahayana movement, aiming at attaining the same enlightenment as Sakyamuni did, realized that it was still impossible for everybody to follow this way because of the necessary conditions required for the purpose of attaining that final enlightenment. In short, the problem lies in the difficulty in performing the religious practices required for the attainment of the ultimate goal. According to Nagarjuna, the best known Indian Mahayana philosopher, and respected as an early exponent of Mahayana Buddhism, there are two ways leading to the stage of non-retrogression. The attainment of the "stage of non-retrogression" means that one is never pulled back or slides back to the starting point, but goes straight to the final goal. The main concern of Buddhists at that time was to attain *this stage*, because then one will never fall back to the starting point.

In "Chapter of Easy Practice," one of Nagarjuna's writings, he mentions that there are two ways concerning the attainment of the stage of non-retrogression:

> In the Buddha's teaching there are countless gates. Just as there are difficult and easy among the paths of this world--for journeying overland is full of hardship while sailing on board a boat is pleasant--so it is with the paths of bodhisattvas. Some engage in rigorous practice and endeavor; others quickly reach the stage of non-retrogression through the easy practice of entrusting as the means [for attaining it].[90]

The phrase, "easy practice of entrusting as the means," is very difficult to understand, but it is a key term in understanding Pure Land Buddhism, especially for understanding Shinran's thought.

The easy practice, as used here in this quotation, is the first definition given to Pure Land Buddhism. The division of the whole Mahayana in this way is not only concerning the way of performing various practices but it also indicates the difference in the structure of attaining the final goal. In Buddhism, in general, attaining emancipation or enlightenment or *satori* through one's strong will and strenuous effort is essential.

Pure Land Buddhism teaches salvation through the working of Amida Buddha. It is generally expressed as being born in Amida Buddha's world, or the Pure Land. Salvation by some absolute being is not found in Buddhism except in the Pure Land tradition. In this sense, Pure Land Buddhism is sometimes regarded as a side stream, not a main stream, of Mahayana Buddhism. In other words, the concept of salvation appeared first in Mahayana concurrently with the rising of the Pure Land tradition. In this sense, Pure Land Buddhism, especially Shin Buddhism, is quite often compared to Christianity because it is a religion of salvation, in which one is saved by some absolute being. For this reason, Pure Land Buddhism is not regarded as main stream Mahayana Buddhism.

Amida is one of the most frequently used religious terms in the Japanese language, but few know its true meaning, except for a superficial understanding that it is the name of a Buddha who takes care of our future destiny after life. For example, people call the name of Amida when they pray for good luck for themselves or their ancestors after they die. You will find that in Japan ancestor worship is very strong. People think that religion is for taking care of ancestor worshipping. In this case, Amida figures prominently in this attitude.

First of all, let us examine the origin of the name Amida Buddha. In Sanskrit texts extant today, we find the Buddha named Amitābha, which means "infinite light," and Amitāyus, "infinite life." Both indicate a Buddha who is living far from this world in the west. Chinese translators extracted only Amita (Skt.: "immeasurable") to represent the various aspects of this Buddha, and called this Buddha "Amita." In Sanskrit texts extant today, we can find the word *amita*, but this is only an adjective and cannot be used independently. The Chinese translators, however, used it as a noun to represent the name of Buddha Amitābha, or Buddha Amitāyus. "Amida" is the Japanese pronunciation of this word, *amita*. Amita, then, is a phonetic transcription of the original Sanskrit word.

Amitābha, and Amitāyus, meaning immeasurable light and immeasurable life, indicate what is infinite, both in space and time. Therefore, we can understand that it is an expression of the ultimate reality as conceived in a Buddhist way. There is a problem concerning the personification of ultimate reality which transcends both time and space, and which is the foundation of our existence. It has been personified as a Buddha who was originally a Bodhisattva called Dharmakara, which was Amida's name when he was a Bodhisattva aiming at the final goal of enlightenment. As Dharmakara, he uttered a vow to save all sentient beings in his Buddha land, which he established through countless eons of time. Amida's wisdom and compassion is said to be boundless in saving beings through their performance of easy practice and faith in Amida. This performance of easy practice and faith in Amida is related to the phrase used by Nagarjuna, "easy practice of entrusting as the means."

Such a myth seems to be no longer understandable to modern Japanese people, especially the contemporary young people of Japan. For example, let me take up a comment by Shusaku Endo, a famous Catholic novelist, with a deep understanding of Shinran's thought. He wrote a novel called *Silence*. Since it was translated into English, it has been often used in American University seminars. Endo's comment goes as follows:

> It is an indisputable fact that Jesus lived in this world and ended his short life by the execution by the Romans. Moreover, though we can know his actual life only vaguely, it is evident that he gave something decisive to the people of his day, and this something grew into faith in him, which has been continually inherited to the present. But Amida Buddha whom the devotees of Shin Buddhism believe in is not an actual historical existence like Jesus, but a concept. Although it is taught that Amida has his own past as Bodhisattva Dharmakara when he performed religious practices to fulfill his Vows, he is not a real historical existence like Jesus. The wonder I find in Shin Buddhism is that they rely wholeheartedly on this concept of Amida as if he were an incarnated being like Jesus. It is this point that I cannot understand at all. I really feel overwhelmed by such words of Shinran's as "I do not know at all whether the *nembutsu* is truly the seed for being born in the Pure Land or whether it is the karmic act for which I must fall into hell," but what surprises me most is that he had such an immovable faith in a concept.[91]

In the last paragraph, *nembutsu* means calling the name of Amida. Endo cannot believe that Shin people put faith in a mere concept. Amida is regarded by Endo as a concept, or idea.

I have some questions about this comment by Endo especially about the very simple comparison of Jesus with Amida Buddha, of an incarnation of ultimate reality with the ultimate reality itself. Endo is at least widening his view of the psychology of Shin devotees who worship, respect and believe in Amida, the savior, as if Amida were a real historical or physical existence. In fact, in Shin piety, Amida is called *oya-sama*. *Oya* means parent, and *sama* is an honorific. They think of Amida as a parent, whether mother or father. Amida's compassion is therefore likened to parental love. Endo says that Shin people have faith in a concept. But they do not think it is a mere concept. They know that Amida is not a historical or physical existence like Jesus, and yet they have deep faith in Amida. In my opinion, when Christians put faith in Jesus, they put faith in an incarnate ultimate reality and not in Jesus as solely a mere human being. In Pure Land Buddhism, the formless ultimate reality, which is generally called *Dharma*, is personified in order to make it an object for worship. *Dharma* (Pali: *Dhamma*) is a very essential term for all schools of Buddhism. It is the key word indicating the fundamental reality of Buddhism.

When Christians have faith in Jesus, they discern more than the humanness of Jesus Christ. In Pure Land Buddhism, we are enabled to personify ultimate reality as Amida Buddha.

In the Pure Land tradition, we do not have any historical event like Jesus of Nazareth. This is the main reason for a criticism from the side of Christians that Jodo-Shinshu, or Pure Land Buddhism, lacks historicity. But, what is historicity? If you put too much emphasis on Jesus Christ then there would be a problem, I think. Jesus is the only manifestation of the ultimate reality in history, only once in history.

The manifestation of the ultimate reality is seen in Jesus in Christianity, but in Shin Buddhism it is revealed at the moment that the devotee of Shin Buddhism has attained *shinjin*. In each moment of a follower realizing the ultimate reality of Amida's compassion, this manifestation occurs. The term for realizing the manifestation of Amida's compassion is called *ichinen*--one moment--of realizing *shinjin*, or the *nembutsu*.

Originally, the concept of "birth in the Pure Land" was regarded as being attained at the moment of death. This is a very traditional teaching. However, Shinran, the founder of Shin Buddhism, said that "birth in the Pure Land" at the moment of death is a secondary matter; the most important thing is to realize Amida's compassionate work at this moment, *ichinen*, which can cause birth in the Pure Land. He uses "birth" at the moment of realizing Amida's working. This, then, is the stage of non-retrogression. Shinran's use of non-retrogression is quite different from the traditional one.

Hisao Inagaki has already mentioned a historical figure called Shan-tao (613-681), a Pure Land monk who lived during the T'ang dynasty in China, and who established the practice of calling the name of Amida, that is *nembutsu* in Japanese. Shan-tao was the first in the history of Pure Land Buddhism to advocate this practice of *nembutsu* as a single practice which can convey the follower or practicer to "birth in Amida's Pure Land." In Shan-tao, however, the "birth in the Pure Land" was still at the moment of death.

This teaching was transmitted to a Japanese Buddhist monk, Honen (1133-1212), who was Shinran's master. Honen, as we have seen, spread the practice of calling the name of Amida as an exclusive practice to attain "birth in the Pure Land." In Shan-tao there were some auxiliary practices leading people to "birth in the Pure Land" at the moment of death, but Honen selected *only* the practice of calling Amida's name for attaining "birth." Honen received sharp criticism by monks holding to what is called the Path of Sages, the ordinary orthodox Buddhist path.

Buddhism is originally a religion or teaching for sages or priests or monks, not for ordinary people. Only Pure Land Buddhism in Mahayana became a school for ordinary people. Honen emphasized the single practice of *nembutsu*, calling the name of Amida, for ordinary people to be saved. For this he was criticized by other outside schools of Japanese Buddhism. They could not believe that merely calling the name of a Buddha, such an easy practice, was effective for achieving the final goal of attaining enlightenment.

In spite of their hard ascetic practices, sometimes even at the risk of their lives, it was still extremely difficult to realize enlightenment for most Buddhists. Even today, as we have seen, there are some monks who are performing ascetic practices on Mt. Hiei at the risk of their lives. It is very hard to perform. Honen insisted on attaining enlightenment merely through calling the name of Buddha. For the people of the Path of Sages, Honen's teaching might have been incredible or stupid. The criticism grew into persecution against him, which resulted in shortening his life.

Shinran was one of Honen's disciples who had performed the practices of the Path of Sages for twenty years on Mt. Hiei, which was the center of Japanese Buddhism at that time. But he gave up performing the practices and descended the mountain because of the impossibility of attaining enlightenment through those prescribed practices. He followed Honen faithfully and accepted the *nembutsu* teaching of realizing salvation through calling Amida's name. Yet, Shinran is often contrasted with Honen in terms of his emphasis on faith in Amida. Even in the academic field of Buddhist studies it is a common view that while Honen advocated the *nembutsu* practice, calling the name of Amida, Shinran emphasized faith in Amida; namely, the two masters taught two different teachings. But this analysis is totally mistaken. It is only one thing that both Honen and Shinran tried to reveal, and that is the working of Amida Buddha's Primal Vow, or his compassion.

Amida uttered a vow, called the Primal Vow. In this vow, salvation for all beings, through simply calling his name, was promised. Therefore, Amida's Primal Vow is none other than the embodiment of Amida's compassion for all beings. It is Honen who emphasized the power of this vow in the practice of calling Amida's name, and it is solely due to this vow that ordinary ignorant beings can be saved and attain "birth in the Pure Land." In this sense, the difficult practices of the Path of Sages and the easy practice of calling Amida's name cannot be made parallel or equated on the same dimension of practice, because the practice performed by the Path of Sages is the practice performed by their own will and effort. The practice of *nembutsu*, advocated by Honen and Shinran, is the practice as the working of Amida's compassion. That is to say, the agents of the practices are quite different.

Salvation through calling the name of Amida is none other than salvation through the working of Amida's Primal Vow, or the working of Amida's compassion, which works to save all beings, and is called Other Power. Shinran emphasized to the utmost this working of Other Power. Of course, he took over Honen's teaching of *nembutsu* practice, but in order to exhaust the true significance of this *nembutsu* teaching, he had to go deeply into the Primal Vow itself, that is to say, we have to realize the depth of Amida's compassion. This is a very essential condition for performing *nembutsu*.

Amida's Primal Vow promises the salvation of all beings through calling his name. This is true, but more important is Amida's compassion which enables beings to be saved simply by calling his name. In other words, Shinran tried to find the driving force behind the act of calling the name. Shinran's emphasis on the Primal Vow, Amida's compassion, naturally led him to the realization of this compassion. For Shinran, the most important condition in performing the practice of calling the name was the realization of Amida's compassion. This realization is called *shinjin*, and it is often rendered as "faith," but we avoid using the word "faith" in translating Shinran's works.

In one of our translations, the problem of translating Shinran's sense of *shinjin* as *faith* is mentioned in a glossary:

> *Shinjin*   The realization of Other Power in which human calculation is negated through the working of Amida Buddha. It denotes the central religious experience of Shin Buddhism, and literally means man's "true, real and sincere heart and mind" (*makoto no kokoro*), which is given by Amida Buddha. This heart-mind has basically two aspects: a non-dichotomous identity wherein the heart and mind of Amida and the heart and mind of man are one; and the dichotomous relationship wherein the two are mutually exclusive and in dynamic interaction. Used as an adjective, shin has the meaning of "true, real and sincere." As a verb, it means "to entrust oneself to the Buddha," an act which is made possible by the working of the true, real and sincere heart and mind of Amida. These two meanings are always inseparable. Thus, while shinjin is an experience on the part of man, its source, its contents and its consummation are to be found not in man but in Buddha.
>
> Shinjin has commonly been translated as "faith," but we have felt that term, so strongly and variously colored by its usage in the Judeo-Christian tradition, would only blur the precision of the meaning of the original.[92]

This is a complicated explanation of the expression *shinjin*. According to Shinran's interpretation, in *shinjin* we find two aspects; one is the true, real and sincere mind of Amida Buddha, and the other is the entrusting mind of beings. In *shinjin*, one entrusts oneself totally to Amida's working. The true mind is given or transported by Amida to beings and it becomes in beings the entrusting mind. *Shinjin* is the total entrusting of oneself to Amida's working of compassion. There can be nothing else. That is why we sometimes use the word *entrusting* for *shinjin*.

If sentient beings can cultivate and raise a firm belief or faith in Amida's saving work, there will be no problem. But, we are not possessed, in the least, of such a true and sincere mind. This is the very reason Amida raised his vow to save beings through an easy practice of simply calling his name. *Shinjin* is the realization of, or awakening to, the compassion of Amida. *Shinjin* is the total entrusting of oneself to Amida's saving work and, what is more, one has been enabled to realize this entrusting by Amida through being given his true mind, and, therefore, there is no way for one other than leaving everything to Amida.

Shinjin is the total negation of self-power mind. *Shinjin* and self-power mind are thus mutually exclusive. Here we can find the final goal of Buddhism, which has penetrated every doctrine from Sakyamuni to the present. This is to say, the concept of non-self, or egolessness, is found in *shinjin*, which Sakyamuni taught us.

I do not know if I am right or not, but self-power mind, which is quite a technical term with Shin Buddhist, is similar to the Christian notion of pride. Pride, in this usage, must mean self-assertion, complimenting oneself as being worthy, as someone who can accomplish great things. Such pride is very difficult to eradicate, as seen in the difficulty of discarding self-power mind.

It is this negation of self-power mind that transforms the Shin followers into a religious existence. Without a struggle with the self-power mind there would be no meaning in following Shinran's teaching. It is regrettable to say that this aspect of *shinjin* is rather neglected among Shin followers over against a sense of positively obtaining *shinjin* just like being given something from Amida. These days, in Jodo-Shinshu schools, people do not emphasize the negation of self-power as the manifestation of *shinjin*; they regard *shinjin* as some present given by Amida, all of a sudden, in their life. As a matter of course, the meaning of *shinjin* becomes shallow and does not lead to a transformation of the self.

Let me repeat the most crucial point of Shinran's thought. *Shinjin* was presented by Shinran as the negation of self-power mind and acts. It is the total entrusting of oneself to Other Power. In Shinran, therefore, self-power and Other Power are mutually exclusive. If there is a bit of self-power, there is no Other Power. If one is occupied with Other Power, there is not the least of self-power.

Now I have to be very careful in using these strange phrases, self-power and

Other Power, because among Japanese people there is an atmosphere in which Other Power is looked down upon and self-power is praised. Of course, this atmosphere has nothing to do with religious piety, but these terms, self-power and Other Power, are so frequently used in daily life, yet people do not even know that these phrases come from Shinran. They take Other Power in the sense of relying on others, doing nothing by oneself. That is to say, Other Power gives them the feeling of always expecting the help of others. This is why the words "Other Power" do not satisfy the feeling of young people, especially. On the contrary, self-power gives them a feeling of being strong willed, or of making one's own way in life. We think we should live by self-power, and so if self-power is negated or denied there would be no room for us to create our lives. This is what we first think of when considering the negation of self-power as well as the emphasis of Other Power. So long as the problem of salvation or liberation of oneself is concerned, that is, the problem of one's whole and entire existence is concerned, self-power attitude is not usable, not effective and is entirely futile. This is what Shinran wanted to say.

Salvation is not only a psychological matter, but it treats the problem of one's whole existence. In addition, self-power, used by Shinran, is, precisely speaking, the human mind or will which comes out of the self-centeredness of human beings. The realization of self-centeredness is the first step toward completing the Buddhist ideal of negation of self. It is therefore an endless negation of self-power mind which is found in the true follower of Shinran's teaching. This is the life of *shinjin*.

Let me attempt to bring this chapter to a conclusion by mentioning a unique personality of Japanese Shin Buddhism, whose name was Asahara Saichi. Saichi lived in the remote country of the northwestern part of Japan, facing the Japan Sea. He was a *geta* (wooden sandal) maker. *Geta* making was considered the lowest occupation in the society at that time. While Saichi was making *geta* every day, he wrote on the plain wood or wood pieces what occurred to his mind about the teaching he listened to in the temple. It was in verse style in a very poor way of writing Japanese. In his poems we do not see any sophistication at all. He was almost illiterate, but he could barely write very simple Japanese. He wrote poems, while making *geta*, on wood pieces, and copied them at night in elementary school notebooks. He died quite unknown about eighty years ago, leaving only these notebooks, which had been totally neglected by his family.

Many years later, the value of his poems was discovered and they were published. D. T. Suzuki quite often used Saichi's poems in his writings. There are a special kind of people who are called *myōkōnin*, which literally means a wondrous, excellent person, among the followers of Shin Buddhism. This title, *myōkōnin*, is used only for Shin followers, not for other people or other schools. These people are all very diligent devotees of Jodo-Shinshu and most of them are illiterate. They worked as farmers, carpenters, fishermen or even beggars. However, their appreciation of the teaching was excellent indeed and their behavior and acts in daily life were noteworthy as simple, innocent and sincere. So, they are likened to white lotus flowers blooming in the mud.

Today Saichi is one of the best known *myōkōnin* for his excellent poems, one of which I would like to share with you.

> Saichi has nothing -- which is joy.
> Outside this there's nothing.
> Both good and evil -- all's taken away,
> Nothing's left.
> To have nothing -- this is the release, this is the peace.
> All's taken away by the "Namu-amida-butsu,"
> This is truly the peace.
> "Namu-amida-butsu!"[93]

This "nothingness" is called *shinjin* in Shinran's terminology. In *shinjin*, Saichi became zero or nothing in terms of his self-power mind. It is the realization of the futility of the self-cultivated mind and will so long as salvation by Amida is concerned. It is, at the same time, the realization of Amida's mind filling Saichi's mind. It is the awakening to Amida's compassionate working in Saichi, and that is the realization of Amida becoming one with him.

In Shin Buddhism, it is never said, as other Mahayana schools say, that a human is originally a Buddha or that he or she is originally enlightened. But the Buddha comes to him and becomes one with him according to Shinran's teaching. The following poem, the authorship of which is attributed to Saichi, clarifies the oneness of the two in the above sense.

> My mind is your mind
> And your mind is my mind.
> It is not that I become one with you,
> But that you become one with me.[94]

Saichi knew that he could never become one with Amida through his own power, but he could not help feeling that Amida was one with him. From that very moment, he realized the futility of his own power and that his self-power was completely negated.

Let me quote some more poems composed by anonymous *myōkōnins* in order to suggest what *shinjin* is.

> The flower of *shinjin* which I cultivated to bloom in my mind
> Has all been picked by Amida, and I have nothing at all to be called *shinjin*;
> Self-power -- I do not worry about it any more,
> Other Power -- it is beyond my knowledge.
> But I am quite at rest in peace,
> Because my *Oya* knows everything.[95]

This poem says that the flower of *shinjin* which the *myōkōnin* had cultivated through his or her own will or efforts, a mind of faith made up by his or her own power through painstaking efforts or listening to the teaching, has totally been picked by Amida. He or she now has nothing in his or her mind to be called *shinjin*. As we have already seen in the poem of Saichi's above, this nothingness is *shinjin*. We can see that there remains nothing in his or her mind other than the working of Amida's compassion.

There is a very well known phrase in the collection of Shinran's words titled *Tannishō*, or "Notes Lamenting the Differences." "Even a good person can attain birth in the Pure Land, so it goes without saying that an evil person will."[96] The concept of good and evil here cannot be well understood or, rather, it can be easily misunderstood if it is formulated on the basis of customary morality. The evil here is an expression of the realization of one's inner self when it is exposed in the light of Amida.

The realization of one's evil nature in *shinjin*, which is similar to the realization of one's sinfulness in Christian faith, should be a key characteristic of *shinjin*. This realization is one with the realization of Amida's compassion, because the compassion works only for saving this evilness, which one can never get rid of through one's own power. However, this is not the evil in a relative sense, but it is, so to speak, an absolute evil for which Amida's compassion works. I will quote another poem by an anonymous *myōkōnin* to indicate how one's realization of evilness is located in Shinran's *shinjin*.

If I had not been possessed of my evils,
Amida would not have constructed his Pure Land.
But only for the sake of saving my evils,
Amida has constructed the Pure Land.
Hey, Amida!
I'll let you save me as you like,
But I will not give my evils to you,
Because they are the source of my joy.[97]

XIV
Other Power and Social Ethics:
The Bifurcation of Shinran's Teaching
Michio Tokunaga

A religious tradition undergoes change and development as time passes. There is an interplay between the tradition itself and persons who respond to that tradition through faith, who respond, nevertheless, not in isolation but in particular historical periods and specific cultural contexts. Professor Tokunaga moves our consideration to a consideration of a horizontal relationship with others in society and seeks to help us see that ideally engagement with social issues is naturally expressive of *shinjin*.

I have introduced the subtitle of this chapter in order to draw attention to the way Shinran's teaching began to be altered because the Hongwanji organization, in its continuing development and phenomenal growth, had to make the teachings fit the mores of the society and the motives of the organization. It is important, as we have noted before, to get some initial idea of the meaning of *shinjin*. Let me refer you to the definition of *shinjin* previously provided on page 141.

According to this definition we can see that *shinjin* has two aspects, that is, "the true, real and sincere mind of Amida Buddha" and "the entrusting mind of a person of *shinjin* to the working of such a mind of Amida." What is more important here is that the latter, the entrusting mind, is made possible by the working of the former, of Amida's power, Amida's power of the Primal Vow. This means that everything concerning our salvation is attributed to the working of Amida. This is *Other Power.*

Here, then, considering the relationship of self-power and Other Power would be instructive. There are schools within the Pure Land tradition of Japan which allocate, for example, thirty percent of self-power and seventy percent of Other Power, or fifty percent self-power and fifty percent Other Power. In a sense, Japanese Pure Land schools can be classified according to the percentage of the dependence on the working of Other Power, in terms of salvation. In Shinran's case, it can definitely be said that our salvation is one hundred percent dependent on Amida. Here occurs a very serious problem concerning the religious life of the followers of Shin Buddhism; partially because of the sense that the term Other Power conveys and partially because of the soteriological structure of Shinran's thought. *Shinjin* is regarded as the source of the very popular image or perception of Jodo-Shinshu, the perception which most Japanese have for Jodo-Shinshu; that is, "the do-nothing school." This is, so to speak, a nickname for Jodo-Shinshu. Even Shin devotees who could not listen to the teaching carefully and could not think about the teaching very seriously have this tendency of viewing their own school as representing the position that one is being saved by doing nothing. This has been a consistent tendency among Japanese Shin people, not only today but also some centuries ago.

A Jesuit missionary named Alejandro Valignano came to Japan in the sixteenth century to make an inspection of the state of Christianity here at that time. He reported,

> Buddhist priests emphasize how great a compassion Amida and Sakyamuni have on beings, and therefore they are easily saved by these Buddhas. Whatever sins one may commit, he or she will be purified only through calling the Buddha's name and having a firm belief in their virtues. Accordingly, one does not need to atone for one's sins. If one did so, it means to insult the amends Amida and Sakyamuni have made for human beings. This is very similar to Martin Luther's heresy.[98]

Although this report reflects some misunderstanding, it is an interesting one. For instance, he does not have any distinction between Amida and Sakyamuni. Amida is not like a historical being, while Sakyamuni is a historical figure. Valignano did not know this. Although his observations were misinformed, there is some truth in them. For example, Valignano was aware that Shin Buddhism was most popular among Japanese people of those days. Further, he regarded Shin Buddhism as the "do-nothing school," which is the very reflection of the perception Japanese people of those days had on Shin Buddhism. He caught the sense of "do-nothing" in Shin Buddhism.

In contrast to the Path of Sages, which requires extremely difficult ascetic practices, Shin Buddhism gives the impression of a very easy going way for final attainment. Therefore the followers of Shin Buddhism can be lazy when seeking for the way of salvation. Such is a serious misunderstanding of Shinran's teaching. For Shinran, *shinjin* could not have been such a static state of mind. On the contrary, it was a dynamic confrontation of self-power and Other Power; namely, an incessant battle against the arising of self-centered wishes and pride for doing something good or efficacious for one's liberation through one's own power. If even one percent of self-power remains in one's mind, it cannot be called *shinjin*. Moreover, this one percent is so strong and persistent that it is hardly possible to eradicate it. It is like lifting one's body with one's own hands.

In Buddhism, in general, doing good for other people is required for the fulfillment of the way; it is an essential condition for attaining the final goal. The main activity of a Bodhisattva, for reaching Buddhahood, is to help others first, leaving his or her own benefit behind. This is the Mahayana Bodhisattva way. But, if the Bodhisattva takes pride in doing good for others, he or she will fall back to the starting point. This is repeatedly taught in every school of Mahayana Buddhism. In a sense, this is regarded as the activation of Sakyamuni's teaching of "non-self."

In the same way, in Shin Buddhism, if one takes pride in doing something efficacious for one's salvation, that state of mind can never be called *shinjin*. This characteristic of *shinjin* should be emphasized in order to make the Shin Buddhist way Mahayanistic and to clarify Shinran's thought as distinctive from other schools of Pure Land tradition, which admit some self-power activity to some degree. Anyway, the source of doing good for others or the source of ethical implications lies in *shinjin* itself, because self-power activity means to do good for oneself and others in order to attain salvation, the problem of which is that this self-power is to be negated by the working of Amida. If there is no self-power, there would be no negation of it; that is, there is no room for the realization of Other Power. There are some people who say that self-power mind itself is *shinjin*, but in our organization, Hongwanji, such is regarded as a heretical view. But I think there is some truth in their claim of self-power mind itself being *shinjin*, because there is no *shinjin* at all without self-power which is to be negated by Other Power.

Shin Buddhist ethics lie right at the confrontation of self-power and Other Power. Unlike Christianity, however, it is quite difficult to find room in Buddhism for ethics, especially with regard to Shin. In addition, it is also very difficult to judge Buddhist teaching, applying the Western notion of ethics. Within the social history of the East, there has not been such a notion as ethics as with the Westerners. In exploring this problem in the Buddhist tradition, such a difference in the way of thinking necessarily has to be taken into consideration. Compared with Christianity, in which social, historical and consequently ethical aspects are highly valued, Buddhism is generally considered to be a religious tradition which is mainly concerned about a very individual liberation of the self.

This tendency of Buddhism was already found when it was first introduced to China and was exposed to severe criticism by the Chinese. The Chinese people are very ethical, in a sense, according to the teaching of Confucianism. Therefore, Confucian ethics were adopted by Buddhism for the purpose of soothing such criticism. Discrepancy between the essence of the Buddhist doctrine and Confucian ethics still remains today and causes numerous problems. This is one of the biggest problems of Japanese Buddhism, even today. We also have had to apply Confucian ethics to Buddhist teaching in order to make it suitable for Japanese society, just as early Chinese Buddhism did. A typical example of the problems is ancestor worshipping applied in Chinese Buddhism and later in Japanese Buddhism. Ancestor worshipping has nothing to do, originally, with Buddhist teaching, but these days, as you may have seen, Japanese Buddhism is closely related to ancestor worshipping.

Returning to the problem of individual liberation through religion and its effect in the society, these look contradictory at a glance and stand against each other. Consider the following passage,

> The rule of the person who renounces worldly life is not to pay homage to the king, not to pay homage to one's parents, not to serve the six kinds of blood relative, and not to worship spirits.[99]

A superficial understanding of this passage is that the world renouncers, that is Buddhists, do not have to respect kings, parents, relatives, or gods, because they are now apart from the secular world. Such an interpretation should be considered biased. It is not right. This statement is very similar to a well-known saying seen in the *Rinzairoku* (Chinese, *Lin-chi lu*),

> Encountering a Buddha, killing the Buddha;
> Encountering a Patriarch, killing the Patriarch;
> Encountering an Arhat, killing the Arhat;
> Encountering mother or father, killing mother or father;
> Encountering a relative, killing the relative,
> Only thus does one attain liberation and disentanglement
> from all things, thereby becoming completely unfettered and free.[100]

These two passages, drawn from the *Bodhisattva Precept Sūtra* and the *Rinzairoku*, both point to the importance of detachment from secular affairs in order to attain the final goal of emancipation. (But Shinran's intention of quoting the former passage is to criticize the pressure of the secular authority upon Buddhists.)

If one is concerned only about secular or earthly desires, one's attainment of the ultimate goal will be beyond reach. Similar passages are found in the *Bible*, too, where Jesus Christ is recorded to have said,

> If anyone comes to me and does not hate his father and mother, wife and children, brothers and sisters, even his own life, he cannot be a disciple of mine. (*Luke*, 14:26).[101]

In another passage, it is said,

> Truly I say to you, there is no one who has given up home, or wife, brothers, parents, or children, for the sake of the Kingdom of God, who will not be repaid many times over in this age, and in the age to come have eternal life. (*Luke*, 18:29-30)[102]

Needless to say, these passages do not simply mean that one is to reject this world for the sake of the attainment of personal liberation, whether it be Christian or Buddhist. Shinran's *shinjin* is often misunderstood from the same perspective. It is, according to D. T. Suzuki, "the culmination of Mahayana Buddhism in the Far East," but because of its too existential or transcendental character, there are some critics who claim that Shin Buddhism lacks social and ethical implications. In other words, it is concerned only with a vertical relationship of "I" and Amida and not with a horizontal conjunction with other people in the society. The vertical relationship of an individual with Amida, this existential and personal aspect of Shinran's *shinjin*, is typically seen in his words recorded in the *Tannishō*:

> When I consider deeply the Vow of Amida, which arose from five kalpas [an extremely long time] of profound thought, I realize that it was entirely for the sake of myself alone!

Then how I am filled with gratitude for the Primal Vow, in which Amida settled on saving me, though I am burdened thus greatly with karma.[103]

This is an exceedingly personal aspect of *shinjin*, and accordingly puts a great stress on the salvific power of Amida's Primal Vow, and naturally leads to the transcendence of good and evil; namely, the transcendence of the ethical level of seeking salvation.

In this context, one would do well to consider other significant passages from the *Tannishō*.

Know that the Primal Vow of Amida makes no distinction between people young and old, good and evil; only the entrusting of yourself to it is essential. For it was made to save the person in whom karmic evil is deep-rooted and whose blind passions abound.

Thus, entrusting yourself to the Primal Vow requires no performance of good, for no act can hold greater virtue than saying the Name. Nor is there need to despair of the evil you commit, for no act is so evil that it obstructs the working of Amida's Primal Vow.[104]

And further,

Even a good person can attain birth in the Pure Land, so it goes without saying that an evil person will.[105]

Moreover,

I know nothing of what is good or evil. For if I could know thoroughly, as is known in the mind of Amida, that an act was good, then I would know the meaning of "good." If I could know thoroughly, as Amida knows, that an act was evil, then I would know "evil." But for a foolish being full of blind passions, in this fleeting world--this burning house-- all matters without exception are lies and gibberish, totally without truth and sincerity. The nembutsu alone is true and real.[106]

These passages reveal the very individual, subjective, and personal character of Shinran's thinking. Here, an important question arises: whether Shinran's *shinjin* is so radically individual and subjective that it is merely a self-satisfaction which lacks the horizontal relation with others. Does it mean that with *shinjin*, described by Shinran in these passages, one should confine oneself to one's internal spiritual world, paying no attention to the external life, or external law; or is *shinjin* a topic taken up only within the circle, so to speak, a circle of faith?

After Shinran was exiled to Echigo province by the Imperial Government at the age of thirty-five, he called himself "neither a priest nor a layman," a well-known phrase. This is usually interpreted to be an expression of his resistance against or escape from the secular authority. It might not be possible, but the depth of his appreciation of the universal compassion is ignored from this point of view.

Nearly twenty years after his exile, Shinran indicated what he meant in the phrase "neither a priest nor a layman."

> In reflecting on the ocean of great *shinjin*, I realize that there is no discrimination between noble and humble, or black-robed monks and white clothed laity, no differentiation between man and woman, old and young. The amount of evil one has committed is not considered, the duration of any performance or religious practice is of no concern.[107]

Notwithstanding the apparently too individualistic appreciation of Amida's Vow, a horizontal conjunction of himself and other people, under universal compassion, is clearly seen in this passage.

So far, I have noted a very complicated character of Shinran's *shinjin*. One dimension is a very subjective character of *shinjin*, the other is the relationship between "I" and other people through *shinjin*, which is usually ignored by Shin followers or by outside critics.

Now, in turning to the notion of a bifurcation of Shinran's *shinjin*, the phrase "Buddha's Law and King's Law" throws into sharp relief the very pure soteriological truth given by the teaching of Pure Land Buddhism, which is the "Buddha's Law," and the "King's Law," which is the law of the secular authorities. Shinran's *shinjin* began to be bifurcated in the process of the expansion of the Hongwanji denominational organization.

Shinran died in 1273, almost unknown to people of his day except for a small *nembutsu* community, which had been organized under his leadership near the Tokyo area, where he lived for approximately twenty years from his early forties to his early sixties. After his death in Kyoto, his grave was entrusted by his disciples to his youngest daughter, Kakushin. The graveyard developed later into the Hongwanji temple.

The bifurcation of Shinran's teaching into the two aspects, "Buddha's Law" and "King's Law," began to appear after the organization of this Shin denomination, centered at Hongwanji. It was Kakunyo (1270-1351), a great grandson of Shinran, who developed the graveyard into Hongwanji temple and tried to acquire authority over the followers of Shinran's teaching. For that purpose, he had to locate or situate the Hongwanji organization within the Japanese society of his time, a process in which, however, he did not succeed. His son, Zonkaku (1290-1373), first cooperated with him toward this objective, but, perhaps because of Zonkaku's too radical compromise with other Buddhist schools and the secular authorities, Kakunyo had to disown him.

Zonkaku's view of "Buddha's Law" and "King's Law," as it is reflected in his behavior, presents a typical picture of the relation of the two aspects which exerted a great influence upon Rennyo (1415-1499), a restorer of the Hongwanji denomination, and also upon the traditional doctrine of Shin Buddhism after Rennyo. In one of Zonkaku's writings, it is stated:

> Buddha's Law and King's Law are to make a pair, just like the two wings of a bird; like the two wheels of a carriage. Neither of the two should be missing. Therefore, Buddha's Law is to protect King's Law and King's Law is to respect Buddha's Law.[108]

This view of Zonkaku's is not his own invention but is based on quite a popular idea which had been prevalent in Japan since the Heian period, when the role of Japanese Buddhism was to protect the nation. For example, the Tendai school on Mt. Hiei was established in order to protect the nation, not to save the people. Put more precisely, it was to protect the Imperial Government, not the ordinary people. The "two wings of a bird" and the "two wheels of a carriage" are phrases commonly used when this topic was discussed. The mutual dependence of "Buddha's Law" and "King's Law" is mentioned by Zonkaku in other writings as well, and it can be assumed that by applying this idea he must have aimed at locating the Hongwanji organization within the structure of the nation. It is to be noted that Zonkaku's notion of the mutual dependence of "Buddha's Law" and "King's Law" is quite different from Shinran's.

Shinran quotes from the *Mappōtōmyōki*, or "A Record of the Lamp in the Last Dharma-age," the author of which is unknown, but usually attributed to the founder of the Tendai School, Saicho:

> Spiritual truth and secular law act in mutual dependence to spread the teachings. Because of this, the profound scriptures pervade the world and virtue permeates the land.[109]

Spiritual truth and secular law act in mutual dependence to spread the teachings; because of this the mutual dependence of "Buddha's Law" and "King's Law" is solely to spread the true teaching within the world. This was the original intent of this passage from the *Mappōtōmyōki*, but later it no longer was precisely understood.

The intention of Shinran's quoting this passage was to protest against the government's way of strictly controlling monks and nuns on the ground of breaking Buddhist precepts. There were many monks and nuns who broke Buddhist precepts in those days. It goes without saying that Shinran's criticism of the government for their despotic control of Buddhists originated for him at the age of thirty-five when the *nembutsu* community, led by Honen, his master, was persecuted by the government. Far from depending on the secular authority in spreading the teaching, Shinran aimed at the independence of the *nembutsu* community from any power of the secular authorities including the power of the other existing Buddhist schools.

Zonkaku, however, states that the *Mappōtōmyōki* was written for revealing the harmony of spiritual law and secular law, which is quite contrary to the original purpose of this book. The purpose of the *Mappōtōmyōki* is to reveal that the Buddha's teachings should spread in the society without having any restrictions or violations by secular authorities.

There is, of course, a great difference between the social and historical settings of Shinran and Zonkaku, but it is true that the Hongwanji denomination and the other schools of Shin Buddhism continued to keep the policy which Zonkaku prepared in compromising with the secular authorities in order for their organizations to survive.

Undoubtedly, it was Rennyo, the eighth Abbot of Hongwanji, who restored the Hongwanji organization which was about to disappear, at that time, from Japan. Hongwanji was a very small school at Rennyo's time. He restored it and made it the biggest school of Japanese Buddhism. He took over the position of the head of Hongwanji in 1457, at the age of forty-three, and during the following forty years he made it an unprecedentedly huge Buddhist organization in Japan. Because of this sudden expansion of the Hongwanji community, Rennyo was forced to meet with various problems of which Shinran would never have dreamed.

Most of these problems were caused by friction between the Hongwanji community and the society at large, which can be roughly classified into two parts: (1) other schools of Buddhism including other sects of Shin Buddhism, and (2) the government in power, both central and local. These two kinds of power were what Rennyo had to call into question. Notwithstanding the frequent persecution and conflicts caused by these powers, Hongwanji continued to grow into a monumental religious community in Japan.

It was solely because of such an abrupt growth of the community that Rennyo had to use skills as imaginative as possible in order to solve these problems. For this he is criticized by some modern scholars as being political, not religious in personality. In order to avoid conflict with outside society, Rennyo had to issue regulations or restrictions (*okite*) for the followers of Hongwanji within the Shin community. Five times he issued *okite*, from 1473 to 1478. The first *okite* issued in 1473 consisted of eleven regulations or restrictions.

(1) Do not make light of other gods, Buddhas, and Bodhisattvas other than Amida.
(2) Do not abuse other teachings and schools.
(3) Do not reproach other schools on the basis of the Shin teaching.
(4) Do not reproach the evasion of impurities [as stressed, for example, in Shinto], though it is meaningless from the standpoint of the Buddhist view.
(5) Do not propagate your own faith without the authentic transmission of the teaching.
(6) Do not make light of the local guardians and landowners.
(7) Do not compete with other schools praising the Shin teaching only.
(8) Do not praise the Shin teaching on the basis of secondhand information about the teaching.
(9) Do not eat fowls and fish in a *nembutsu* gathering.
(10) Do not drink so much as to lose your temper in a *nembutsu* gathering.
(11) Do not gamble among the *nembutsu* followers.[110]

In addition to these restrictions, the *okite* said that those who violated them were to be banished from the Hongwanji community. A total of thirty-five regulations included in the five *okites* can be summarized as follows: (1) Observance of the governmental law is taken to be essential and one should keep the Buddhadharma to oneself. (2) Make the point of obeying the social morals and never make light of other schools. Many expressions of this kind in Rennyo's letters may be summarized in such a sentence as "Externally, the observance of King's Law is essential, and internally, keeping Buddha's Law is fundamental."[111]

So, in Rennyo, "Buddha's Law" and "King's Law" are completely bifurcated, separated. This kind of expression very frequently appears in Rennyo's letters to the followers. With this teaching, Rennyo seems to have divided the life of *nembutsu* followers: life in the secular society outside the Shin community, and life in a religious circle within the community. The clear contrast of the two, a dualistic opposition of "Buddha's Law" and "King's Law," is usually said to be contradictory to Shinran's way of living. This is the main reason for the criticism of Rennyo. But without Rennyo, there would not have been any Hongwanji organization.

Shinran, too, had to face a problem similar to Rennyo's, concerning the relationship between the *nembutsu* community and society. He returned to Kyoto when he was sixty-two or sixty-three. When he was about eighty, a very serious dispute concerning the interpretation of the teaching occurred among his disciples and followers in the Kanto area. As a result of this dispute, the *nembutsu* community in the Kanto area split into two: one was a group called "Licensed Evil," which roughly stressed the inconceivably deep compassion of Amida's Primal Vow, and consequently an idea began to prevail in the Kanto area that Amida's compassion is so deep that it is never hindered by any evil. This perspective can naturally develop into an idea that the more one does evil, the greater the possibility that one can be saved by Amida. This is undoubtedly a misunderstanding of Shinran's thought as recorded later in the *Tannishō*, as we have seen; "Even a good person can attain birth in the Pure Land, so it goes without saying that an evil person will."[112] and further, "the evil person who entrusts himself to Other Power is precisely the one who possesses the true cause for birth."[113] This description of Shinran's was misunderstood. Some intentionally did evil in society. People of licensed evil intentionally dealt in wrongdoing in the society. This caused an intervention into the Shin community by the Kamakura Shogunate government.

Shinran sent letters often to the disciples in Kanto warning them not to disturb the society outside their community. We have to admit that there is a decisive difference between Shinran and Rennyo. In Shinran's case, his warnings to the followers were closely connected with the teaching, while in Rennyo's case, a bifurcation of "Buddha's Law" and "King's Law" can be clearly observed. This, of course, is only a rough sketch of Rennyo's view of "Buddha's Law and King's Law." Many other aspects must be taken into consideration in order to grasp his thought.

The Hongwanji community restored by Rennyo went through the kaleidoscopic changes of the Japanese nation, sometimes standing against the ruler, sometimes compromising with the government. It is during the Edo period that not only Hongwanji but all the other schools of Buddhism had their backbone taken out by the government and were tamed, just like a dog. This lasted for about 260 years.

This political skill was first demonstrated by TOKUGAWA Ieyasu (1542-1616), the founder of the Tokugawa Shogunate government. For instance, very early in the Edo period, the huge denomination or organization of the Hongwanji community was forced to split into two, forming West Hongwanji and East Hongwanji. This move was caused by TOKUGAWA Ieyasu in response to the enormous power of the riots initiated by farmers (*ikkōikki*) led by Hongwanji members. TOKUGAWA Ieyasu had experienced the terror of the *ikkōikki*, as a local ruler when he was young. The Hongwanji community was forced to split into two, and hence they could not cooperate anymore to lead in further *ikkōikki* riots.

After Ieyasu, the Tokugawa Shogunate protected all schools of Buddhism in Japan and placed Buddhist priests at a highly ranked status within the social classes. This meant that there was no need for Buddhists to protect themselves. It was, so to speak, like a wise bird being caught in a cage and being kept under a careful watch. Shin Buddhism was no exception.

Under governmental protection and supervision, Hongwanji lost its power to expand its horizontal influence in society. In addition, it began to strengthen the relation with the secular authorities. In this setting, the study of Shinran's teaching was greatly encouraged within the Hongwanji organization. However, the study progressed only with the focus on the subjective and individual aspect of salvation--that is, the vertical relation between the aspirant and Amida. The relation with other people within society, which is indispensable for the Mahayana Bodhisattva path for its fulfillment, was not emphasized in the study of Shinran's thought. This grew into a scholastic tradition of Shin Buddhism. Even today, we can observe that the study of Shin "theology" is focused mainly on the vertical relation between the "I" and Amida.

It can also be said that only the passive acceptance of Shinran's teaching was applied and urged, and the active aspect was intentionally ignored. A good example of what has been ignored is the matter of "being equal to Buddhas." Shinran, especially in his late years, repeatedly emphasized that the person of *shinjin* is the same as a Bodhisattva and equal to Buddhas.

> Now, the *Larger Sutra* speaks of the "stage next to enlightenment, like that of Maitreya." Since Maitreya is already close to Buddhahood, it is the custom of various schools to speak of him as Maitreya *Buddha*. Since the person counted among the truly settled is of the same stage as Maitreya, he is also said to be equal to Tathagatas. You should know that the person of true shinjin can be called equal to Tathagatas because, even though he himself is always impure and creating karmic evil, his heart and mind are already equal to Tathagatas.[114]

This roughly says that a person of *shinjin* is equal to Maitreya Bodhisattva or Buddha, which means that he or she is right on the path of the Mahayana Bodhisattva way. In the Mahayana Bodhisattva way, doing good for others is the necessary, first condition, to attain the final goal. This assertion by Shinran, however, was completely ignored in Shin scholarship during the Edo period, though it was treated with great importance in his writings, especially in his letters. What is more surprising is that even today, it is missing in the doctrine which is supposed to be authentic at Hongwanji. Shinran's emphasis on the Mahayana Bodhisattva way, that means the very active way of living for Shin followers, is not accepted by the Hongwanji, especially by the elders.

So long as a person of *shinjin* is equated with a Bodhisattva or a Buddha, and if it is stressed as it was by Shinran as an active phase of *shinjin* focused on the horizontal relationship with people in society as an essential condition for the Mahayana Bodhisattva path, Shin ethics will naturally come out of the teaching. In this sense, during the Edo period, Shinran's *shinjin* fell down to the ground of self-satisfaction, which is even today observed as the major attitude of Shin followers of "the do-nothing school." *Shinjin* is a topic concerned only with the topic of faith. Shin followers confine themselves to a small community which appreciates the boundless compassion of Amida only on the occasion of gathering or listening to the teaching in temples. All that is seen is the passive acceptance of the teaching. There must be, of course, some passiveness in any religious tradition to receive the teaching, but what is important is the natural outflow of the truth or reality presented in the form of teaching, through the entire personality of the listener, or of the follower. The confinement of Shin Buddhists themselves in a special circle is chiefly because the teaching has been and continues to be presented in a way that is accepted only passively.

In Rennyo's day, in the Edo period, and in the period after the Meiji Restoration to the end of World War II, social ethics in Shin Buddhism were more focused on the harmony of the community with the outside society than on a follower's individual participation in social issues. It was mainly due to the visible and invisible pressure on the community from the side of the secular authority or governmental power. Today, there is hardly any pressure on the communities of Shin from the governmental side. Therefore, the members of the community can act freely in social issues as they wish.

There are several social movements in which Hongwanji has been taking leadership, such as the anti-Yasukuni Shrine movement--involving the Japanese government's attempts to make Yasukuni a national shrine. Other religious schools too are strongly against this policy. Also, Hongwanji is involved with anti-nuclear weapons movements, and anti-*buraku* discrimination movements. Regarding the last one, Hongwanji has the longest history of involvement. They have been trying to solve the problem for many years. It is, however, very ironic that Hongwanji is criticized these days for doing anti-*buraku* discrimination movement activities.

What is more important is a voluntary participation of the members in these movements, not the organization as a whole but individually, personally. Each person must participate in what he or she thinks is important for solving social problems. Also, if their commitment to these social issues has nothing to do with the realization of *shinjin*, there will appear another bifurcation of Shinran's teaching as observed in the bifurcation of "Buddha's Law" and "King's Law." The most important thing is that the commitment of Shin followers to resolving social problems should be connected with *shinjin*.

XV

The Role of Women in the
Buddhist Tradition in Japan
Kyoko Motomochi Nakamura

We have glimpsed important dimensions of three major strands of the Buddhist heritage in Japan: the important contributions persons have been enabled to make in response to the *Lotus Sūtra*, the fresh breezes of Zen, both Rinzai and Soto, and the subtlety of reflective thought on questions of the religious life in the True Pure Land Sect. Issues of more comprehensive scope now will hold our attention. Fully aware of the core Buddhist soteriological affirmation of liberation into freedom and creativity, Professor Kyoko Motomochi Nakamura turns our attention to the role of women in the Buddhist tradition in Japan, and reminds us of the importance of historical self-consciousness while enabling us to share her vision of freedom from gender discrimination.

This topic seems to me to be very significant, not only historically but in its relevance to our contemporary problems. It is true that women and religion as such is a recently developed area for Westerners as well as for Japanese. But there have been quite a number of works on the religious lives of women in this country. The contribution of women in the history of religion in Japan has been too significant to be ignored, and, hence, many researchers have studied female religionists as well as their male counterparts. This does not mean that there has not been sexism in our religious tradition. As you may have noticed, Japanese women do suffer from sexual discrimination in spite of legal equality, given after the end of World War II. Nevertheless, we cherish the tradition in which the study of women has been carried out, not only by women but by some men. Our sincere hope is that such men will increase in number, and men and women will cooperate for a better understanding of sexism and of each other, and eventually create a better relationship between the two sexes.

The First Nuns

You will probably agree that any social group has some archetypal images of women as spiritual figures. In order to discuss women's role in the Buddhist tradition, we will point out first the three images of women in our mythological and legendary traditions, in other words, the pre-Buddhist religious traditions. They are as follows: (1) Woman as Mother Goddess, (2) Woman as Guardian of Her Kin, (3) Woman as Divine Wife or Maid. These three archaic images are persistent all through Japanese history and are alive even today with some new additions.

As you know, Buddhism was transmitted from Korea to the Japanese court in 538 or 552, according to the tradition. Some immigrants from the continent might have brought it earlier, and could have kept it privately at home, without formally introducing it to the court. Therefore, when the issue of accepting a new religion was debated at court, the immigrant families naturally favored Buddhism over against the nationalistic ethos of the indigenous families. It caused even a domestic war resulting in the victory of the immigrant families, or the cause of what one might call liberal internationalism.

After the emperor's sanction in favor of its introduction, Buddhism was heavily patronized by the upper class. The court chronicle gives an account of three girls of the immigrant families who renounced the world to become Buddhist nuns.[115] It might be more exact to say that they were made to be nuns to serve the Buddha under the guidance of their fathers for they were all in their teens and did not seem to have much knowledge of Buddhism. At that time in Japan there were only six monks sent from Korea with Buddhist scriptures and images. In the meantime, the three nuns entreated the authorities to send them to Korea to study Buddhist scriptures and to be ordained in the authentic ceremony which needed ten monks and ten nuns. Eventually they were sent to Korea and, after studying there for two years and being ordained formally, they came back, in 590, and lived in the first Buddhist temple in Japan. They are, however, not mentioned thereafter in the chronicle probably because of the overthrow of their patron family.[116]

You might wonder why women were chosen to be the first renunciants. In fact, they were chosen to serve the Buddha, the deity of the foreign countries, such as Korea, China and India just as indigenous *kami* were served by priestesses. They represent woman's images as divine maid and guardian of her kin.[117] Therefore, we may assume that the influential immigrant families sent their daughters to serve the Buddha following the traditional model. The three nuns, however, were not so passive, and wanted to be enlightened through devotion and scholarship as full-fledged members of the Buddhist *sangha*. It seems to me that this is a Buddhist innovation of the traditional roles of women, namely, *Woman as Pursuer of the Way to Enlightenment*, which I would like to stress was well accepted in the sixth century.

Prince Shotoku, a great patron of Buddhism at court, is said to have built more convents than monasteries in the late sixth and early seventh centuries, but we lack solid historical evidence. In 624, one century after the introduction of Buddhism, there were 816 monks and 569 nuns residing in forty-six monasteries and convents.[118] Although we do not have the regular statistics of the exact number of monks and nuns, it seems that more and more men were ordained or sent abroad by the government to study and to pray for the welfare of the nation as well as for the imperial family. We have to add that the statistical numbers do not reflect the religious zeal of the Japanese men and women, because the right to ordain "people of right conduct" was in the hands of the emperor.

In 741 Emperor Shomu and Empress Komyo, a devout Buddhist couple, issued an edict to have a monastery and a convent built in every province in order to pray for the prosperity of the nation. This system had a precedence in China since 581. Although there were differences in the number of monks and nuns in residence, namely two to one, and the sizes of the estates offered to the monastery and to the convent, monks and nuns were expected to live in state temples and attend the state rites. In return, the state supported and controlled them to a certain extent. Therefore, we may conclude that women were not so discriminated against socially or institutionally in the beginning, but there were economic and numerical inequalities already present.

Sexism and the Theory of Women's Sinful Nature

A change, however, was soon to come. As I have already indicated, the legal system of society was made patrilineal. Both Buddhism and Confucianism introduced sexism and established a male-dominated hierarchy in religious organizations as well as other social institutions. As society became more complicated, specialization developed, and social status became hereditary, many household heads came to carry out all significant roles allotted to the family. As the place of religious rites moved from temporary sites, such as open fields, woods, waterside, fireside and the like, to permanent constructions, such as temples and shrines, charismatic women gave place to professional male priests and monks assigned by the government. In many Buddhist scriptures, women are looked down upon as being inferior to men in their ability to practice the discipline that leads to enlightenment because of their evil *karma* or sinful nature. For instance, the *Lotus Sūtra* was popular among women as the sole *sūtra* to save women, but even in it, women have to be turned into men first in order to attain buddhahood.

Such a view of woman's nature was new and obviously unacceptable to the Japanese, women in particular, in the first few centuries. As an illustration, let me share a favorite Buddhist legend. This is partly historical, partly legendary. In 771, in Kyushu, a charismatic nun known for her wisdom and charisma went to attend a series of lectures on the *Garland Sūtra* given by a learned monk sent from the capital. When she was seated among the monks and accused thereof, she protested by saying "Buddha promulgated the right teaching out of his compassion for all sentient beings. Why do you restrain me in particular?" As her wisdom and faith overwhelmed the monks in attendance, nobody dared to restrain her and the laity paid tribute to her. You will find this legend with similar ones in the first collection of Buddhist legends compiled in the early ninth century.[119]

As you find in this legend, sexism is evident, but there is not a little resistance on the side of women. The qualification of the ordained nun was knowledge of Buddhist scriptures as well as the right conduct or discipline, the same as that required of the ordained monks. Gradually, however, nuns were not encouraged to study and practice for enlightenment. One reason, it seems to me, is the shift from urban Buddhism to mountain Buddhism, which resulted in preventing women from the straight path to enlightenment.

Traditionally, mountains were regarded as sacred places and retreats to the mountains were very popular among shamanistic ascetics. Furthermore, because of the patronage of the upper class, the monastic community in state temples suffered from so much secular interventions that elite monks emphasized withdrawal to the mountains for a meditative and disciplined life. Hermitages were soon built on the mountains where monks could live detached from the secular world, including the court. As the mountains became the sacred places for monks to concentrate on Buddhist studies and spiritual exercises, women were prohibited from stepping in, for, by then, the Buddhist view of women's sinful nature permeated the society so much that women, including nuns, were regarded as a distraction for monks on their way to enlightenment. Nuns as well as laywomen had a great longing to go up to the mountains arising from their aspiration for salvation, which we can note in the writings of female poets, essayists, novelists, and the like, from the tenth century onwards.

Another factor contributing to a decline in encouragement for nuns to pursue the practice is the nuns' eventual loss of official status and economic support. Owing to a new law in 927, nuns were not invited to participate in the state rites, which had been the main source of income for the convent. This caused immediate economic deficiency and further discrimination. Ordained nuns decreased rapidly if they could not secure financial support from their families. Because of economic need, nuns had to work for monks by cooking, washing, sewing and so on, and monks became their spiritual leaders as well as financial supporters. The economic deficiency of the convent was so great that ladies preferred to remain at their homes even after their renunciation without formal ordination; princesses or daughters of influential families were welcomed to head the convent because of their own estates or income. In this way the role-playing of the sexes was established in the Buddhist *sangha* as well as society at large. Sexism became more and more explicit and taken for granted from the 11th century onwards, and it became worse and worse in the medieval age.

The Legendary Cycle of E no Ozunu, Mountain Ascetic

To illustrate such a transition in history, let me note the development of the E no Ozunu legend. E no Ozunu was a wandering ascetic and legendary founder of the mountain cult, who was believed to have lived from the seventh to the eighth century. The first version of his legend in the *Nihon ryōiki*,[120] compiled in the early ninth century, reveals an obvious Chinese influence in the text written in Japanized Chinese. Although he was pictured as a Buddhist lay ascetic, he was more like a shamanistic Taoist sage. When he was slandered by a native deity as a usurper of the throne, the emperor dispatched messengers to capture him but they found it hard to take him due to his own mysterious magical power. So they captured his mother instead. In order that his mother might be freed, he gave himself up and was exiled to an island.

In a version of the legend, compiled a century later than the first version, a new element was added to this legend concerning his mother. There is a kind of legendary cycle developing and many stories related to him. According to the *Sanbō ekotoba* (Illustrated Tales of Three Treasures) edited in 984, he flew to T'ang China on a reed mat with his mother in a big begging bowl. In the late eleventh century it became more realistic and he crossed the sea with his mother in an iron bowl. Strangely enough, nothing is heard of his father except the name and title. But his mother follows him everywhere, even crossing the sea to China or, according to a twelfth century version, climbing the high mountains. It relates that he erected a thousand stone *stūpas* for his parents.[121] On Mt. Omine, where the entry of women is still forbidden, mountain ascetics have paid respects to the former residence of the founder, E no Ozunu, as well as that of his mother in the shape of a *stūpa*. This *stūpa* is a very small one, not large like the ones in India. Thus we know filial piety and deification of motherhood developed during medieval times.

Symbolically, the sacred mountain which has forbidden women to enter is the earth mother whose "womb" ascetics enter in order to receive rebirth after a period of initiation into the cosmic mystery. Those who are reborn out of the sacred womb are endowed with supernatural power to work for others. In rituals you will find the symbolic play of death and rebirth through mother's womb, the mountain. The E no Ozunu legend reveals the close mother-son relationship mythologically, while the sacred mountain and the reborn ascetics represent the symbolical and cosmological one.[122]

Devout Mother and Eminent Monk

In the medieval age women were respected only as mother, as is well exemplified everywhere. Women were named after their sons then. There came into being a group of Buddhist legends, which I have designated "eminent-monk-devout-mother type." We will cite another example from the monastic community at the Enryakuji temple on Mt. Hiei, the headquarter of the Tendai Buddhism and the original center of mountain Buddhism.[123] Its founder, Saicho (767-822), is the one who moved his temple apart from Kyoto. Today we can reach the temple on Mt. Hiei by car in an hour or so, but we must go back, in our imagination, to the ninth century when people had to climb the mountain on foot, and the city of Kyoto then was far smaller than the present city. Saicho, who had set up a hermitage there, petitioned the emperor to allow him to ordain monks with Mahayana monastic rules and to open a new rigid curriculum for student monks. They were required to study scriptures for twelve years on the mountain after ordination and then "those who are capable in both action and speech" were chosen to remain permanently on the mountain as leaders of the order. Those "who are capable in either action or speech" were sent to the provincial temples to be local religious leaders. For the first twelve years Saicho ordained twenty-four, ten of whom remained with him but fourteen dropped out. We learn that two monks deserted the community to take care of their mothers. Although renunciation and the secluded life of the monastic community signify separation from home, it does not mean that a monk must cut off the ties with his family. Some legends show that filial deserters, let us call them, did not incur any censure and that they, due to their faith, could also prolong their parents' lives.[124] Monks not only played the role of spiritual guides for their families but sometimes provided their material needs, food and shelter at the temple or convent, especially for mothers and sisters, since women were dependent on the male family members economically. From many legends we learn that monks were given a leave of absence to pay visits to their aged parents, even after they had chosen to live a meditative life in mountain temples like Enryakuji on Mt. Hiei.

Roughly speaking, there are two types of mother-son relations: one is a closely attached one, and the other a detached but spiritually corresponding one; in other words, a natural, overt type and a stoic, covert type. A kind of tension existed between the two lifestyles; the former gained popular support, while the latter was a more elitistic one. The cases of two eminent monks present a marked contrast. The former is Ryogen (912-985), the eighteenth supreme executive of the Tendai school,[125] while the latter is Genshin (942-1017), the author of *The Essentials of Salvation* and a leader of the *nembutsu* cult.[126] Ryogen made his mother live at the foot of the mountain where his temple was situated. This place was later called *Chino*, meaning *field of milk*. Tradition has it that young Ryogen would come to suck the mother's breasts there (He is said to have entered the monastery at the age of six or seven.). It might be folk etymology, but it reminds us of a correspondence with a hermitage as a mother's womb in which a baby grows, later to be fed on mother's milk. As I have mentioned, the convent he built for her stands now with her tomb, a *stūpa*, at the back. After death, she was deified as a Bodhisattva of the North Pole Star, which was believed to control the lives of people. Her image was wood block printed and distributed as a talisman in medieval times, just like Ryogen's. Ryogen started from the bottom of the clerical hierarchy and climbed the ladder of success to the top, owing to his learning, dexterous management of the community and close ties with the court and peers. On his mother's sixtieth, seventieth and eightieth birthdays, he held ceremonies at which scriptures were copied, doctrinal debates held, alms offered, and so forth, for merit making. On the anniversary of her death he held a big memorial service and paid homage to the tomb of his parents. He encouraged filial piety and showed deep concern for the mothers of his disciples, too. This is not completely a legend; it is quite well historically documented.

Not all the monks on Mt. Hiei or elsewhere were happy with Ryogen's practice.

The tension was felt between this master and his serious-minded disciples. One of them, Zouga (917-1003), left the temple, protesting against the excessive aristocratic patronage and condescending ways of his master. He sought a secluded place to live like a hermit and devoted himself to the way of faith. Some say that Ryogen deliberately extended the influence of the Enryaku-ji and brought about a great revival of branch temples in Yokawa and Tounomine by sending his disciples. But this sounds like an apology.[127]

Another disciple, Genshin, stayed in the monastic community on Mt. Hiei but lived in a hermitage and devoted himself to studying and writing. Despite his great scholarship he was not promoted to a high rank but remained as an ordinary monk. According to tradition, Genshin's mother was devout, while his father, although honest in nature, was not pious at all. She was known to have admonished Genshin when he had sent her a portion of the offerings given to him at the religious rites and court. She said her intention to allow him to become a monk was not to see him elected to officiate the court ceremony but to make him a sage, ready to save others. When six years had passed, he wrote to her asking whether or not he should see her, only to get a negative answer. When nine more years had passed, he suddenly felt uneasy and anxious to see her. He took this to be an omen of her impending death, or his own, and immediately started home. On his way, he met a messenger from home, who begged him to visit her without delay. He hurried home to find her in her death bed and helped her to recite Amida's name and to die a peaceful death. His family was regarded as an ideal Buddhist family with his two sisters as nuns, both known for their faith and learning.[128]

Ryogen and Genshin, two eminent monks on Mt. Hiei, were both believed to be a gift child of Kannon (Avalokitesvara) to whom their mothers devoted themselves with daily prayers. Although Ryogen's mother was deified and venerated by local people, she depended so heavily on her son's success and merit-making acts that she was not counted among eminent Buddhists. On the other hand, Genshin and his mother, as well as his sisters, were recorded with the compiler's high praise. In other words, the elitistic tradition supported the stoic relation between the mother and son, while the popular support might have gone to Ryogen's filial acts. Confucian ethics were the standard of evaluation in this case.

The Split Between Elite Nuns and Popular Shamanistic Women

During the warlike age, warriors and noblemen fought frequently to win power, but the Kamakura era (1185-1533) saw the flowering of Japanese Buddhism. Zen Master Dogen of the Soto school was exceptionally sympathetic toward women, criticizing the negative attitudes toward women of the monks who would prevent them from the religious quest. He emphasized the equality of men and women in attaining Buddhahood. His ideas, however, were neither understood nor transmitted by his successors and contemporaries. Dogen was a unique exception in his age.

Warriors were conscious of their sinful deeds of killing, and became very good patrons of temples for merit-making. In such an age of disorder and power struggles, Buddhist temples served as a sanctuary for some who sought protection and isolation from wars and turmoil. Convents were the sanctuary for the princesses of the dethroned emperors or the widows and daughters of defeated warriors. Although men renounced the world for their salvation, women were not allowed to leave the family to do so. Once they became widows, however, renunciation, formal or private, was encouraged to pray for merit-making for their deceased husbands and other family members. Women of the upper class often became nuns and, in the meantime, heads of the convents.

Common women, however, could not enjoy such opportunities to satisfy their desire for salvation. In the feudalistic Tokugawa period, from the seventeenth to the nineteenth century, the leading ideology of the government was neo-Confucianism adopted to suit the Japanese society. The institution of *ie*, family household, was the primary political, economic and social unit of the static feudal society, and it became increasingly so rigid in time that women suffered from it. By *ie* I mean the patrilineal household institution that includes family members, estate, social status, profession or trade, reputation, and so forth. Spiritually, it is a temporally extended commune consisting of ancestors and descendants all tied by karmic chains. Women were taught to adjust themselves to any given situation for they would have to leave their family and marry into another family. It was necessary for them to devote themselves to the service of this new family and to give birth to an heir.

As to religious activities, women were taught not to frequent shrines and temples, but to stay at home in the service of the family. They should not be deluded by the arts of male and female mediums, nor should they divert their attention to invisible spiritual beings, because there were many wandering shamanistic women, particularly in rural areas. Their main functions were communication with spirits, deities and the dead; divination and fortune telling through possession; healing; purification of houses, wells, stoves, and hearths; preaching by telling tales, singing hymns, dancing, and the like. They were called nuns and they provided entertainment as well as religious messages to the common people who were banned from paying tribute to many state-supported or private temples. Deprived of opportunities to study for a religious quest, women's religiosity tended to find outlets in the spirit world or shamanistic activities. Even after the Meiji Restoration in 1868, when the Shogunate system of government was overturned and modernization started, the fundamental principles regarding female education remained unchanged until the end of World War II.

Women Religionists in Modern Japan[129]

Name	1st Revela- tion	Marriage (Termi- nation)	Chil- dren	Edu- cation Yrs.	Organization (No. Members)
Miki NAKAYAMA (1798-1887)	1838	1810-1833 (death)	6	0	Tenrikyo (1,839,007)
Nao DEGUCHI (1837-1918)	1892	1855-1887 (death)	8	0	Omoto (172,460)
Fusa MIZUNO (1883-1970)	1911	1901 (divorced) 1905-1912 (divorced)	0	6	Kannagarakyo (24,346)
Chiyoko FUKATA (1887-1925)	1919	1907-1908 (death) 1909-1922 (divorce)	1	0	Ennokyo (419,452)
Myoko NAGANUMA (1889-1957)	1939	1914-1925 (divorce) 1930-1944 (divorce)	1	6	Rissho Koseikai (6,348,120)
Esho MIZOGAMI (1892-1984)	1930	1915-1950 (divorce)	1	12	Nanayokai (no membership)
Sayo KITAMURA (1900-1967)	1944	1920-1967 (death)	1	6	Tensho Kotai Jingukyo (439,001)
Mitsu MIYAMOTO (1900-1984)	1932	1918-1945 (death)	3	6	Myochikai (962,611)
Kimi KOTANI (1901-1971)	1929	1917 (death) 1926-1929 (death)	0	5	Reiyukai (3,202,172)
Hisako HOZUMI (1907-)	1933	1934-1961 (divorce)	6	12	Taiwa Kyodan (56,374)

After briefly considering 1,400 years of Japanese history, we now are poised to understand contemporary problems. So far, we have discussed historical changes of women's religious life, as well as some archaic models and symbols. Perhaps you will be surprised to find all of them alive in our present society. In this sense, we have no severance with the past. It is said that our country has achieved modernization within one century, and with success. It may be true with technology but the people have had a hard time catching up with the rapid changes. You have heard about the emergence of many so-called New Religions since the end of the last century. One striking feature of these new religious movements, in general, is the fact that women have often initiated and contributed significantly to the development of these religions. This table of women religionists is by no means an exhaustive list of modern charismatic women in this country, there are many more, but it is, I believe, a good representation.

These women are all known for their extensive spiritual influence. They represent a wide variety in terms of life span, locality, social status, religious background, education, etc. They have one thing in common, however. They all lived a life of religious devotion after their revelatory experience and did so in spite of the various hardships that resulted from discrimination and the conflict in roles of wife, mother and religionist they were forced to assume.[130]

Much sociological research has been done on various aspects of these movements but little attention has thus far been paid to the question why there were so many female founders or co-founders in spite of adversity. For instance, some say that a sudden rise of new religious movements was a response to the chaotic disorder into which the Japanese were thrown by the military defeat in 1945. It is true we experienced a total reversal of values. Women were recognized as equal to men in our new constitution; freedom of faith was also established for the first time in history. Thus, there was a "mushrooming" of new religions.

However, I should like to turn our attention to the table of women religionists again. You will notice that most of these women have led a life of devotion without any benefits of post-war Japan. They were discriminated against just because they were women, and they were suppressed by the police just because their charisma attracted too many people. Some of them fought fiercely against the establishment, in which they had been given no place: some criticized the government and willingly went to prison. Having little to lose, they endured hardship.

I interpret the emergence of female charismatic religionists as the revival of the age-old tradition of women as mediums and the embodiment of life, mercy and power, which have survived on the popular level in spite of sexism. Since clerical professions and official titles have actually been inherited in both Shinto and Buddhist establishments, nearly excluding women or allowing them niggardly mere nominal or suppressed existence, the female religionists did not have any choice but to find self-expression in new religious movements. Strong female leadership is sporadic and is generally limited to the founder's own lifetime. The women religionists have never advocated dramatic changes in sex roles or in the power relationship between women and men. As women's maternal functions and family responsibilities are considered of paramount importance, their role in society as individual human beings is secondary, even if they are given a chance. This might be the reason why no constructive contribution to women's self-realization has yet been made by the so-called new religious organizations here, in spite of the fact that women members usually outnumber men and the missionary zeal of women has most often been responsible for the expansion of the new organizations.

There are still many hindrances for women to overcome. First and foremost is the theory of their sinful nature or inferiority. In the feudal age, childbirth and menstruation were thought to be the source of women's pollution. Younger generations are getting free of these theories, which are still visible in older generations. Religionists used to utilize them to convert women. Second, the *ie*, patrilineal household institution, is still a social and religious unit although non-existent legally, while faith is becoming more and more a personal matter. Buddhist temples and their supporters are tied with a family tomb, funerals and memorial services, but women in particular are getting critical of such a system and seek for a loosening or cutting of such ties. Third, both feudalists and modernists were critical of women's involvement in the spirit world and shamanistic activities. There are some businesses flourishing today which take advantage of such women. One of them is *mizuko kuyō*, memorial service for aborted babies. Women, including younger generations, have been made targets of contemporary commercialization of the traditional cult.[131]

As you can see, we have a long way to go, looking for a new cooperative way of men and women in every sphere of our lives.

XVI
Reflections on the Notion of the Inward Quest in the Japanese Buddhist Experience
Dennis Hirota

One engaged in a study of the Buddhist tradition in Japan might see in the practice of Buddhists a focus on an inward quest with a primary emphasis on realizing one's liberation. Professor Bando drew our attention to the life-flow pulsation of the universe, of wisdom and compassion, with which one becomes identified in a salvific realization. Professor Tokunaga indicated a natural extension from the core of the *shinjin* realization into supportive social involvement for humankind. Dennis Hirota thinks carefully about the notion of "the inward quest" and lets his reflections lead us into a more critical appraisal of our assumptions and to a deeper understanding of the religious life of Japanese Buddhists.

In some respects the notion of "the inward quest" seems transparent. We all have some sense of what this might mean when we reflect on who we are really and try to probe inward beneath our social identities, formed through our relations with others and our entanglements with society. When we wonder about what our lives are really about we have some sense of reflecting inward into something within us, something close to our real existence.

It is hard to bring this notion into central focus in a Japanese Buddhist context. I am not sure why it seems so difficult to have a clear concept of "the inward quest." I do think that there are elements of this notion of the inward quest that are not appropriate or that do not really express the way Japanese Buddhists think about what in English we might call the inward quest. This is what I will now attempt to consider.

There are two problems that might be raised. One is the idea of the inward, suggesting a dichotomy, a split or distinction between inward and outward. I think this is not the kind of perspective that a Japanese Buddhist would ordinarily bring to the problem. At least, it is not expected that Buddhists would stay with it. The other issue is the idea of the quest, the idea of exerting effort and will towards a goal. This also is something that is not stressed in the thinking of Japanese Buddhists. There is, of course, the idea of the path, which is broader than the notion of "inward quest," and may be seen to incorporate the idea of a quest. In the end, I think this idea of a quest is also to be abandoned. It is sometimes said that in life, the journey is more important than the destination. Here we have two contrasting ideas: the idea of getting there, reaching the goal, and the idea that how the journey is undertaken, how it is experienced, is more important. There is a slightly different perspective in the idea of the path that Japanese Buddhists uphold. It is neither of the two. Finally, the goal becomes, or has to become, present at every point along the path. It is not that the journey is more important than the goal, but perhaps that when the goal is reached we find that we are on the path and the goal is manifested at every step.

In order to attempt to deal with this idea of the inward quest, I would like to present as briefly as possible, two very widely known Buddhist depictions of the path and to look at them within the framework I have just suggested.

The first is the Ten Oxherding Pictures, which are widely used in Zen. The second illustration depicts a parable of the two rivers and the white path. Both of these illustrations are of Chinese origin.[132] The Oxherding pictures are from the Chinese Zen tradition, and the parable, itself originally a Chinese narrative, is from the Chinese Pure Land tradition. I think this is significant because although both of these illustrations are widely used in Japan, I know of no native Japanese attempts to do something like it.[133] It seems to me that this is partly due to the way larger literary structures are built in Japanese thought. We tend to see, rather than complex narrative structures, a kind of episodic or serial structure. I think the Japanese have found it easier to borrow this kind of depiction of progress on the path from China than to develop depictions themselves, although the interpretations do express this Japanese view of looking at a series of frames, each frame a moment that embraces the whole while nevertheless remaining a part. There is a total form, a view of the path, that is a view of both a part and the whole at the same time. There is, therefore, an attempt both to represent and to transcend the temporal process of the path.

The Ten Oxherding Pictures

The dualism of inward and outward that is suggested by the notion of the inward quest does not fit the Japanese experience precisely, and yet it is easily recognizable. To clarify how the situation is perceived in the Japanese Buddhist tradition, I will turn first to another paradigm, one stemming from ancient India. This is the model of four stages of life.

The first stage is that of the student, starting from about the age of nine. According to some sources, ideally this phase would last about twelve years. During this time the student would leave his family, his parents, and go to the house of a master or teacher. He would serve the master and undergo a period of study, leading a celibate and austere life. After completing study under his master, he would return to his parents' home, marry, and start his own family. This is the second stage, the householder. After he had established and maintained his own household and seen his own grandchildren born, he would have fulfilled his social obligations and would go off into the forest to meditate, to perform religious cultivation and discipline. This would be the third stage, the forest dweller. After living the life of a hermit in the forest and reaching some religious attainment, he would then, as a very old man, leave his hermitage and take up the life of a homeless wanderer, the wandering stage.

In this very idealized ancient Indian scheme, we can sketch two basic phases. As a student and householder, a person would fulfill mundane obligations. After completing those two first stages, one would be free to go off and devote oneself to religious practices. This second phase corresponds to an inward aspect in which one turns away from society and social involvement and pursues a solitary existence in the forest as a wanderer.

The Buddhist tradition might be seen as stemming basically from the latter two stages. We can see this in the biography of Sakyamuni Buddha who left his palace, went out into the forest, performed austere practices, attained enlightenment under the bodhi tree, and then, for about thirty-five years, took up a mendicant existence, wandering and teaching. Sakyamuni was thus a typical mendicant practicer, a not uncommon figure in his day.

If the paradigm is looked at in this way, we would expect the idea of an inward quest to be a dominant feature in the Buddhist tradition. However, in looking at Japan, we find something very different. For one thing, the Buddhist temples are, as a rule, passed on from father to son. In essence, for a temple family, there is no difference between the household and the temple. Almost all Buddhist priests who have temples in Japan have been born into their temples and now, in almost all the Buddhist schools, they marry, rear their family in their temples and then pass the temples on to their children like a business or hereditary trade.

Originally, it would appear as though the Buddhist tradition emphasized a kind of truncated scheme of this version of life in four phases, concentrating only on the final two phases and seeing little essential meaning in the first two phases. One of the strongest expressions of renunciation in the case of Japan that I recall is that of Dogen, a contemporary of Shinran. A monk came to Dogen and said that he wanted to concentrate on his religious practice but that he was supporting his elderly mother. He was the only child and his mother had no other support. He was undertaking a life of practice but at the same time he maintained his ties in society in order to provide a meager existence for his mother. He asked Dogen's advice whether, since he strongly wished to pursue the Buddhist practice, he should immediately go off to his hermitage and leave his mother, or support his mother and wait until her death before devoting himself entirely to his practice. Dogen answered that while, of course, it was a decision the monk had to make himself, it was not necessarily certain that the mother would die before the son. If she were to live longer than her son and if, for some reason, he was unable to devote himself completely to practice, it would be unfortunate for both of them. So, Dogen suggested that the monk might make what provisions he could for his mother and then go off and devote himself to his practice. I think we see in this a very sharply drawn dichotomy of the first two phases and the final two.

What has happened in Japanese Buddhism, however, is that instead of the first two phases being truncated and the Buddhist tradition focusing on the final two, it is almost as though the inward quest has been lopped off and the temples have become households. There is a very mundane, practical reason for this: many temples have become almost completely secularized and, to a considerable degree, this phase of the inward quest has been much too much forgotten. But there is also, as I hope will become clearer as we consider the two illustrations, a basis for this in the Japanese view of the path.

One can gain a general idea of the ten oxherding pictures by considering briefly the titles of the pictures.

[1]

Searching for the ox. In the center of the picture is a young oxherd who has lost his ox. It is said in commentaries that the ox is a symbol for the true self. Although the meaning of this becomes clearer as we progress through the pictures, if seen in this way, the opening picture may be understood as a beginning of the inward quest of the oxherd as he awakens to the fact that the ox is gone and he begins his search for it.

[2]

Seeing the tracks. As the oxherd proceeds with his search he is able to locate the tracks of the ox but does not see the ox itself. It is said that the tracks are the Buddhist teachings--the *sūtras*, the Buddhist literature.

[3]

Seeing the ox. As the oxherd continues following the tracks, he is able to glimpse the ox. The tail of the ox appears at the left side of the picture. This first glimpse is a kind of awakening, an apprehension of the true self, perhaps.

[4]

Taking hold of the ox. Here the oxherd continues his search, his practice, especially seated meditation. He has been able to attach his rope to the ox.

[5]

Taming the ox. Although the ox resisted, the oxherd is now able to lead the ox through his attainments in practice and discipline. He has the strength to lead the ox.

[6]

On the ox's back, returning home. Now the ox is completely tame and will bear the oxherd on its back and will, of itself, return home.

[7]

The ox forgotten. There is only the oxherd. Here, the series of frames as a unified narrative seems to break down. The ox disappears, but the oxherd has now returned home. In contrast to the first picture, where the oxherd is filled with anxiety with having lost his ox, here he is totally at home with himself. There is no longer any concern about something missing.

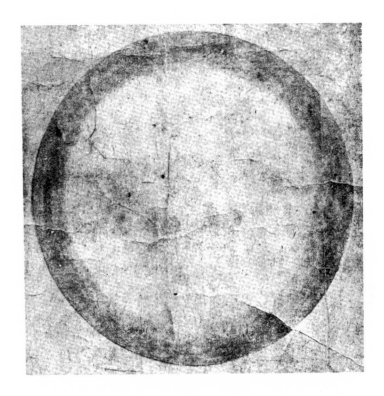

[8]

The ox and oxherd are both forgotten. This is an empty circle, widely employed in Zen. Now, both ox and oxherd are gone. The original metaphor of searching for the true self has totally dissolved.

[9]

Return to the source. Here we see blossoms and a river flowing by, a scene from nature.

[10]

Entering the marketplace, with loose hands. Here, *loose hands* means without any particular purpose or intention, without doing anything. The figure is no longer the oxherd but a kind of beggar saint figure, the beggar who is in possession of great wealth which he carries in the large sack, and gives to others. We see another figure here and the two are engaging in some kind of interaction.

In the set of pictures, we have a presentation of some kind of quest, perhaps an inward quest, even. However, this narrative motif falls away part way through, and we end up with something completely different. At first, we see the oxherd heading out into the wilderness alone, which, perhaps looks like phase three of the old Indian notion of four stages of life. At the end, we have a beggar, perhaps something like stage four, but also, significantly, in engagement with others in the world. Here we see the practitioner going to the wine merchant, going to the fish market, going to places traditionally off limits to the religious practitioner. He is freely involved in society, appearing actually closer to the older Indian idea of a householder.

It is necessary to impose a kind of interpretation on the whole set of pictures by dividing them into three frames in order to try to grasp comprehensively the entire meaning.

Pictures *1-3* may be said to correspond to the inward quest. Pictures *4-7* correspond to the practice and realization. Pictures *8-10* correspond to the activity of wisdom-compassion, perhaps the activity of Zen, of the true mind, the true self, or no mind. Let us look at the pictures in these three sets.

The oxherd pictures as traditionally handed down include, in each frame, the picture itself and commentary in the form of a verse and a prose note, which was added later.

The commentary in the first frame, under the first picture, begins, "Never lost from the very beginning: what need to seek and search?" This is a theme that runs throughout the pictures and throughout much of Buddhism in Japan. It is connected with the idea of Buddha nature, the potentiality of enlightenment present in all beings, even though we may be ignorant of it. This is a rhetorical question--what need is there to search, to search for the self, when actually if we knew, if we were "awake," we would know that we are not lost? Nevertheless, unless we search we cannot really find ourselves, and we feel lost. In one sense there is no need to "seek and search" and in another sense, of course, we can never find ourselves unless we do undertake the quest.

Although there are many depictions of the ten oxherding pictures based on the commentary and the verse, traditionally, they are all drawn, like these, within a circle, and the circle may be seen to act in two ways. One is that it is a motif--the purest form is in picture number eight, which is an empty circle--and represents true reality or the true self. Even with the very first picture, this stage does not occur separate from or apart from the eighth picture, the circle, the depiction of reality. So, when we reach the final stage of running through the ten pictures, in a sense we have never left the first stage, and we can truly grasp the first line, that we are never lost. Further, the ten pictures are circular in this way as well--the end of the path is present at every step along the way.

Let me begin a kind of running interpretation of the commentary. We can see in the first picture one who is turning his back on awakening, turning away from the true self, perhaps, with face to the dust, the dust of worldly involvement, of mundane life, of entanglements in society, being totally concerned with others and with making a living in the world, with temporal concerns. With face to the dust, totally absorbed in mundane life, suddenly it is gone and he has lost track of himself. He suddenly discovers that he does not know who he is. The sense of a "home on the hill, ever farther, farther," speaks of his alienation and anxiety, and for us a feeling of not being at home where we are. Then, reasoning where the trail forks, he instantly errs: there is a decision based on gain or loss, a decision between right or wrong. This is a reference to the source of the problem, which is his ignorance, his mistaken view of himself and the world. "Gain or loss, right or wrong, smoldering into flame"--this is a kind of shorthand for false thinking, false discrimination, the perception of the world based on the perspective of the egocentric self, or thinking based on self-attachment. Basically, involved here are discrimination of the self and world, and then judgments about things. This is the problem of not seeing things in the world as they really are, but seeing them only from the perspective of the concerns of the self. This is the Buddhist notion of the three poisons--desire, aversion. and delusion--the attitudes that we take towards the things in the world, the judgments that we make about them based on what good, what value they have for us, or what kinds of threats, menace, they seem to present to us. Our vision of things is colored by this kind of view, centered on the egocentric self and self-attachments. In the same way, then, we make the self into a kind of object, we see ourselves with a certain level or position and place in society, with a certain amount of wealth, number of friends, etc. We try to bolster our own existence by gathering possessions around us, keeping at a distance whatever threatens us. This is the gain or loss, right or wrong kind of vision, the vision of ordinary life in society.

The next phase clarifies the state of mind:

"Aimlessly, endlessly, he parts the grass, seeking.
Waters widen, mountains loom far off, the path goes deeper.
At strength's end, weary at heart, and with nowhere to begin to search,
He hears only, in ghostly maples, cries of late autumn cicadas."

He hears the hints of anxiety stemming from all attachment to ourselves, that we cannot manage to cling to what we gain, that all our efforts to support and maintain our existence must ultimately fail, and the hint of an impulse of the awakening to the need for the inward quest.

In the second picture, he comes across the tracks, the Buddhist teachings, or perhaps finding a teacher. He receives instruction and he is able to proceed along the way. But, of course, the teachings themselves remain only abstractions unless one is seriously undertaking and following the path, through practice in *zazen*, seated meditation, devoting oneself to that discipline, an attempt to still the mind, to free oneself from the false thinking of one's self-attachment. There can be no progress until finally through one's study and practice one is able to see the ox, as in the third picture. This is a kind of attainment. This initial seeing of the ox can perhaps be called a kind of *satori*. It is not, however, that the path can end here. In Zen, there is a great stress upon practice after realization. The Edo period Zen master Hakuin stated that he experienced several great awakenings and small awakenings without number. Perhaps this third picture might represent a kind of small awakening. In any case, although the image of the path and the idea of searching for the ox are applicable here, the sense of the oxherd and the search for the ox representing the inward quest follow well the narrative to this point. In all forms of

Buddhism, there has to be practice after this kind of realization, and practice continues throughout life.

We see this clearly in the second set of pictures, numbers *4-7*. I would like to look at these schematically, dividing them into frames *4* and *5*, and frames *6* and *7*. I would view these as dialectically interacting. Pictures *4* and *5* represent clearly the idea of diligence and practice, the necessity for continued discipline, for constant vigilance and effort. Pictures *6* and *7* show the realm of fulfillment; the ox has been completely tamed and there is no need at this point for the discipline. I think these four pictures, taken in pairs of frames, might be said to represent a kind of practice after attainment, a practice that is itself attainment. Master Dogen maintained that practice and realization are one. One does not perform the practice in order *to gain* realization. *Practice itself is the manifestation, the presence in the present, of realization itself.* These pictures here effect the same thing--the fusion of these two ideas. They reflect very clearly the Buddhist thinking of a kind of phase of the path that might be beyond what we normally think of as an inward quest.

Now let us look at the final three pictures (*8-10*). The ox and oxherd have vanished. There is a kind of self-contradiction in representing the path in terms of an oxherd searching for an ox, searching for the true self. After all, who is it that searches for the ox? Finally, the ox, as with all conceptions or images of the self, completely disappears. One view of meditation is that it is the practice of eliminating objects. Ordinarily, we perceive the world falsely, in ignorance. We objectify things. We put labels on them and we judge from the perspective of the self. We perceive our own conceptions. We project our own desires and fears, we do not see things themselves. The usual image is that of a flower. We look at a flower and see that it is a rose, that it is red or white, we see that it is in full blossom or is fading, we make judgments about it. None of those conceptions, abstractions, are really what it is that is there before us. What is there is not a rose, the image that we have gathered, learned, used, with identity imposed. What it is is itself unique, uniquely there. That it is there is part of its definition. So, the Buddhist in meditation practices by eradicating that kind of objectifying, thinking that objectifies things from the perspective of the self. When the image and the image of the self are eliminated, there is no seeing of things. There is no false deception, false thinking about things. This state, the awakening that is attained at that point, is spoken of as wisdom. This is described as emptiness--there are no objects to be eradicated. This might be the circle, as in picture *8*. It is an empty circle and there is nothing in it. It is also the wisdom attained when all false thinking has been eradicated.

This is one aspect of wisdom. Since there is no dichotomy between seer and seeing, this wisdom is the wisdom of totality--reality. This is the circle. This wisdom is always, in Buddhism, not simply a nothingness, not simply a complete blank. So, there are two other aspects of the true mind that are illustrated here, the true mind is also reality and is also things not conceptualized but things as they really are. This is what is illustrated in pictures *9* and *10*.

You have studied Zen thinking, and know that there is meditation leading to awakening through a kind of eradication of false thinking, but not to a blankness. There emerges a kind of seeing, a perception, and this is stressed very much in Zen; "No thing in mind, no mind in things"--meaning no false objects--the two sides of the wisdom that is attained with the true mind. As the false, conceptualized, mental object is eradicated, there arises a kind of perception that perceives things and is active in the world. This discrimination is never separated from the fundamental realization. It is a kind of perception in which, since fundamentally there is no dichotomy between what is the seer and what is seen, it may be said things emerge to be perceived, from outside of themselves but, by an elimination of the self that stands apart from things, are perceived, by entering things, are seen from within themselves.

This is a kind of ideal that is very common in Japanese aesthetics and other cultural activity and I hope to be able to touch on this on another occasion in speaking about the tea ceremony. For example, there is a statement by Basho, a master of *haiku*: "To learn of the pine tree, you must ask the pine; to learn of bamboo you must ask bamboo." Through his own Zen discipline, and the discipline of poetry, he attempted to enter this realm in which, with the elimination of the false self, there was a perception of things that arose from within the things themselves so that the things could be perceived as they truly are and not as divided from, distinct from, the perceiving mind.

In terms of Zen, this is depicted in pictures *8* and *9*. It is very evident where Zen has played a very prominent role in the development of the arts with the great concern for the beauty of nature, and also in contributing to the aesthetic ideal of perceiving things as they are, and letting things emerge by themselves without imposition from the artist onto the depiction.

There is also one other aspect which has not been stressed very much in Zen, though Zen masters today are becoming more aware of the need to develop this aspect. It is suggested in picture *10*. This picture depicts a figure, a kind of beggar-sage entering a market place. Although a beggar, he is nevertheless dispensing wealth out of a huge sack. This is a popular image known to Japanese as Hotei, a folk figure. This represents an aspect that I think might be called compassion, one aspect inseparable from wisdom. When one perceives the world and sees things as they are from beyond the stance of self-attachment, when one sees other beings in the world and sees them not as supports for one's own existence but as beings in suffering and in so perceiving them from knowledge of the essential identity of oneself with beings in the world, one experiences the suffering of beings as one's own suffering. It is from this experience of the pain of ignorant beings, the pain suggested in the first picture, perhaps, and even before that, of beings who are lost and suffering from their own ignorance in the world, that one cannot but go out into the world and seek to aid them and lead them to awakening. This is the activity, the compassion, that arises directly from wisdom, as indicated in the last sentence of the commentary: "Wine seller and fish monger--these he transforms and brings to buddhahood."

There are two dimensions that should be noted here. One is that there is a return to the world and a direct engagement with beings in the world. This is not simply the idea of the wandering sage but a real involvement, a direct involvement, on the one hand. On the other hand, there is a smaller figure incorporated within the circle. From the stance of the Bodhisattva, the practitioner who has again the true realization, the beings in the world are not separate, not divided from the self. He sees that in essence they are both held within the circle, from the realization that is depicted in picture *8*, the circle. Although the Bodhisattva goes out into the world to save other beings from the pain in the world, these are not just *other* beings. There is also a point of oneness! He sees the other beings while standing beyond the stance of his own self-attachment. This is the other meaning of the sentence, "Never lost from the very beginning: what need to seek and search?" This is the view of the man in picture *10*, looking at the beings who have yet to traverse the path. On the one hand he experiences their pain, on the other hand he encounters them with *loose hands*, knowing that they are never lost from the beginning. He does not take his task overly seriously.

In the Pure Land context, this recognition is stated by an early Chinese master, T'an-luan: "In saving beings one perceives no object of salvation." The Bodhisattva, in observing sentient beings, sees that in the final analysis they are nonexistent, meaning that they are also ultimately, in fact, embraced in picture *8*. Although he saves countless sentient beings, in reality there is not a single sentient being who realizes he or she is never lost from the beginning. This manifests the act of saving sentient beings as being like play. In the Pure Land tradition, from early on, we see something very close to this Zen picture *10*, though this is not the most emphasized aspect of Zen.

Ultimately, we see here a sense of path as perceived by the Japanese Buddhists that runs a risk of being compressed when summed up in the notion of "the inward quest." The inward quest might be seen as part of the path, but ultimately the quest drops away: there is a quest but *the goal is also present at every step along the way.* There is an inward quest and when the inward quest is achieved, then there unfolds a vision of all beings. The practitioner becomes able to see all beings and things of the world as they truly are.

The Parable of the Two Rivers and the White Path

The illustration of this parable is a Kamakura painting. The story related to the picture is as follows:

Suppose there is a traveler journeying one hundred thousand li toward the west, when suddenly, along the way, he comes upon two rivers [in a single channel]--one of fire, extending southward, and one of water, extending north. Each river is one hundred paces across, immeasurably deep, and endless to the north and south. Dividing the fire and water is a single path four or five inches wide. This path, from the eastern bank to the western bank, is one hundred paces in length. Billows of water surge over the path and flames sweep up to scorch it. Water and fire thus alternate without break.

Now the traveler has already gone far in the vast and solitary wilderness; there is no one to be seen. But bands of brigands and wild beasts lurk there, and seeing the traveler alone, they vie with each other to kill him. Fearing for his life, the traveler at once flees toward the west, when without warning the great river appears. He reflects, "I can see no end to this river, either to the north or south. In the middle is a white path, but it is exceedingly narrow. Although the two banks are but slightly separated, how is it possible to cross? Assuredly this day I shall die. If I turn back, brigands and wild beasts will press closer and closer upon me. If I run north or south, beasts and poisonous insects will contend with each other to attack me. If I venture on the path westward, surely I will plunge into the two currents of water and fire."

There are no words to express the terror and despair that fill him at this point. He thinks further to himself: "If I turn back now, I die. If I remain here, I die. If I go forward, I die. There is no way for me to escape death. Therefore, I choose to go forth, venturing on this path. Since this path exists, it must be possible to cross the rivers."

When this thought occurs to him, he suddenly hears an encouraging voice of someone on the eastern bank, "O traveler, just resolve to follow this path forward! You will certainly not encounter the grief of death. But if you stay where you are, you will surely die."

Further, someone on the western bank calls to him, "O traveler, with mind that is single, with right-mindedness, come at once! I will protect you. Have no fear of plunging to grief in the water or fire." The traveler, having heard the exhortation on his side of the river and the call from the other, immediately acquires firm resolution in body and mind and decisively takes the path, advancing directly without entertaining any doubt or apprehension.

When he has gone one or two paces, the brigands on the eastern bank call out to him: "O traveler, come back! This path is treacherous and permits no crossing. You are certain to meet death. None of us address you thus with evil intent.

The traveler hears the voices calling him, but he gives no backward glance. Thinking only of the path, he advances directly forward with mind that is single, forthwith reaches the western side, and is free forever of all afflictions. He meets his good friend, and his joy is boundless.[134]

The author of the parable, Shan-tao, was a Chinese Pure Land master. In Japan, the parable is widely known. I understand there is a calligraphy of the *kanji*, "the white path" at Chapel House, on the Colgate University campus. It seems to me that the parable itself and its depiction give us a sense of what is going on. The explanation makes it less complex than it actually is. D. H. Lawrence makes the comment that we should trust the tale, not the teller, and I think this is perhaps the case here.

The west is chosen because that is the direction in which the Pure Land lies. This world is at the bottom of the picture, and there are scenes depicting ordinary life. Above this is the wilderness with the bandits and wild beasts. The rivers are the rivers of greed and of anger stemming from our basic ignorance. The path arises from our ignorance, which binds us to a life of pain, blinded to the way things really are. The two figures on the banks are Amida Buddha and Sakyamuni Buddha, who has taught us about the Pure Land and Amida's Vow. The two Buddhas are friends who encourage us on the path. I think we can imagine the traveler alone, heading into the wilderness from the world, beginning his inward quest, similar to the oxherd. There is a basic difference here, however, between Zen and Pure Land traditions. Twice, Shan-tao says the river *suddenly* arises before the traveler. This is a puzzling part of the narrative, but I think it must express Shan-tao's own experience. He states that the river suddenly arises and that the traveler is chased by the bandits and beasts into suddenly coming to the river without warning. The bandits and beasts and poisonous insects are symbols for things of this world, our six senses, our false perceptions and images of our own ignorance. These false images pursue us. When we leave our concerns of the world, we come to feel we are pursued by these "falsenesses," we are driven to confront the anger and greed within, the two rivers that block our path.

I think that we can take two perspectives of this scheme. One reason I like this painting is that it is highly geometric, tending itself to a kind of schematic view of the path. There is a sense of progress, of pursuing the path, but again I think this image breaks down if we interpret it as Shinran sees it. It then expresses a complex image that cannot be simply understood as pursuing the path. When Shan-tao interprets the path he says it is the good mind of aspiration. If we look at it in that way, we can see that from the very beginning we already have the traveler heading west. There is a teleological element here, a goal, a sense that he should go west, that he is heading toward his true home. Perhaps this is the inward quest and he has some sense of direction toward his true self, his real nature. As he perceives the bandits and the things of this world, mundane entanglements, they become clearly threats to his progress. He finally comes across these two rivers and he does not know what to do. He decides that since the white path lies before him, there must be a way to cross. But this white path, according to Shan-tao, is the good mind of aspiration itself, and so I think it may be seen as an extension of the early impulse that the traveler has had from the very beginning. It is what is good in his mind, even though there is always raging evil. There is the narrow path, four or five inches wide, and if he undertakes it, with the support of the Buddhas, it is possible to cross and to reach the Pure Land, the land of life and purity beyond the two rivers.

What is important here is making it to the end of the path, and the practitioner must strive along every point of the path to keep his resolve in terms of *nembutsu*, to say the *nembutsu*, to worship Amida, to maintain the aspiration and not to be tempted by the calls of the world, which would draw him away. If he succeeds in this way, then at the very end of his life, when his karmic bonds have come to an end and he is across the river at the point of death, he will attain birth in the Pure Land. This is the crucial point, here at the end of life. I think this might be seen as one vision of the parable. Although the parable seems very clear on the surface, it has been open to various types of interpretation. In that vision, then, this life can be seen as one continuous path, that would be the kind of inward quest that leads to the Pure Land at the time of death.

For Shinran, however, I think it might be said that the entire depiction itself, perhaps like the last three pictures in the ten oxherding pictures, emerges at the point of the realization of *shinjin* and is seen as a representation of what it is like to realize *shinjin*. For Shinran, the concept of birth is used in the Pure Land in two ways: one would occur at the very first step onto the white path because the white path is not the person's own good mind but Other Power (*tariki*) or the power or Vow of Amida. This is the crucial step for Shinran, this step onto the white path. At that time, in some sense, the person has already attained birth, although it is at death that one attains the Pure Land and enlightenment.

For Shinran, it might be said that this whole image itself is, in its entirety, an image of the truth of *shinjin*. All of this in the lower part of the picture becomes true, becomes seen as it is, becomes a recognition of these passions working within one's self and the Pure Land becomes true, becomes present, extends itself into this life as Other Power which becomes a part of one's own personal use in this life.

I have presented these two depictions of the path to try to sketch what might be thought of as the inward quest, and to try to show a kind of complexity in the thinking of Japanese Buddhists, a kind of interfusion of contrasting elements that can only be brought together and discerned in illustrations such as these.

You will recall the Mahayana idea of the Bodhisattva, who, in one sense, looks on or perceives all beings as they are, and in doing so he also perceives that the beings of the world and himself are essentially one, inseparable. In a sense, he comes to experience the suffering of beings in the world as his own suffering, his own pain. At the same time, because he has transcended the usual thinking about the self, the usual egocentricity, self-attachment, and has realized the transcendent that pervades both his own existence and that of all beings, he also realizes that while he works to save all beings, in fact, there are no beings that he saves. In this sense, he is free of his own intentional activity. He has no designs to save other beings. He undertakes his compassionate activity as a kind of play.

One might raise a question concerning this kind of vision, of beings in pain and suffering, as essentially non-existent. I was reminded, as I thought about this, of a slightly different question--the question of this ideal of compassion that Buddhists hold and the tendency not to move from this into a kind of activism. Once D. T. Suzuki was asked about this. I have only read his response but I have assumed that it had to do with this kind of question--of social activism and its relationship with compassion, the Buddhist ideal. Someone asked him whether this sense of compassion was not extremely fragile and whether it had something really concrete to say to us in our existence in the world.

I first came across this, as it was recorded in a poem, which I assume to be a poem about Vietnam. I came across it at a time when much of the world was horrified at the self-immolation of Buddhist monks and nuns in Vietnam. There was a kind of incomprehension about the religion in which this kind of act would be taken as a means of communication and expression of the anguish that the monks and nuns felt at what was happening in their country. Suzuki's answer was, "You talk to me, I talk to you, is this fragile?" I puzzled over this at the time. It seems to me, now, that this idea, though it seems simple if taken at the usual level of conversation in daily life, to be rather superficial or even sentimental, when seen on a deeper level, this idea--"You talk to me, I talk to you"--this seems to lie at the very heart of what many Japanese Buddhists have thought to be the very foundation of our existence in the world. It is this kind of speech, conversation, that we come to when we seek the true nature of our existence in the world or what it is that our lives are really about. In this sense, it is perhaps what lies at the end and also along the way, of the inward quest as perceived by Japanese Buddhists and it is at the core of the vision of the ways as arts and in particular, or perhaps most apparently, in the art of *chanoyu*.

So, this kind of talk that Suzuki was referring to is of course not our ordinary use of language. It arises out of some realization, some attainment of our true self. It arises only where both the self and the other at once stand opposite each other and at the same time both have emerged from the shadows of delusional thought and perception, the kind of thinking based on self-attachment. It is the kind of talk that is also a kind of perception, it is talk in which the self and others emerge from a realization of a deeper interrelatedness or, perhaps, a deeper non-duality. It is a kind of talk, then, which is a seeing, a perceiving, of things in the world as they are, removed from our own designs and impositions of calculations, impositions of our own conceptions, values and judgments. It is the emergence of the self into self-awareness in the process of the conversation of the talk with the other.

To give one kind of example of how this thinking might develop, we might consider the air that we breathe. This is a fairly common example in Buddhism but there is a deep sense, and I think this is the case in many religious traditions, of our own life as our breath, our basic living activity, our breathing, perhaps related to our other living spirit, what lies at the heart of our activity of living. There is a reflection about the air that we breathe, our breath as a breath is in fact shared with everyone else, everyone in the room, for example. We share the air that we are breathing now. The breath that we breathe becomes your own breath and mine. This is true of course not only with human beings but also with animals, plants. The air that we all share forms an environment, a sphere, a kind of world, in which we all have our own existence and in which we all carry on our own life and activity of breathing. In this sense, there is a deeper, broader unity that we can easily perceive when we move beyond our sense of only our breath and our own life.

Of course, this extends to all things in the world. In Buddhist reflection, for example, with Ippen, a Pure Land thinker, a younger contemporary of Shinran, there is the sense also of the saying of the name of Amida as breath, and Amida the Buddha of immeasurable life as inhabiting that breath itself, which is shared by all beings. Ippen goes on to speak of the wind, the rushing wind, rising waves, the sound itself as no different from our own utterance of the *nembutsu*, our own breath as not different from the sound of waves, the sound of the wind. This is taken even further--the wind sometimes is identified not only with Amida but with the emptiness, the transcendent itself. The image of wind, sky, air and emptiness stands at the heart of Mahayana Buddhist practice. So, all beings in fact have a single existence, related by their breath and connected by the same air.

I think, perhaps, if we look at the two paradigms of the ten oxherding pictures and the white path we can connect them with some unified sense of the self and the world.

We start with what is most familiar, the world in which we carry out our ordinary lives. This would be the world of *saṃsāra*, the world of ignorance, the world of self-attachment, where the self and the things of the world are not as they actually are. The images and the concepts are what we have formed through our hopes and fears, our own clinging to what we think of. Perhaps we might see in the ten oxherding pictures the fact that we have tried to see our genuine selves, our lives as they really are, perhaps in an inward direction, to the true self, while we are on this path, and then the true self is symbolized in the pictures as the ox. Of course, even the image of the ox concept of the true self is that which we have in our ignorance before we have awakened, is that which itself comes to be abandoned, vanishes, with true attainment beyond the limits of the world as we have conceived it, way beyond the limits of our view of the world, delusional and deceptive, when we go on to realize what in the pictures is represented by the circle. To use Buddhist terms, perhaps this would be the world of forms and concepts, and the true self which is formless. The empty circle is that which is not conceptualized, not perceived as an object. It is now beyond perception, into "suchness," a positive term for formlessness, for things just as they are without the possibility of our imposing any concepts on them. Nothing more can be said.

The other model of the inward quest, the parable of the white path, signifies the Pure Land--the image of what stands beyond our own delusional world, what we come to pursue on the inward quest. Another world, the Pure Land, a world of enlightenment, genuine wisdom, compassion, stands beyond our egocentric view.

In this image of the path, it is said that when awakening is attained, then again, there is a re-emergence of a kind of perception and seeing. The path itself is a kind of practice of bringing us out of delusional thinking. With attainment, there is again a kind of re-emergence of perception of the world, and this time it is a world free of division of subject and object.

When considering the last three frames of the oxherding pictures--the empty circle, the images of blossoms and a river and trees, and the figure of the beggar with a large sack, distributing his wealth in the world--we see the image of the true self that emerges upon breaking out of the circle. All of these together form the true self. The first (8) can be seen as the foundation, and the last two (9 and 10), as the re-emergence of the world that occurs at this point. It is this that might have been what Suzuki was referring to when he said "You talk to me, I talk to you. Is this fragile?" *Talk*, here, is not from the tenth stage, but perhaps even before that. It refers to a new perception of the world that is based on a deeper non-duality. It is a perception in which the practitioner perceives the things of the world as inseparable from himself or herself, in which the very perception of the things of the world is itself the awareness of the self. This is also effective, perhaps more clearly cut, in the tenth picture where this conversation is depicted as an exchange in language; again, a conversation which stands upon a deeper awareness, a deeper sense of that which unifies the self and the other.

In this model, essentially there is going out of the world into a realization of that which is transcendent, that which transcends any concept we might hold, an apprehension of a true reality that is beyond any conception. Then, this turns into a re-emergence of the forms of the things of the world, of the self and others in the world, in this time a new relationship that is often referred to as something like two and yet one, one and yet two, a kind of contradictory structure. There is conversation, there is talk, there is a perception of things and this occurs only on the basis of an awareness of unity. So, there is a kind of movement from form to formless, and again a re-emergence of the world in which these two are unified, these two are one.

Regarding the perspective of the scheme of four stages of life, which I have mentioned: student, householder, forest dweller, and wandering sage, I noted the situation in which Indian Buddhism seemed to be focused on the latter two stages exclusively, but that in Japan, now, it seems there is a concern with the first two. Perhaps the idea of the world of forms might be identified in the first two, and the pursuit of the formless, the transcendent, in the latter two. I think, ideally, what happened is that in Zen, or in the oxherd pictures, there is a process of growing through the four stages and then returning to the world. In the oxherd pictures this would be considered the process of practice.

In Pure Land Buddhism, essentially there is no process of practice that can be taken by a person. Shinran speaks very clearly on this: practice is not pursued by a person, it is given by the Buddha. There is no going through these stages and returning as there is in the ideal pattern of Zen. Essentially, there is in Pure Land Buddhism nothing that corresponds to pictures *3-8* in the oxherding pictures: the empty circle, the beginning of practice, the sense of being lost, the finding of the tracks, the finding of the teaching. Pictures *3-8* convey the process by which a person begins to take up the practices and to pursue the practice. In *8*, there is the culmination of that practice: the idea of the empty circle is essentially the concept of practice. It is not fundamentally a metaphysical principle but it is an expression of the practice that the practitioner undertakes in meditation when he seeks to eradicate the delusions, the attachment that ordinarily fills our minds.

As you know, in Pure Land Buddhism, particularly in Shin Buddhism, there is little attention paid to the concept of emptiness because this entire frame showing the individual pursuing practice is not necessary.

In the depiction of the parable of the white path, the Pure land is depicted at the top. The river channel with the rivers of passions and desire and hatred are running horizontally across the picture and the white path, a narrow line, running up and down across the river. At the bottom of the picture are images of worldly life, the bandits, poisonous insects and the wild beast, the things that make life miserable in this world. We see the practicer moving vertically from this world toward the other world.

There are basically two ways of reading the painting. While we are still pursuing the path with our own images--the Buddha, the Pure Land--while through some sense at the very beginning of the parable in Shan-tao, we of course find the practicer already making his way westward toward the Pure Land. There is no explanation for this, but there is probably something at the beginning showing a sense of the inward quest, the need to move toward some authentic sense of our own life and existence in the world. Before we actually step on the white path we engage in this kind of movement--fleeing the beasts and bandits--and we attempt to pursue the path toward the Pure Land. Then, suddenly, the white path emerges before us with the two rivers. It is at that point in the parable, it is said, that the wayfarer sees death all about him, he sees that he cannot escape death that pursues him from behind and from either side, along the river. He is led to step on the white path. At the moment that he steps on the path, he hears the voice of the Buddha, first Sakyamuni and then Amida, calling him.

I think this is an interesting moment in the parable. Before we step on the path, of course, we believe we are being called, being led, that we have seen the traces of the teaching, and we seek to follow our own idea of the teaching by making ourselves worthy by trying to form a strong resolution within ourselves. This is what Shinran calls *self-power within Other Power*. It is a kind of engagement, distorted by attachments to our own images of ourselves, of the Buddha, of the path, of attainment, of birth in the Pure Land. In this case, before we step on the white path, we seek to move through our own aspiration and we sense that we must carry on our endeavor to the moment of death and to the moment that we can finally leave this world and escape from the dangers and pitfalls, and attain the Pure Land.

For Shinran, however, the white path is defined in two ways: (1) the white path is *shinjin*, the mind of wisdom, of compassion, that we realize as the entrusting of ourselves to Amida's vow and, (2) it is the power of the vow. To enter the white path is to be pervaded by the power of Amida's wisdom and compassion, in the form of *shinjin*. It is at this point that this occurs, it is becoming free of self power which is our own image again of the path, the path now being approached from beyond the boundaries of our world by Amida, by Other Power, by the power of Amida, as the form of that which is formless, moving and manifesting itself in our lives. So, it is at the moment that we enter the path that we are filled with Other Power, that the Buddha speaks to us. I think perhaps that this also may be what Suzuki meant when he said "You talk to me . . . ."

Because the power of the vow fills us at the moment we enter the path, Shinran says that it is at this point that our birth in the Pure Land becomes settled. There are two things that happen at this point, at the point of the realization of *shinjin*. On the one hand, it is the point that we have touched the transcendent and it is the point at which all of this, all of our paths and entanglements in the world, have been severed, so that it no longer has any power over us to bind us to our former existence. The idea of *saṃsāra* is defined as the bonds that tie us to meaningless repetition of painful existence. All of this is cut off and loses its power to bind us. In a sense, we are free.

At the same time, Shinran states that we have already attained birth, that our birth has become settled, as one part of this. But in a sense, to have touched the transcendent in the form of the entrusting of ourselves to Amida's vow is in itself to be pervaded by the power of that which transcends this world of ignorance. So, when Shinran says that to realize *shinjin* is the attainment of birth, I think we can take this to have a more literal sense, not merely that the future is settled but that we have come into the working of Amida. In this sense, the future that we have looked to also becomes present in our ongoing lives and it can perhaps be said that the future also has lost its ability to generate in our perception a sense of anxiety, concern. The future also is severed, no longer the object of worry. It has lost that kind of hold on our lives. We are free to live our lives in the presence of the future, which is already settled.

Shinran is recorded to have said,

> Therefore, as regards myself, I have no idea as to my destiny whether I am bound for the Pure Land or for hell. According to my late master (that is, Honen Shonin of Kurodani), "You just follow me wherever I may be." This being what I have been told by him, I am ready to go wherever he is bound for--even for hell be it.[135]

The same kind of words occur in the *Tannishō*. "I have no idea whether the nembutsu is truly the seed for my being born in the Pure Land or whether it is the karmic act for which I must fall into hell."[136] This is explained in different ways in the traditional Shin scholasticism. I think we can take this literally, in some sense: the future has ceased to be a problem. On the one had it has already become settled, on the other hand it is simply lost--the Pure Land has simply lost its sense and so also all that lies in the future.

In this sense, there is a kind of transcendence of this world. A person has broken out of the circle, the circle of ignorance which has bound him or her in this life. The white path is itself Other Power, and this life is a life in which the Buddhas speak to the practitioner, it is the place where words like "You just follow me wherever I may be," can arise. It is, in other words, the site where in an authentic sense "You talk to me, I talk to you . . . ." At the same time, there is an awareness of the vow made in the infinite past, and there is the sense of it having been grasped. The life of the vow shines from the infinite past on to us in the present, so that while the life that is depicted in the lower part of the picture--the mundane life, the pursuit of bandits and wild beasts and insects--has been severed by the white path, at the same time all of this has been redeemed and begins to emerge at the present toward us for the first time. It is no longer the world from which we flee. It is the world that is illuminated by the Buddha of compassion, the world that we begin to see as we cease to flee from it.

It is the emergence, perhaps, that gives us our actual self which has emerged from the infinite past and in infinite numbers of births and existences in the world, which has related us to all other beings, all other beings who presently share the world with us and all other beings with whom we have been connected as parent and child through states of existence through infinite fields. It is this kind of world that begins to emerge and at the same time the Pure Land remains, it has become settled in some sense. We have already attained birth and at the same time the Pure Land, the world of enlightenment, lies in the future, and we awaken a genuine aspiration for that Pure Land through the realization of *shinjin*. The aspiration for the Pure Land is also the aspiration to save all sentient beings, the aspiration to lead them from the world of pain and bring them to the Pure Land.

So, in one sense we have attained the transcendent, we have gone beyond the simple circle of our own making and at the same time we have returned to this world, the world in which we continue to live out our existence, which has its roots in the past, and to look to the future to our destiny, as the activity of saving all sentient beings. Our life is the traversing of the white path, opening out in both directions.

XVII
Religiousness and the Way of Tea
Dennis Hirota

Completing our series of lectures, Dennis Hirota, drawing upon both the Zen and Pure Land strands of the Japanese Buddhist heritage, lets us see a unique feature of Japanese religiousness, a natural harmony of the religious and the aesthetic, bringing our focus to the way of tea, a way of aesthetic practice that leads to an attained simplicity unfolding into an expression of religiousness when human beings meet as persons living life in the present moment--"one lifetime, one meeting," (*ichigo ichie*).

The question of the relationship between aesthetics and religious pursuits is of course a basic one. In this chapter I would like to venture a few comments about the aesthetic thinking in the way of tea, the practice of what is commonly known as the tea ceremony, considering the kind of thinking that has occurred historically.

To begin with, I would like to pick up a few threads from my previous chapter and to pursue them into this question of the traditional arts and practices in religion.

There are different Japanese terms for the way of tea. One is *sa-dō*, or sometimes *cha-dō* (*dō* means "the way," *cha* is the character for "tea"). Another is *chanoyu*. Many practitioners prefer to use the term *chanoyu* instead of "tea ceremony," which is often used in English. I think that *religiousness* as it is referred to here has a certain dynamic quality, a sense of activity--perhaps a mode of life--that seems very appropriate.

Perhaps the idea of "the inward quest," which we have considered, also conveys the idea of religiousness, the religious element as found in tea. The way of tea, the practice of tea, is itself a traversing of the path, of the inward quest. Also, the practice of tea can be seen as the goal, the realization or the manifestation of what lies at the end of the quest, the object of the quest itself.

Many of you have read descriptions of, or have seen, *chanoyu*. Basically, it is nothing more than the preparation of a bowl of tea. Here, the tea is powdered *macha*, the tea leaf ground into a fine powder. In the serving of tea itself, the water is boiled and the tea is taken from a small container with a bamboo scoop and is put in a large tea bowl. It is mixed with the boiling water and is served to guests. This is the basic activity that takes place in *chanoyu*. The activity as a whole consists of a gathering: a person invites a small number of guests to join with him or her in a small tearoom. The standard size is traditionally four and a half *tatami* mats, but rooms as small as only two mats have been used by accomplished masters. Commonly today, larger rooms are used for larger numbers of guests. The ideal number of guests is three, so there would be a total of four people in the tearoom. I think you have seen rooms of the kind used, having an alcove in which a scroll is hung. The entire occasion takes about four hours, beginning with the preparation and the laying of the charcoal in the hearth (a small sunken hearth or brazier is used where a kettle is placed and water is heated). The guests are served a meal and then after the meal, two kinds of tea are prepared. One is a thick tea. This is the most formal part of the gathering. The tea is made into a very thick mixture, probably about the consistency of honey. All the guests drink from the same bowl. After that, there is a sort of finishing with a more informal serving of tea. This time, each guest drinks from an individual bowl, and this is a thin tea. After that, the guests depart.

Every aspect of the gathering is rigidly determined by rules concerning the behavior and the order of the service and the procedure. For example, the meal is served on a tray with utensils that are placed in a certain way. The rice is in a certain kind of vessel, the soup in another kind. The vessels, the tea bowls and so on, are of a determined shape. Placement on the tray is specific. Even the conversation that occurs during the ceremony is restricted and in general follows a pattern with which the host and guests are thoroughly familiar. It includes asking about the nature of the utensils in a specific order with specific questions. Even in the more informal periods of the session, the conversation is restricted to matters directly dealing with tea, with its history, with the utensils, with stories of tea masters, and to topics relating to Buddhism. No other kinds of conversation are allowed in a tea room.

I think you can see that the tea, though it is surrounded by a code of rules, is basically little more than the most ordinary of daily activities: the preparation of a meal and the serving of it to a group of friends, and the serving and enjoyment of a bowl of tea--usual, daily activities but raised to a level of artistic accomplishment, insofar as the concept of Japanese arts is concerned.

In its ordinariness, its focus on daily activities, I think the tea resembles other arts, like flower arrangement. Its raising of a fairly ordinary activity to an artistic level as a group activity closely resembles arts like joint composition of poetry, which is very common in Japanese literature, culminating in the art of linked verse, in which a small group of friends would come together in a small, carefully designed and arranged room and they would compose poetry together, according to strict rules. There is also the art of incense where people come together to enjoy different kinds of incense together. Again, this would involve some similar rules of propriety, manners, specific topics.

All of these arts developed at about the same time. They were common among the warrior aristocracy. They were dominated by a Buddhist aesthetic influence, and they were considered ways in the sense of *dō*, a *way* of religious practice, both the practice and the activity itself as the manifestation of one's deepest religious nature.

The traditional arts, such as *chanoyu*, performed by small groups, share a kind of pattern of practice. There is the practice carried on which consists of a process of learning. In tea, this is considered a life-long kind of engagement. If you see tea being prepared, I think it is true of everyone, you wonder how or why learning tea should be considered a life long endeavor. Also, among tea practitioners themselves, there is an insistence that tea, the activity of tea, is fundamentally very simple. It shares this kind of structure in the sense that there is the requirement of a great deal of learning, practice, but all of this is aimed toward the present moment, toward perhaps even severing the past and the future and coming to stand in the immediate present, which is the present in which "You talk to me, I talk to you . . . ." as we discussed before, which is the immediate present in which the things of the world emerge to be seen clearly and to be perceived so that that perception is also the self-realization, the emergence of the self of the practicer.

In the practice of *chanoyu* the tearoom is, as I said, quite small. It is modelled on the hermitage of a recluse, perhaps, a simple hut away in the mountains for religious practice. It has been called a kind of mountain hermitage built in the city. It gave a sense of entering a special environment, entering the enclosure, the environment of the secluded existence away from the world. The passage into the room is called *roji*, a small garden, usually without flowers but with shrubs, small trees and stepping stones. Among tea practitioners the passage is said to lead to a sense of departure, separation from the world. Within the tearoom one undertakes a cultivation of all the senses. There are the sounds of the water boiling, the lingering fragrance of incense used to purify the room, the sounds of the small movements, all of this receives great attention. Of course, the room is so small that even standing up effects all other people in the room. They can not only sense it visually but also in the sound in the movement of the air within the room. All of this is the subject of much practice.

Although the tearoom is modelled on the life of the hermit, it has involved a large number of crafts and arts traditionally. Just to mention some of them, *chanoyu* has played a large role in influencing Japanese architecture, probably the typical features of Japanese residences now, like wall to wall *tatami* mats, the use of an alcove, the split level shelving, all of these derive from the world of tea and the kinds of art that were undertaken. There are also ceramics--tea bowls considered and labelled national treasures in Japan. Some of these tea bowls were originally imported from China and Korea. Such bowls no longer survive in those countries, but in Japan they have been treasured and maintained. Many are in private hands. Of course, in the tea ceremony, one would not only be expected to recognize these utensils but to know them individually. One of the many interesting features of these utensils is that they have names. A significant tea bowl would have a name, sometimes based on a poetic allusion, sometimes based on the name of the owner. It would be an individual name. It is somewhat different from a title of a painting, for example, that would identify its theme or subject. The name of the tea bowl is used as a kind of personal name, and tea practitioners would know the tea bowls by name. The bowl would have the sense of a front, of course not that there is something that looks like "eyes" on it, but a sense of being a single unified being, having its own personality, its own breath and spirit of life.

Ceramics has been raised to a high art in Japan because of the appreciation in the tea ceremony. One of the interesting features about ceramics is that there are limits to what can be accomplished through the technique with which the artisan or potter makes the tea utensils. Many of the early bowls found were not originally made as tea bowls, certainly not intended for use in the tea ceremony, but were recognized by tea masters as possessing their own life. A potter can seek to make a tea bowl but in the end, it depends on the fire, the kiln, the interaction of the clay and air. This kind of natural process is very important in that it allows for a vision of something made through craft but viewed as living.

There is a saying in tea, *ichigo ichie*, "one lifetime, one meeting." The rule for behavior in the tearoom for the host or hostess and the guest when they sit down together is expressed in these terms. That is, people come together in the spirit that that particular meeting will be the only meeting in your lifetime. I think there is some resonance here, in the sense of "You talk to me, I talk to you . . . ." This may be true here, in a classroom, also. We may never meet again. Of course, in the tearoom you invite people who are close friends, or who become so. Still, the attitude is that although you may have met outside in various worldly contexts, as student and teacher, business associates, and so on, when you go into the tearoom, that meeting, that moment is the moment when you meet as a human being, as a person living life in that present moment. This extends not only between host or hostess and guest, guest and guest but also with the utensils that are used. In other words, it deals with the relationship with the utensil; the seeing that emerges is the kind of seeing that can only emerge in the present moment and the present as a moment will not repeat itself.

This kind of feeling is expressed in a quotation of linked verse, which explains how the meeting for creating linked verse (*renga*) is to be arranged at one sitting (*ichiza*) in a room. It refers to how the atmosphere of the entire meeting is to be appropriately arranged. This kind of concern passes directly into tea, and I think it has basically a religious dimension, a sense of being in the present, living life in the immediate present without distractions, the extraneous concerns that we usually go about with.

> If you are thinking of holding a renga meeting (ichiza), first decide on the hour and select a site with an appropriate view. On an evening of snow or moonlight, or where there are flowers and trees, the participants will be moved inwardly as they gaze on the changes that come over the scene with the passage of time, and their feelings will take on expression in words . . . . By all means avoid a crowd of people, a very large room, and any heavy drinking or boisterous talk; these will all impair the atmosphere . . . . A proper session is one for which the time and occasion have been carefully considered, and all who gather are devoted to the art, composing themselves and making the session concentrated, and producing excellent verse with complete attention.[137]

There is an explanation of this phrase, *ichigo ichie*, "one lifetime, one meeting," which gives the restrictions on what can take place in the meeting.

The attitude of the guest is part of the foundation upon which the meeting (ichiza) stands
. . . . From the moment you enter the roji until the time you depart, you should hold the
host in most respectful esteem, in the spirit that that session will be your only meeting
with him in your lifetime. Worldly gossip has no place here.[138]

I think there are two perspectives on the environment of tea that might be taken.
One is derived from the Pure Land Tradition, and one from Zen. The one stemming from
the Pure Land Tradition passes through the tradition of the wandering monks who often
are mentioned in medieval literature. These are frequently men who have left the established temples because they have not been able to gain attainment through the traditional
scholasticism or the practices in those temples. They have found the temples to be corrupted by social entanglements and political involvement. They have fled those temples
to carry out their own pursuit in isolation without government restrictions, without being
plagued by social concerns.

There were many such wandering monks, and many of them carried on the Pure
Land tradition, going throughout the countryside, living in isolation, building their thatched
huts, teaching the common people. There also came to be men who imitated this kind of
life, even while carrying on their careers in society, and one is mentioned here--a Vice-
Governor:

Vice-governor of Dazaifu, Sukemichi, a skilled biwa player . . . did not perform any of
the usual practices for attaining the world beyond. Going into his private chapel each
day, he simply played pieces on the biwa while having someone keep count and directed
the merit accruing from this toward his birth in the Land of Bliss.[139]

This of course is a kind of practice, a religious pursuit based on the Pure Land practice of
recitation of the *nembutsu*, reciting the name of Amida. He would go into his chapel,
modelled perhaps on the dwellings of hermits, and play his *biwa*, offering his artistic
pursuit as a kind of spiritual discipline in place of the *nembutsu*. Someone would count it
in the same way that the recitations of the *nembutsu* were counted, and this he would see
as merit leading toward his religious aspiration of birth in the Pure Land. Further, there is
an explanation given by Kamo no Chomei, who is best known for his work, "Ten Foot
Square Hut" (*hōjōki*). This quotation is from a collection of tales that he wrote in 1216.

Religious practices are [essentially] acts accomplished through effort and aspiration; hence,
one should not necessarily think of such [performance on the biwa] as ineffective. We
find here the spirit of artistic dedication (*suki*), in which a person ceases to delight in
joining socially with others, or to sorrow at declining fortune. He is moved to deep
compassion by the opening and scattering of blossoms, and his mind is made lucid wherever he thinks of the moon's rising and setting, so that he seeks above all to remain
unstained by worldly defilements. Thus, the reality of arising-and-perishing naturally
manifests itself to him, and attachments to fame and profit completely die away. This is
indeed the gateway to freedom and emancipation.[140]

Here we find one cornerstone in the idea of the arts, dedication to an art, the cultivation of a sensibility necessary for an art like poetry, incense, playing the *biwa*, when it is pursued in a larger context, defined by the hermitage, the recluse in his thatched hut with his aspirations, becoming indeed a kind of substitute for more traditional religious practices.

Because of this ideal--the hermitage and the wandering monk as ideals of life dedicated to arts -- and because the arts were so often dedicated to a kind of cultivation of a sensitivity to nature and the changes in the seasons, to a sense of impermanence, some of the features of the hermit's life came to take on a positive aesthetic quality.

Another important dimension of human sensitivity cultivated in the arts can be seen in the notion of *wabi*. The term, now appearing in *wabicha*, is commonly used to mean tea in the spirit of a kind of poverty or austerity. The tea practiced by the largest schools of tea now is in the style of *wabi*, as opposed to the tea that was carried out by the warlords, which was a more opulent, aristocratic form. Originally, *wabi* was not at all a positive term. It meant wretched, miserable, forlorn, lonesome. The verb form is *wabiru*, "to feel wretched, to feel forlorn." This term, which was originally used in the classical Heian literature--in the *Tale of Genji*, for example, and the literature of the court ladies' romances--expressed the sense of desolation in being abandoned by a lover. This word gradually came to take on a positive meaning through being associated with the lives of poverty, the wandering monks in the thatched huts. Then, gradually, when that kind of life became an ideal for those who pursued the various arts, it gradually came to take on a positive, aesthetic sense, as we can see in the following quotation, which is from *Tsurezuregusa*, ("The Essays in Idleness") by Kenko, considered one of the classics. This is from the early fourteenth century:

> Someone once said, "It is distressing (wabishiki) the way coverings of thin-woven silk [affixed to the outer ends of scrolls] become worn so quickly." Ton'a replied, "It is after the silk has frayed at the top and bottom edges and the decorated roller has lost its mother-of-pearl inlay that it has elegance."[141]

Ton'a comes out of the tradition of the wandering monk, like Kenko, the author. Here we can see the beginnings of this transformation. Something that looks *wabi*, miserable, depressing, outwardly impoverished, takes on a positive sense, the patina of age and use, carrying a positive, aesthetic feeling. It is also seen in the following quotation, from a Noh play, *Matsukaze*. This came slightly later, in the fourteenth century:

> Moreover, a sensitive person would surely choose to live in poverty and solitude (wabite) here at Suma. Yukihira composed the poem,
>> If, by chance, someone ask of me,
>> answer that I live forlorn (wabu),
>> sleeves wet with the bitterness
>> of the dripping seaweed,

on Suma's shore.[142]

Yukihira was a court noble in the Heian period who was exiled to Suma. This, of course, shows a sense of forlornness of the court noble coming to carry the positive sense of harmony and solitude. This enters into the way of tea.

This is one source of the aesthetic notion of *wabi* that is present in the *wabicha*, in tea. The other source would come from Zen. It also has Chinese roots, a certain somberness. The most common example is the monochrome ink paintings where there is a large paper, and in one corner a flower is suggested by brief strokes of the brush. The rest of the paper is without anything at all. Here, there is the sense of one's attempt to paint the flower as emerging out of the formless, as in the oxherding pictures, emerging into the form of becoming visible, seen as it is in the instant. All that is extraneous, the use of color, etc., is eliminated. The flower, in its "suchness," appears, clearly emerging as perceived by the artist who has awakened. There is a kind of reduction of the usual concepts, the usual images of flowers and the portrayal of the flower in its actual presence against a background. The flower is severed from time, from involvement in the world, from its own thinking of its own existence and emergent present. This kind of aesthetic sense leads to, for example, the dimness of light within the tearoom. Light from small windows is filtered through paper, and extreme care is taken regarding what can enter the room and meet the senses: touch, sound, taste, smell, sight--all are under strict control. Probably, this sense can also be seen in the next quotation, both in its Chinese origins and perhaps in a Zen approach:

Tu Fu, the foremost poet of the T'ang dynasty, wrote only poems of grief; hence he is known as "Tu Fu, of a lifetime of sorrows." Hsu Hun, speaking of three thousand kinds of water, devoted his whole life to the poetry of its forms. Indeed, what can stir us so deeply, with such coolness and lucidity, as water? Speak of the water of springtime and the heart is set at ease; reflections drift to memory, giving it always a plaintive air. In summer, the cold persists at the spring's source, where the crystalline stream wells up. The very thought of autumn waters draws a chill calm over the mind. And nothing is more exquisite than ice. The stubbled fields of early morning, with needles of ice formed where sleet has glazed the cypress bark of the roof, or the dew and hoarfrost frozen upon the withered grasses and trees of the meadow: what is there to match this loveliness, this beauty?[143]

This is what intrigues me here, the great sensitivity to water. It is said that the finest verse is like plain water: it has no particular flavor and yet one never tires of it. This shows a sensitivity to what is most common. All of these notions, "leanness or meagerness" (*yase*), "chilled, withered" (*hiya*), are all used as aesthetic ideals. From the Pure Land side, I think there is a kind of plaintiveness, a sense of sorrow that comes through this, along with compassion. From the Zen side there is a sense of reduction to the essence--touching of things as they truly are in this chill, withered state.

Rikyu is considered the person who perfected *wabicha*, the spirit of tea in the style of poverty, the spirit of the chill and withered. He lived in the sixteenth century. His descendants still carry on the way of tea and are still the heads of the largest schools of *chanoyu* at present.

APPENDIX I
The First Round-Table Discussion
Professors Gadjin Nagao, Michio Tokunaga, Nobuo Nomura, John Ross Carter, and Students

Often discussions following upon lectures open new vistas, providing a group dynamic that gives rise to new directions for inquiry and further reflection. At about the half-way point of the course of lectures, just prior to departing for Tokyo, a round-table discussion was held. The logistics of the course, requiring travelling from place to place, made it impossible to integrate into a comprehensive round-table discussion all of our distinguished colleagues from both Kyoto and Tokyo. This explains an obvious lacuna regarding matters related to Shinto in this round-table discussion and the subsequent one held at the end of the course, again in Kyoto. When the first roundtable discussion was held, the students had heard lectures forming chapters: I, II, VII, IX, XII, XIII, and XVI.

Abbreviations:

GN: Gadjin Nagao
JC: John Carter
MT: Michio Tokunaga
NN: Nobuo Nomura
Q: A student's question
SR: A student's response

Q: I have a question about ministering to marginalized people in Jodo-Shinshu. It would seem, from what has been said, that marginalized people are the most likely to have a chance to enter the Pure Land. Does this extend to women, and how do women fit into Jodo-Shinshu, as far as entering the Pure Land? And further, how do you minister to women as opposed to men?

MT: There is no discrimination between men and women, concerning the priest's work. But, we are now being criticized by outsiders for having sexual discrimination, because in the *sūtra* women have to be reborn first as men before entering the Pure Land.[144] This is a big problem for our days. It is very hard to change a *sūtra* expression. But women's liberation groups always criticize this, so we have to reinterpret it according to their claims. We have to have thorough discussions among our priests and scholars about this.

Q: What about other marginalized people--homosexuals for example? What is the attitude about the ministry to this group of people?

MT: In Japan, it is not a social problem. Unlike America, Japan is still regarded as not believing in homosexuality. We cannot be serious about this problem since it appears there are not so many people involved. In this sense, Japan is still old fashioned.

GN: We must first exist as men--everyone must first become a man to practice the Buddha-way. These people, women and homosexuals, are physically made, not spiritually made, if you understand. Transforming ourselves into a male is not discriminatory, it does not involve discrimination. It is a symbolic expression of the qualification for practicing the Buddha-way. In this sense, being a man or a male is a symbolic expression.

Q: The topic for my seminar presentation in this course is the notion of dependence in the religious life and the role dependence plays in the Buddhist tradition. I have been told that Shinran basically says that a person must have one hundred percent dependence upon Amida. This is the point the person wants to get to. Yet it was said that different Pure Land schools allow for different degrees of dependence. Can you address the role of dependence on Other Power, and how important it is in the different schools or sects?

MT: There are many schools which teach dependence on Amida Buddha and Other Power. We can classify the schools of the Pure Land tradition according to the degree of the dependence on Other Power. Jodo-Shinshu is well known to be a school teaching total dependence of oneself on Other Power. There are some other schools that teach, say, a kind of fifty percent/fifty percent dependence on Other Power and on one's own power; for example, the Jodo school (Jodo-shu), a very traditional Pure Land school in Japan. Shinran is very well known for teaching total dependence on Other Power. Only the working of Other Power is the source of our salvation or of being born in the Pure Land. Even one percent of self-power, one's own power, is enough to disturb the working of Amida, the Other Power. This is Shinran's teaching. This one percent is a problem. It is a very strong power of dependence on ourselves. In other words, it is a kind of self-centeredness, as Shinran says. However, Buddhism, in general, does not teach dependence on something other or outside of us. Buddhism is a religion of developing our life through our own power. The Pure Land school is an exception. If one can say there is an orthodox teaching in Buddhism, generally, it is that you have to realize your own true nature through your own power.

JC: I don't think so.

MT: You don't think so?

NN: Even one percent of self-power can disturb Amida's power.

MT: This is my interpretation. One percent of self-power is the problem.

NN: This can disturb Amida's work.

MT: It hinders.

GN: So strong is our self-power?

MT: Yes. This is what Shinran called into question. This is my interpretation of Shinran's thought.

GN: I don't know precisely . . . .

JC: Buddhists have been affirming that we do not save ourselves. We prepare and we follow the practice and we discipline ourselves and we meditate, but when the insight arises, it is not directly caused by us, whether we want to call it Other Power or whether we want to call it the limits of self-power.

MT: Is this the Theravada understanding?

JC: Yes, of course. It seems that if Nirvana is the extinction of the passions and the purifications of one's mind, then how can one's own mind purify itself? There must be "a happening," "a realization," that is not the direct product of one's own consciousness.

MT: That you call Other Power?

JC: That I call *not* self-power, arising or coming not from me. Whether it is outside or not is a different matter. This, it seems to me, is mainstream Buddhist thought.

MT: In Mahayana, the general teaching is that we all have Buddha nature inside, deep inside, of our existence. It is hidden by something, by passions or desires. We call them evil passions. We eradicate by our own self-power these hindrances or coverings. Then our own Buddha nature appears naturally. There is no Other Power in this way of thinking. Pure Land Buddhism is quite different from this teaching. Shinran did not teach that we have Buddha nature. This is opposite to the general Mahayana understanding.

JC: I think our Theravada brothers and sisters and others are very subtle not to describe what brings about that transformational moment. Even with the idea that we have Buddha nature and we have to rid ourselves of passions, it is still the tainted mind that is supposed to rid itself of the taints. How can that happen? Even with the so-called "*self-power* schools," self-power seems to be effective only up to a point.

GN: I think the notions of self-power and Other Power are specifically used in the Pure Land Buddhist tradition. In most general Buddhism there is power, of course, but without discriminating self-power or Other Power. We are trusting always to some energy or power, which is, in Pure Land Buddhism, especially in Jodo-shinshu, differentiated or discriminated into self-power and Other Power. In that context, self-power is nothing at all, really no power. This is emphasized. But all powers are coming from outside, or from something, but not from within -- since we are always "made to live" by others. "Coming from something other" is my understanding. In other words, all are embraced by Amida's power.

Q: Professor Nagao, do you believe there is one percent self-power or are you saying that that one percent does not exist?

GN: It is not that powerful. It is negative power, but not power in the true sense.

Q: So it is not useful to talk about this. Can people who possess no self-power still be saved by Amida? Is it that they don't need the impetus, the beginning of their own effort, to receive Amida's compassion? They don't even need a small amount of self effort, or do they?

MT: I think the core of Shinran's teaching is the denial or negation of self-power. We are taught that self-power is not efficacious, is not effective at all. We try to eradicate or discard our own self-power. We diminish the presence of self-power even up to one percent. This is the problem of self-power. Shinran says it is the hardest thing to eradicate. It should be eradicated by realizing Other Power. It happens at the same time, eradication and realization. This is the realization of salvation.

Q: It is very hard for me to understand how one can say the realization of Other Power, Amida's compassion, is not self-power. How do you know? It seems that all efforts to eradicate self-power are self-power. It is a vicious circle. I just don't understand how anyone can realize Amida's compassion and discard self-power without their self-power.

MT: But, on the realization of Other Power, Shinran says, we realize at the same time the thankfulness for Amida Buddha. The thankfulness accompanies the mind. This is the realization of Other Power.

Q: So you definitely need at least a little bit of self-power.

MT: It is a very individual problem. We cannot objectify it. Our innermost feelings prove it, I think.

Q: You said before that one percent of self-power inhibits Amida?

MT: Even one percent of self-power means one hundred percent of self-power.

Q: That one percent inhibits Amida from letting us have the realization of Other Power. So, consequently, is the one percent of self-power evil because it is inhibiting Amida? Paradoxically, does this make Amida's work easier because, as our group during this course has become very fond of saying, a good person can be saved, so much more an evil person? So then, is that one percent evil because it is inhibiting and, because it is evil, making it, paradoxically, easier for Amida?

MT: You are classifying self-power with evilness. Self-power is our own effort to attain realization through our own power. Evilness is ours by nature. Evil cannot be eradicated. We are evil until we die. Self-power can be eradicated, Shinran says, can be discarded, should be discarded.

GN: I believe self-power and Other Power are both investigated or studied with regard to our final realization or final salvation. But, actually, we are living with our own power, at least we are believing that by our own self-power we are doing something: study, everything. Actually we are relying on such self-power. But, from Shinran's perspective, as far as our own salvation, our own realization, is concerned, such a power is nothing. I was thinking about the notion of *pratītyasamutpāda*; everything is dependent on everything.

MT: We are living on, depending on our own power. We are living through our own power, but as far as our liberation or realization of final attainment is concerned, self-power is not effective and we have to realize this at the final point of our life.

NN: Self-power--whatever it may be for each person--you have to get into it very deeply. But as far as we are concerned, we have complete insight into it. Other Power is needed when we come to know what self-power is. At the crucial point, at the same time, we need Other Power to throw this self-power away.

Q: Do we destroy self-power by Other Power, in other words, is there some sort of grace that comes?

NN: If you can throw this self-power away by yourself, the crucial emphasis is put on your power. But you cannot make it by your self. This is why Other Power is necessary for our self even to try to forsake one percent of self-power in us.

Q: If I could move away from how the defilements are gotten rid of once the true mind arises within a person, so that a person moves from *A* to *B* and back to *A*, as you noted Professor Nomura, and how a person's activity takes on wisdom and compassion, how a person sees things truly as they are, my question is how, then, is one to act in this world with all of the atrocities being committed around the world? How does a Zen Buddhist or Jodo-Shinshu Buddhist act with compassion, now that their Zen eye is "opened" or Amida's grace has risen within them? I have difficulty understanding this in a world that is so horrible.

NN: This is difficult for me. For me as a Jodo-Shinshu Buddhist, Zen priests can attain Buddhahood by Other Power, not by themselves. Even Zen priests need Other Power. In Zen Buddhism, the priests just sit and realize what Other Power is, by sitting. There is their own strenuous effort which is performed so. In a sense, they say, a Zen Buddhist needs one hundred percent of self-power to attain Buddhahood. But, from my perspective, I believe that even they need Other Power to realize what reality is. Buddha's compassion alone can perform altruistic activity in this world through those who sit or say the *nembutsu*. The point is how you see those practicers.

MT: I think this is similar to what Professor Carter said. Something occurs. Even Tendai Buddhists need Other Power.

JC: If religion is solely our human construction, then we are in real trouble. Whatever religion is, it requires transcending self. But, the question still stands, wherein are Jodo-Shinshu's social ethics grounded?

MT: This is a problem.

Q: It is not indifference is it? What an outsider might say is that Zen people just sit. They seem indifferent to what is going on. I would not imagine that it is a selfish, self-centered objective, being an enlightened being and leaving it at that.

MT: The problem of social ethics is a question always raised by Westerners. We cannot sufficiently answer it because the first problem is the concept of *social ethics*. We

Easterners do not have *society* in your Western sense of society. No ethics in the Western sense of ethics--we have our own but you cannot measure it by using Western concepts of society or ethics. The measure or ruler is different. It is very hard to understand. When I am at Harvard, they always criticize Buddhism for lacking social ethics. Harvard Christians especially talk about social ethics. Theology is a talk about social ethics. When I am asked the question I always answer in this way: the ruler for measuring what we mean is itself different. You have to use an oriental ruler in order to criticize Buddhism.

NN: When American students speak of social ethics, do you use the term only in the phase or position *A*, that is, the ordinary mode of being? Or are you using the term for both positions *A* and *B*?

SR: I am not sure.

NN: Do you understand my question? If you take social ethics to apply only in *A*, it is not a religious problem. If you take it as a religious problem, you have to discuss social ethics in both *A* and *B*. So how do you understand social ethics if you take it to apply both to *A* and *B*?

SR: When I asked the question, the context I had in mind applied to *A*.

NN: This enables you give yourself the answer to your question.

GN: In thinking about social ethics we have to go back to the very starting point of Buddhism, *pratītyasamutpāda*, interdependence; we are all related. This is the basis of social ethics. This is a kind of principle of Buddhism which is quite different from the Western principle I think. All are related. All are dependent on other people. There is no one substantial being who can do something with his or her own self-power independently. Always we are depending on others, being related to each other. *Pratītyasamutpāda* means universal relativity, mutuality, and therefore "no-self" (*anatta*, *nairātmya*), "emptiness (*śunyātā*). It denies thus the existence of any absolute being, all are relative. This is the Buddhist principle underlying all doctrines, I think. I think Shinran's notion of Other Power also comes from this basic idea of *pratītyasamutpāda*. Everything is relative, all are others -- there is no self, no self-power. In spite of this, it is also true that we have an idea of self or individual being, an idea of our commonsense in daily life. How and why can one say so? Because "no self, therefore self everywhere," if I put it in a way in accord with the *Prajñāpāramitā Sūtra* . "No self" is *paramārthatas* (as the ultimate truth), while "self everywhere" is *saṃvṛtitās* (as conventional truth). There are many individuals living together, and this may be called society which will be characterized, again, as *pratītyasamutpāda*. Social ethics also will be established in terms of such a community. But it seems to me that almost all philosophies in the West are established on the basic conviction of substantial, absolute existence of the self: though selfishness may be negated in its ethics, the self itself is usually not denied. At this point Buddhism departs from the West. Self is a temporary name, provisional designation (*saṃvṛti*). Only after radical negation of self, it revives as nominal being, as negated being, with the name *self*. By "mutuality" said of *pratītyasamutpāda*, I don't mean that substantial beings first exist and then they enter into mutual relationship. I mean all are from the beginning relative, therefore universal relativity.

MT: Professor Nagao, that is a very basic doctrine of Buddhism. We understand it theoretically. Yet, we think we are living in this way, as substantial beings. This is a problem. The overcoming of the sense of a substantial self is a real problem.

GN: Buddhism is no self.

MT: We hear that, but we think we are living here by our own power, our own consciousness. We think there is something that can be called *we*. This is the problem. How are we to overcome this?

GN: Yes, there is something that can be called *we*. But it is just temporary being, nominal being. Because self does not exist as substantial being, it is temporary. The real question, I think, is how are we to get to the realizationa of no-self, or the realization of non-existence of substantial self.

SR: In considering your point, we all ask that question from the Judeo-Christian point of view, where we say we act from the goodness given by God, but we do it all as individual selves. We do not negate the self. It is hard for us to ask that question, as you say, with a different ruler or means by which to measure because we see it from different points of view. We see ourselves as being given power by God to do good work on earth, in the world, instead of letting go of that power and letting Other Power take over. This seems to be the crux of the problem. We sit back and say "How come no one does anything?" We tramp into a situation, sometimes doing more damage than good. We bring our selves with us.

MT: There is exactly the same way of thinking in Jodo-Shinshu, too. The eighth descendent of Shinran, named Rennyo, who re-established Hongwanji, who is actually the founder of Hongwanji as a denomination, says the same thing. Everything good is through the power of Amida. Everything evil is our own fault.

Q: Does one have to know who Amida is in order to be saved?

NN: I don't think so. Who can know what Amida is, or what he is like?

Q: I mean, for example, if I am living in South America and I have never even heard of Amida Buddha, can I still be saved by him?

NN: For me, the answer is yes. I can say that. You can be saved by Amida, wherever you may be. But this is your problem, if you question whether one will be saved by God or Jesus Christ. For me, you are saved by Amida. The point is one of self-consciousness of who you are. If you are Christian, you will be saved by God. If you meet with the Buddha, you will be saved by Amida.

MT: That is the question of the oneness of the ultimate reality, whether it is one or not. Some people say the ultimate reality is one throughout the world. Others might say there are many gods in the world, many ultimate realities in the world.

Amida is Amida. Amida is a name. Shinran says we have to realize the meaning of the name, not only *Amida*; we call his name: *Namo Amitābha*. *Namo* means the oneness of Amida on high, Amida, who comes down, or who becomes one with me. At least, we have to listen to that teaching. We have to understand the meaning of *Namo Amitābha*, Amida's name. We have to realize Amida through words, through human words. Everyone who hears, who understands the name can be saved.

Concerning people who are outside of the teaching, I am not sure. This is the problem with religion, but what is religion? When I teach Pure Land Buddhism to my students I equate Amida with the universe and the working of the universe, the energy of the universe. He is always with us. We are living in the universe, under the working of the universe. Everyone has the possibility of being saved by Amida. We are embraced by the energy of the universe. The problem is the realization of that energy, that working. This comes through words. In Jodo-Shinshu there is a frequent misunderstanding--that we are already saved, because Amida is always with us. Amida is everywhere at any time, so we are already saved. This is a typical misunderstanding of Shinran's teaching. We are embraced by Amida's grace and compassion, energy. This is true, but it is not called salvation. Shinran says: when our self-power effort is negated, we realize Amida's compassion is always with us. Doing nothing is not salvation. People say, we are already in Amida's embrace, we do not have to do anything. This is not the religious way of living.

Theoretically, everyone is within the embrace of Amida. This is a problem not only in Jodo-Shinshu, but in Christianity, too. God reaches everyone. This is not faith or salvation. Faith is the realization of God's embrace. In this sense, Shinran says that we need *shinjin*. *Shinjin* is salvation. Without talking about *shinjin*, we cannot talk about salvation.

JC: For Shinran to say that we need *shinjin* seems to be a statement that emanates from knowledge and wisdom, but for me to say we need *shinjin* would seem to be an expression of faith.

MT: Yes, an awakening to the compassion and working. This is my understanding of *shinjin*.

JC: This is a momentous occasion, it seems to me. Professor Nomura are you saying that a person is saved by Amida but that this person is saved by an idol, as it were, that must be destroyed?

NN: You can be saved by something different from idols, when you can break through idols. I have no idea who will save me, but I will be saved. This is a key point. The moment when I realize the agent of saving, or salvation, is Amida, I can be a real Buddhist. If you realize the agent is Jesus Christ, or God, you are a real Christian.

Q: But is the realization by our self-power or by Other Power? If Other Power, then why isn't everyone saved?

NN: Theoretically, the world is filled with Amida's power. The power or energy from Amida, or something absolute, does reach everyone in this world. Theoretically, people are saved by Amida. This is the attitude in position *A*.

Q: Regarding salvation, do you think a comparison can be made between Christ dying to save persons, thereby being the vehicle for salvation and the Eighteenth Vow, the Primal Vow, in which Amida Buddha, as the Bodhisattva Dharmakara, saves all living creatures?

NN: The equivalent in the Jodo-Shinshu tradition to Christ would be the *nembutsu*, it seems to me.

Q: The act?

NN: Yes as far as function is concerned.

Q: That is the concept that most followers of the Jodo-Shinshu tradition see as a parallel?

NN: Yes. But you know, Jesus Christ is not merely a name. He died to save. One would think also of *Emanuel*. How would you understand this *Emanuel*? How would you reconcile the life cycle of Jesus Christ as the agent of salvation in *this* world, in *this* moment here and now?

SR: It is certainly not as easy to understand the *nembutsu* as a concept. I can't answer that.

NN: This is my purpose--to raise the quest for the answer.

Q: Those of us in the Christian tradition have always been taught that yes, Christ died on the cross. But, the Christ, through the spirit, is supposed to be present in the world today, still acting, delivering the divine message through the course of time. In the Biblical setting when Christ told the apostles to pray, one of the things that stands out is "Our Father who art in heaven," and "thy will be done on earth as it is in heaven," meaning that God's will, whatever it is, should be seen through Christ and then carried out, through history. My first question would be does Amida have a similar type of will, and does Amida wish for that will to be done both in the Pure Land and here and now?

NN: I must say, Amida has a will, he/she has a will, and at the same time I must say it--it has a function of salvation. Without salvation, Amida does not mean anything. The function itself is the essence of Amida. In this sense, he or she may be in the Pure Land but at the same time he or she is always here and now. Amida is just function, he or she is not an existence in our sense--we cannot see or grasp him-her-it. We can realize the function of Amida.

Q: A follow-up question is: Of that will that both God and Amida possess, Amida's compassion I equate in some respects with the love of God--*agape*. In the Christian tradition, however, we hear a great deal about God's justice. Is there something comparable in the Buddhist tradition.

NN: Justice as a social norm in Christian society?

SR: Not necessarily in a Christian society. In the Biblical record there is the dialectic between God's mercy and what God will expect of us.

NN: I would say that there is no *justice*, in that sense, in Jodo-Shinshu or the Pure Land tradition. There are no general criteria by which to live in our society. We each must have our own criteria.

JC: Do you discern a sense of mercy in justice?

MT: We cannot understand the meaning of justice as such.

NN: Yes, what is the meaning of justice related to *agape*?

JC: I did not have *agape* in mind, rather the sense of mercy. Speaking theologically, a just God is also merciful. There could be deities in our human experience who are all powerful, capable of doing anything they wished to do, both just and unjust acts. But, a just God seems to reflect a human affirmation that there is in justice a quality of mercy.

MT: When the Christian notion of justice is translated from English into Japanese it appears as *seigi*, in a sense that is very limited and special. So, I don't trust the translation *seigi*. I am always at a loss how to understand justice in Christian terms. The Japanese translation of justice is used only by gangsters. It is very limited and shallow. Japanese Christians must change the sense of the word or find another one.

Q: One of the things that Judaism and Christianity are wrestling with now is the task of rewriting the Bible using non-gender specific pronouns. Is there a revisionist theology or movement to rewrite the *sūtras* and, where possible, to use non-gender specific pronouns?

NN: We usually use "parent" as beyond gender.

Q: As a follow-up question, one of the things that Christianity and Judaism are facing as well is that the texts were written by men, and women feel that men have recorded the experiences of men with God, and that they do not represent women's experiences. Is there a similar movement among Buddhist to reconstruct the accounts in order to reflect women's experience?

NN: There is one movement to reinterpret the phrase in a certain vow. It is now fairly widespread.

Q: Which vow is this?

MT: The thirty-fifth vow among the forty-eight. First, you have to become men in order to be saved, in order to be born in the Pure Land. This is a very problematic vow these days.
        May I ask a question? What sense do you have for the discrimination against women in Buddhism? Do you think that there is such a discrimination in Buddhist teachings, or in the Japanese context?

SR: I see some similarities between how women are discriminated against in Christianity, in that women are excluded from the priesthood, as in the case of Catholicism. This has begun to be questioned. In some Christian denominations there are women ministers. Also, looking at the texts, it seems that there are regulations which discriminate against women. I see it more as a problem that human society faces and not something established by God. The testaments and *sūtras* were written by men and that is where the problem seems to have originated, not that God only saves men. I do not think that God discriminates, but the people who wrote the texts did.

Q: I believe you said, when discussing the thirty-fifth vow, that there was a problem because men wrote the *sūtras*. I just do not understand. If this is a human construct, how are we supposed to know where human constructs end and truth begins? How do we know that the whole thing is not a human construct? For me, at least, this seems like a pretty big thing to quickly cover over by saying, "men wrote it, so it is a small problem." How do we know that the whole thing is not made up by man?

NN: Why are you living? How? Do you live by yourself? Do you control every part of your body? Can you stop your heart? No, you can't. Why do you live?

MT: I don't think religion is a human construction. But, theology, or religious doctrine, is a human construction. The religious expressions, the *sūtras* or the Bible, are the reflections of the society or scene at the time of the recording. Religious expressions are always limited by the social conditions in which they are written or recorded. In this sense, we maintain the thirty-fifth vow. It is not discrimination against women. It is our intention to include or save all women then and now. But, women of the liberation movement always attack the thirty-fifth vow. They say it is an expression of discrimination We cannot cooperate in this. When I asked Professor Carter, many years ago, about the Biblical account of God's creation of this world, he answered, that it was primarily an expression of the worldview of the Biblical writers, of the world in which they lived and of God, rather than a propositional assertion of the actual causal sequence of creation itself. I understood very well. God is the maker of heaven and earth. I understand the thirty-fifth vow also in this way of thinking. It is a reflection of the social conditions of the time. We have to reinterpret the texts according to the needs of our days.

Q: Nomura Sensei's question, "Why are you living?" is a grand question. I feel its force. At the same time, how do we know whether Jodo-Shinshu is the way or whether Christianity is the way? It is all a personal decision. Yet they are still human constructs, at least in my mind, and I don't know how one can justify all the different constructs and determine which is, or which are, true.

NN: Every form of religion could be true to yourself. I am not saying this objectively. The truth is to be very personal. Every form could be true.

Q: Tomorrow, we are going to Hiroshima, where, I hear, a large number of Jodo-Shinshu followers live. One of the things that we talk about is faith after the holocaust, and the effect that the holocaust had on Judaism and Christianity. What effects did the bombing of Hiroshima have on the Jodo-Shinshu tradition? Did it have no effect or did it fundamentally change certain lines of thinking?

NN: Priests think about the facts. What is the fact? The atomic bomb makes priests in Jodo-Shinshu realize that in a sense we cannot save our own selves or the people who are victims. We priests cannot give our hands to them, all we can do is to put salve on their skin. We realize that human beings are really weak.

Q: You realized the limits of what you can do as priests? Since the war Christianity has tended to be peace centered. Has the same occurred in Jodo-Shinshu?

NN: It was somewhat that way. Jodo-Shinshu was the first denomination which began the peace movement in Japan. We are always opposed to discrimination against people. In Japan there is discrimination against the *buraku* people. This discrimination is very strong. Hongwanji was the first and the strongest denomination which led in the movement of aiding the *buraku*. We have done this for many years.

Q: Would you describe the difference between the experience that a lay person has on realizing Amida and the experience had by someone who has already reached the stage of nonretrogression during this life?

MT: The stage of nonretrogression is not known by us. It is a synonym for the realization of Amida. The realization of Amida's compassion is the same as attaining the stage of nonretrogression because Amida's compassion will never change. People who have *shinjin*, who have realized Amida's working, have transcended this relative world of living and dying. They have already transcended.

SR: I was misusing the idea of nonretrogression.

MT: No, you used it in the right sense.

Q: What I am asking is, when a physical being stops working, when someone dies, is there a difference between what a lay person like me experiences at death and what someone who has already achieved enlightenment in this life experiences?

NN: I do not think there is a difference between the two. Death is death for anyone. The situation after death could be described in position *A*. You expect there is a future when you ask the question. No one can tell, no one can send a letter back. We can not know what death is until we experience it ourselves. We may be in the Pure Land, in any case we will know where we are.

MT: Your question is very serious and it is one of the biggest problems of Jodo-Shinshu, because in Buddhism, in general, we do not think of any substantial self which lasts forever. We are beings of interrelated conditions, yet we speak of being reborn in the Pure Land. *What* is reborn? This is a frequently asked question, because Buddhism talks of non-self. There is nothing which is substantial, which is everlasting, like the soul in the Christian sense.

What, then, is *reborn*? This is something no one can answer. We are told by our teachers that we do not have to answer this. We should keep silent. We have to find an answer in Professor Nagao's comment. We are beings, living on the basis of *pratītyasamutpāda*, interdependent, correlated. Everything is interdependent. Nothing is independent. On this basis you have to find the answer.

Shinran simply says we are reborn in the Pure Land. People who have *shinjin* assuredly will be reborn.

Professor Nagao, what do you think about the subject of birth in the Pure Land? Who is born in the Pure Land? On the one hand we speak of birth in the Pure Land. On the other, we speak of non-self. This is a contradiction.

GN: Rebirth is continuing always, from second to second. To be reborn somewhere is to be reborn constantly.

MT: Do you mean we are being reborn at each moment?

GN: Yes, each moment. Therefore, *pratītyasamutpāda*. Always we are being reborn. *To be reborn* is our idea, a human idea. *To die* is our idea. *To die* is from the viewpoint of the medical doctors. But, from the ultimate standpoint of Buddhist thought, to die and to be reborn is the same thing, both are only in *saṃsāra*.

MT: So, we are always dying? Always being reborn?

GN: Yes. And this idea is applied to the *somewhere* which is called the Pure Land. We must conduct ourselves with our own self-power and with our own concepts. We must wish to be reborn in the Pure Land sometime, which is equal to the realization of the ultimate reality. From the Buddhist viewpoint, we are always being reborn. To realize the ultimate reality is also to realize our own life. Shinran has also used our concepts, our Japanese language, and in the same way, *to be reborn, to die, to realize everything* are our concepts. So, what is death? What is rebirth? This will be explained from various viewpoints--from the medical, ethical, physical, spiritual--we can say something *about* death or rebirth or realization. One way Jodo-Shinshu is expressed through our language, is by saying that when we are reborn by the power of Amida, it is our final realization. Such is my own understanding. Whether it is Jodo-Shinshu or not, I do not know. Actually, the birth issue, or the matter of being reborn, is not such a serious problem. You are to be liberated, that is the main point. Probably you have some fear of death. It is not unnatural to have such a fear.

MT: Nagao sensei, traditionally, for many people, Pure Land Buddhism was regarded as an escape, a way of escaping from the fear of death. I think it is okay, if people think in that way. If they can escape from the fear of death, then Jodo-Shinshu functions in this sense.

Nagao sensei has already overcome the fear of death so he is a Buddha already. For us, ordinary men, we are afraid of death.

APPENDIX II
The Second Round-Table Discussion
Professors Minoru Tada, Michio Tokunaga, Nobuo Nomura, John Ross Carter, and Students

From a brief consideration of the attitudes of Japanese young people toward religion to an inquiry into what constitutes a proper understanding of religion, the round-table discussion, held at the end of the course, moves to a more general consideration of religious living. It represented the last opportunity to work together in seeking understanding.

Abbreviations:

JC: John Carter
MT: Michio Tokunaga
NN: Nobuo Nomura
Q: A student's question
SR: A student's response
Tada: Minoru Tada

Q: We have traveled around Japan and have had lectures from scholars, and met with Zen masters, and people who have dedicated their lives to the different traditions we are studying. My question is, what do we say when the Japanese say they are not religious? What do we reply when they ask, "Why are you studying religion?" It seems so peculiar to the average Japanese person. In what ways are Japanese religious and why do they say they are not religious? Before we left the United States, people asked me why I was studying Japanese religions--the Japanese are not religious, or they have almost no interest in religion. I still hear something like this from the Japanese themselves.

MT: There are many standards as to what religion is. From our standpoint, it is not very admirable to see the Japanese people's daily life. For instance, when they are born, in 3 months or half a year, they go to a Shinto shrine. They go to Shinto shrines every New Year's and on special days. They go to many temples or shrines to pray for their happiness. When they get married, they have their ceremony in Christian churches. When they die, they come to Buddhist temples. Foreigners see this and say that the Japanese are very religious.

From my viewpoint, it is not religious. Jodo-Shinshu is comparatively too genuine, or pure. It is not easily understandable for ordinary Japanese people. We prohibit going to Shinto shrines or other temples to pray for one's own happiness. Jodo-Shinshu is isolated in this sense. But, we Jodo-Shinshu priests are somewhat corrupted because our main source of income is from the performance of funeral services or memorial services. We receive income from this type of service, but we cannot stop this because our denomination could not support itself without it. We are in a serious dilemma because of this.

Yet, we are proud of having many temples. Even the one denomination of Nishihongwanji has more than 10,000 temples all over Japan. In each of the temples we have services, we give sermons or teachings, at least once a month. Many people come to listen to the teaching. This is the only thing about which we can be proud.

Tada: Do you think the Japanese are religious? Are they not so religious?

SR: I would probably say the Japanese are religious but they just do not show it in the same ways we do. Just because a lot of Westerners are Catholics and go to church every Sunday does not at all mean they are religious. One of our group brought up a great point in her seminar presentation the other day: you see thousands of bicycles on the street, some locked, some not--none of them are ever stolen. This is an example of the faith the Japanese have among themselves. This is, I think, religious. So, it is manifested in different ways. I do not understand why so many people say the Japanese are not religious. Even the Japanese themselves say they are not.

SR: I think they do not separate it from the rest of their lives the way most people in Western nations do. A lot of people in the United States do not practice what they preach; they go to church on Sunday but bring pencils home from the office. I think the Japanese do not say to foreigners that they feel religious, they do not think they are doing anything special because being religious is part of their everyday lives. They do not think of it consciously as a separate part or dimension of living.

MT: We have read pamphlets put out in the United States about religious pluralism. In one person, here, there are many religions. This is the problem. Often Japanese are not very serious. Japanese religions are family religions. "Our family belongs to Hongwanji," "our family belongs to so-and-so." In this country, religion is not a spiritual support for one's life; it is a kind of custom, a habit.

JC: One reason some of our young people in Japan are having trouble finding their way in religious living is because the religious traditions have been expressed through the families and in the villages. Demographic shifts are occurring very quickly now, with urbanization and associated adjustments, and, at the same time, there is not much intellectual articulation for the young people. Now they have no place to turn. The family is dislocated. There are not a great number of Buddhist or Shinto intellectuals, it seems, trying to interpret the threshold of the twenty-first century for young people.

MT: Some students are going to the so-called "New Religions" because of these reasons. Some also go for entertainment, some go to fill a vacuum in their lives.

Q: My homestay brother said that many Japanese people feel religion is what society says. Society says respect your elders, or your friends are going to the festival, so you go. Is this an accurate evaluation of the situation or just one person's opinion?

Tada: I would like to say that this is not a religious attitude. Religion is supposed to be part of all aspects of life. Some people use religion to avoid unhappy things in their lives, they are actually afraid to have unhappy things occur in their lives. They try very hard to avoid them. This is the only reason for their being interested in religion.

MT: When we speak about religion, we have to make a clear distinction between indigenous folk religion and true religion. We have many customs derived from folk religions. Many of the folk religions are embedded deep in the structure of Japanese society.

NN: I feel that Japanese people are scared to be in real religions. They play around with pseudo-religions, being only superficially involved. In one sense, we Japanese are very religious, in another sense we are not. Many Japanese are keeping their belief just as tradition, perhaps.

MT: Young people want to live by their own power and their own will. One announces that one is independent from Other Power. This means one has lost one's way in this life, willingly. It is a weak way of living. In this sense young people are afraid of Other Power. They are afraid of saying out loud that they are dependent on Other Power. This means they are not yet really *human*.

    Actually, they are dependent on many kinds of other power, Shintoism, Inari, many *kami*. There is some discrepancy. These days especially, young people are interested in religion but their tendency is to escape from traditional religions with long histories, and they go to the New Religions. These days, the New Religions attract people through mysticism. There is a popular, well-known New Religion whose founder can "float in the air." This kind of thing attracts young people.

    When I was young, New Religions attracted people by getting money and becoming very wealthy or by healing illness or other auspicious things. These days, the Japanese people are rich, and they are listening to superstitions, and are attracted by mystical things.

Tada: What do you mean by traditional religion?

MT: Buddhism, some schools of Buddhism.

Tada: I think when one is young, usually one is optimistic and eager to learn and prefers not to feel Other Power. "This is my own way! I am powerful!" "I can do it!" "I must do it in my own way!" Towards the end of life, when someone is thinking deeply or comes across a disaster, one then is ready to feel something beyond self-power. This is my experience.

When I was young, I felt only a little of Other Power, "I can do it!" But, I am already over 60 years old and nowadays I feel a sense of Other Power very strongly. Do you think this is the general tendency of human beings? Some religious geniuses can feel the ephemerality of the world when still young. Most ordinary people, like myself, it seems, could not have a sense for such Other Power when they were young.

MT: I can not agree totally with what you say. If what you say is right, then there is no room left for young people to participate in Shinran's teaching. I agree that one's appreciation of Other Power deepens with age and experience, one's appreciation of life, of health, and of Other Power. Beyond that there must be persistent truth in one's life.

JC: I wonder if something like Professor Tada's observation was to some degree behind professor Nagao's comment that one percent of self-power is power, but not so powerful. Professor Nagao is in his mid-eighties's.

MT: One percent is not very powerful, but it is persistent, because that one percent is polished by one's mind frequently. Every time one listens to the teachings, one polishes one's mind, elevating it to a comfortable and distant place. But, if one is caught by even one percent of self-power, one cannot see the true working of Other Power. Objectively it is not powerful, subjectively it is indestructible.

JC: Your position, Professor Tokunaga, is very clear, is dynamic, creative and catalytic. But, I wonder when we approach our mid-eighties, if we be so fortunate, whether we will see one percent of self-power as being very powerful. My hunch is that the dialectic which you reflect might be discerned more readily, say, when we are between thirty and sixty years old.

Tada: Unfortunately, young people nowadays detect little feeling in Buddhism--just ordinary monks working as servicemen, or with funeral ceremonies. Also, Buddhism was conservative through the years, during the Edo period, even after the Meiji restoration, during the war years and after, even though it seems, superficially, to be thriving. Young people do not like to have much to do with even such things as the smell of incense.

MT: Buddhism sounds and looks very old and conservative. This is true. If young people are serious about their own lives they can transcend that kind of feeling, the superficial feelings, and get into the teaching itself. What you say is very true, though. Japanese Buddhism was tamed by the Edo Shogunate for 270 years. Before that, Jodo-Shinshu people were very active and tried to reform the government system. The founder of the Edo period was afraid of that kind of power held by Jodo-Shinshu and he set up a policy to tame and to maintain the Buddhist schools of Japan. During those 270 years, Japanese Buddhism became totally corrupted. This influence still remains now. This is the reason for Japanese Buddhist priests not being very active in society, or in spreading the teaching. They can make a living if they perform funerals, and rituals for ancestor worshipping. This is the main reason.

As you may know, during the Edo period, Buddhist temples were like city offices. The family was expected to register in a temple near their home. One should belong to one temple. The priests certify the person, as, for example, he is the second son of this family, etc. Buddhist priests did not have to do true religious activities. We can make a living when we perform services.

JC: May I ask a question of each of you in turn, if you wish? What, in your thinking, constitutes the religious life and why have you chosen to become involved in it?

NN: If you ask me whether I am religious or not, I would answer that I am not religious, because I am trying to be religious. I want to get into the religious quest. I am struggling in getting from position A to B. In that sense I am not religious. What constitutes my religious life? It cannot be expressed easily.

I can learn from studying others, about their religious life, like all of you--to me you are religious. You are my teacher. You all may make me very religious. When I see you lead your lives, when you attend ceremonies in Christian churches, I see you and your difference, and from that scene I learn much about religion. Not as knowledge, but as a feeling. So far as I am concerned, I am trying to be very religious, and I am not, not yet.

MT: Professor Nomura and I are both from temple families. When I was a student, I studied subjects quite different from Buddhism. I majored in English literature, and he was a navigator for JAL. I do not know why he decided to study religion. In my case, I was about to become a journalist and I took the examination. I read many Japanese and English novels to find out about life, to choose a life. I also read some books about philosophy. Still I could not find my way.

I disliked Buddhism when I was young. I did not want to become a priest. I happened to read one of the scriptures and it gave me quite a different sense, a deeper sense. It was written in Japanese, but the Japanese itself was different, the depth was different. And I began to be attracted to Buddhism. I started to study Buddhism, at the age of twenty-three or twenty-four.

There is no special religious life. Every day is to be religious. To live as a human being, I believe, is to live religiously. This is my belief. We cannot force our way of living on others.

NN: Can you draw a line between the sacred and secular life?

JC: One can do this with regard to the religious orders in the Christian tradition, or any orders for that matter in any religious tradition. However, apart from that, I think a person's life is out of balance when a precise line is drawn between the sacred and secular life. There is little continuity, little integrity, little coherence, it seems to me, in that kind of life.

MT: D. T. Suzuki made an interesting comment: When we compare Zen Buddhism and Shin Buddhism, everybody says that the Zen way of living the religious life is much more difficult than Shin, but it is not. In Zen, there is one path. In Shin, there is no path. You have to find your own way. This is interesting. I agree with Suzuki because in Zen, one can become a monk and become confined from the secular world. You can center yourself on the way. In Shin, we have to live religiously at the same time as we are living secularly. To live an ordinary life is to live in this way. I think it is more difficult than the Zen way.

Tada: To be real to Shin Buddhism is difficult. To live not following a set way, just to live genuinely, religiously, is very difficult. Many years ago, Shinran told us that this is an easy way to attain Buddhahood, but it is the most difficult way.

I myself do not like to appear "religious," but maybe I am religious after having come through some very crucial experiences. Many relatives of mine died in the war, and one was executed as a war criminal without understanding in what way his subordinates had done something considered wrong. Also, many of my family members and relatives were destroyed in Hiroshima. My relatives disappeared from this world. Those were crucial experiences for me.

After World War II I was at a loss what to do. I struggled this way and that. I tried many things. Finally, I came across Buddhism and Christianity. I hated "Buddhism" and "Christianity," because I was the usual young man: "I have power!" "Why don't I depend on myself!" I wanted to revolutionize everything after World War II. I resorted to a political party for a short time, then gave it up for I realized that political campaigns were nonsense. So, I came to my true voice in my mind. I went to many people and asked what is the truth. I read many books, including D.T. Suzuki's. I liked to read such books, by Suzuki, Nishida, Hyakuzo Kurata, and many other really religious people and philosophers.

I want to be a simple man and seek to attain the "precious pearl." To attain such a state, I have to go to Christianity, sometimes to Shin Buddhism, and I have to practice Zen. I myself feel religiousness embedded in human beings, regardless of which religious tradition they endorse.

MT: Have any one of you read Shusaku Endo's *Silence*? This is a very interesting novel. It is translated by William Johnston. We can find a notable transformation of Christianity in Japan. Shusaku Endo is attacked by many Japanese Christians even today. Few people accept his understanding of the Christian faith. This transformation can be equated with the Shin Buddhist way of thinking.

When we accept Western thought or ideology, we become stiff. We think too much of what is Western, we become too formal. We cannot be frank with what is Western. This is the reason, I think, for Japanese Christians being only about one percent of the population. Endo is a very brave man. He transformed his faith in a Japanese way. He elaborated another view of God, one very similar to Amida. I like Endo very much. This kind of transformation has never been done by Japanese Christians. It is interesting.

What is tragic is that many Japanese critics cannot find Endo's true intention. They say that the major topic of his novel is the death of God, because God kept silent when Japanese Christians, four hundred years ago, were tortured by the Japanese government officials. But this is not it. What Endo wanted to say was that even those who run away from God are the objects of God's love. Even Japanese critics cannot understand this main theme. This indicates the non-religiousness of many Japanese intellectuals.

Tada: Have you had a chance to meet Vietnam veterans?

JC: Yes, I think all of us have.

Tada: What is the general mentality?

JC: It varies a good bit. It is very hard to see a person as a veteran of the Vietnam War until that person begins talking. Some are very religious in the traditional sense and are active in the church, and among them, the ones who decided to re-enlist are very active in the churches near the bases. Some have been very negative about their experiences. They feel no need whatsoever to go into traditional Christian lives. Almost universally, the veterans are much appreciated. At the Fourth of July parades in the little village of Hamilton, New York, the group that receives the warmest applause is the Vietnam veterans.

Wars wound people, the wounds are there. Why did you ask?

Tada: It is just as with Japanese soldiers who returned after World War II. Lots of people did not believe in Buddhism nor Christianity nor Shinto at all. Many people then, especially young people, were very skeptical and nihilistic. I have a sympathetic feeling with such people.

JC: My question for these colleagues was designed to see whether we could drop "Shin Buddhism," drop "Jodo-Shinshu," drop "Zen," drop this and that descriptive label, and just talk about religious living, to see whether we were beginning to understand that perhaps the only English adjective that can stand, in the final analysis, before the English noun *faith* is the English word *human*. Eventually, upon reflection, Christian, as an adjective might drop. *Christian* as an adjective so used seems problematic. Insofar as *Christian* faith is exclusive or divisive, the adjective poorly serves the noun. Insofar as such faith is Christlike, it would tend to lead to some embarassment were one to use it to refer to oneself. It would appear to be the same with *Buddhist* so used, and so on, until we find that faith is characteristically human, or rather, that the character of what it means to be human is seen when humans rise to the level of faith. I think maybe we nudged this as we listened to the responses. Perhaps some of us in this program of study discerned consonance with what you men of Japan were saying. We did not hear a religious tradition saying something, we heard you, each one speaking to us. We have traveled a long way to hear this. We have come a long way, too, in recognizing it.

Tada: To be human, we are always to be religious. Is this right, don't you think so?

JC: I agree. To be religious is to be authentically human.

Tada: God is not dead.

NOTE TO CHAPTER I

1. *Barrack Room Ballads And Other Verses*, 1890.

NOTES TO CHAPTER II

2. *The National Geographic Magazine*, June, 1927, no page number.

3. December 10, 1990, Special Advertising Section, "Grand Tour of Asia and the Pacific," no page number.

4. *Mainichi Daily News*, April 1, 1991, p. 12.

5. *Miyako meisho zue* [Pictures of the Famous Places of the Capital] 1780 and *Shūi miyako meisho zue* [Continued Pictures of Famous Places of the Capital] 1787 were originally issued in respectively six and five Japanese style stitched volumes. A modern reprint combined the two works in a single volume totaling 1,354 pages. Harada Kan, ed., *Miyako meisho zue zen* [Complete Pictures of the Famous Places of the Capital] (Tokyo: Jimbutsu Oraisha, 1967).

6. Edwin O. Reischauer and John K. Fairbank, *East Asia: the Great Tradition* (Boston: Houghton Mifflin, 1958), p. 169.

7. Quoted by João Rodrigues, *This Island of Japan*, translated by Michael Cooper (Tokyo: Kodansha International, 1973), p. 110, n. 125.

8. *Ibid.*, p. 119.

9. *Ibid.*, p. 121.

10. *Ibid.*

11. Englebert Kaempher, *The History of Japan* (originally published, 1727; New York: AMS Press, 1971), vol. 3, p. 21.

12. As of August, 1992, after much controversy, the builders decided to continue with their original plans for a sixty meter tall Kyoto Hotel

NOTES TO CHAPTER III

13. I have translated this passage from Karl Ludvig Reichelt, *Fromhetstyper og helligdomer* (Oslo, 1948), II, p. 78.

14. Heinrich Dumoulin, *Zen Buddhism: A History,* (New York: Macmillan, 1990), p. 263.

15. *Ibid.*

16. Robert Bellah, *Beyond Belief: Essays on Religion in a Post-Traditional World* (New York: Harper & Row, 1970), p. 105.

17. C. Skovgaard-Petersen, *Fren nutidens Japan* (Stockholm, 1919), p. 139.

18. G. W. Lindeberg, *Protestantismen i Japan 1959-1913* (Lund, 1918), p. 146. See also Aasulf Lande, *Meiji Protestantism in History and Historiography* (Uppsala, 1988), pp. 126-128.

19. C. H. Germany, *Protestant Theologies in Modern Japan* (Tokyo: IISR Press, 1965), p. 25.

20. Uchimura Kanzo, *How I Became a Christian* (Tokyo: Kyobunkwan, 1971), p. 18.

21. Raymond Hammer, *Japans religioner i smä ltdegeln*, (Stockholm, 1967), p. 94.

22. Richard H. Drummond, *A History of Christianity in Japan* (Grand Rapids, Michigan: William Eerdmans Publishing Company, 1971), p. 210.

23. Germany, *op. cit.*, pp. 36-37.

24. See Notto, Reidar Thelle, *From Conflict to Dialogue: Buddhism and Christianity in Japan 1854-1959* (Honolulu: University of Hawaii Press, 1987).

25. D. T. Suzuki, *Mysticism: Christian and Buddhist* (New York: Macmillan, 1969), p. 14.

26. See Nishitani, Keiji, *Religion and Nothingness*, translated, with an Introduction by Jan Van Bragt, Nanzan Studies in Religion and Culture, (Berkeley, University of California Press, 1982).

27. This essay appears in *The Future of Religions: Paul Tillich*, Jerald C. Brauer, ed. (New York: Harper & Row, Publishers, 1966).

NOTE TO CHAPTER IV

28. Translated from the original declaration by Naofusa Hirai. This declaration was presented at the Tenth Anniversary of the founding of the Association of Shinto Shrines, and since then has been recited at the beginning of many gatherings of Shrine Shinto.

NOTES TO CHAPTER V

29. *The World of Shinto* edited by Junichi Kamata and translated by Norman Havens (Tokyo: Bukkyo Dendo Kyokai, 1986), p. 31.

30. *Genponsogen* literally means "origin." Kuni-no-tokotachi-no-mikoto is the first and original *kami* in the *Nihonshoki*. Therefore, the Shinto which worships and emphasizes the original *kami* may be called the original Shinto.

31. Kazuo Oosumi, editor, *Chūsei Shintō Ron* (Tokyo: Iwanami, 1977), p. 222.

32. Nihon Koten Gakkai, ed. *Yamazaki Ansai Zenshū* (Tokyo, 2nd ed., 1977), Vol. 5, p. 27.

33. *The World of Shinto*, p. 62.

34. *Kokutai no Hongi* was issued by the Ministry of Education in 1937. The title means "Principles of the National Structure or Polity." It was translated by J. O. Gauntlett (Cambridge, Mass., 1949).

35. Kokugaku is one of the Shinto schools. KADA Azumamaro (1669-1736), KAMO Mabuchi (1697-1769), MOOTORI Norinaga (1730-1801) and HIRATA Atsutane (1776-1843) are the most familiar. Kokugaku, beginning with painstaking study of ancient philology, attempted to make clear the mentality of the ancient Japanese and thus to discover the essence of Shinto.

36. KOUNO Seizo, *Shintō no Kenkyū* (Tokyo, 1930), p. 1.

37. NISHIDA Nagao, "*Jinja no Kigen no Furusa*" ("The Oldness of the Origin of Shrines") Nihon Shintoshi Kenkyu (Tokyo, 1978).

38. ANZU Motohiko, *Shinto Shisūshi* ("History of Shinto Thought") (Tokyo, 1955)

39. ONO Susumu, ed., *Motoori Norinaga Zenshū* (Tokyo: 1968), Vol. 9, p. 54.

40. *Chūsei Shintō Ron*, pp. 31-32.

NOTES TO CHAPTER VI

41. *The systematic Collection of Historical Documents (Shintei Zōho Kokushi Taikei)*, New Edition, Part I, No. 10, edited by Katsumi Kuroita, Yoshikawa-Kobundo, 1955, p. 5. The translation of the passage quoted is mine.

42. We have an intriguing situation in Japan. As was the case with the formation of the word for *nature*, we originally did not have any equivalent word for the Western words *matter* or *material*. As it happened, we applied this word *mono* as the translation word for *matter* and *material*. As a result, the Japanese began to show what appeared to Western eyes as unreasonable behavior, as you can easily imagine, in thinking a machine is only a tool, on one hand, and, on the other, to purify it with a prayer in order that it will work well. Most Japanese cannot explain this contradiction. If you ask them the reason, they will say something like, "We do this just for the peace of mind. Do not take it seriously." This reply, I think, suggests that the old disposition toward what we today call nature is still living in their mind, even though it might be unconscious.

NOTES TO CHAPTER VII

43. In conjunction with the *Lotus Sūtra* one must mention Nichiren, who founded the Nichiren school. Nichiren based his teaching on this text, but his approach was quite different from that of Saicho. The Tendai approach was more meditative, whereas Nichiren's stressed chanting or the recitation of the title of the *sūtra*. Nichiren's approach

in many ways is like that of Pure Land Buddhists who emphasize chanting of the name of Amida Buddha.

44. There are three mountains considered sacred in the Tendai tradition: one is in India, the "Vultures Peak" (Grdhrakuta), this was the place where the *Lotus Sūtra* was expounded. This is a very famous sacred mountain. The second mountain is Mt. T'ien T'ai in China. The third one is Mt. Hiei just outside Kyoto.

NOTES TO CHAPTER VIII

45. Nikkyo Niwano, *Buddhism For Today* (New York: Weatherhill, 1980).

46. Yoshiro Tamaru, *Hokekyō* ("The Lotus Sutra"), (Tokyo: Chuokoron-sha, 1969), pp. 62-120.

47. See *Myōhō-renge-kyō: The Sutra of the Lotus Flower of the Wonderful Law*, translated by Bunno KATO, revised by W. E. Soothill and Wilhelm Schiffer (Tokyo: Kosei Publishing Co., 1971), pp. 82-86. See also Niwano, *op. cit.*, pp. 56-59.

48. See John Hick, *Problems of Religious Pluralism* (London: Macmillan, 1985).

49. The Bodhisattva, in this way, practices the six perfections: donation or generosity, keeping the precepts of morality, maintaining perseverance, diligence, meditation and wisdom.

50. Niwano, *op. cit.*, pp. 177-183.

51. See *Myōhō-renge-kyō: The Sutra of the Lotus Flower*, p. 292.

52. Niwano, *op. cit.*, pp. 179-180.

53. *Myōhō-renge-kyō: The Sutra of the Lotus Flower,* p. 317.

54. Yoshiro Tamura, *op. cit.*, p. 115.

55. Niwano, *op. cit.*, pp. 306-310.

NOTE TO CHAPTER IX

56. Shibayama, Zenkei. *Zen Comments on the Mumonkan*, translated into English by Sumiko Kudo (New York: Harper & Row, Publishers, 1974).

NOTES TO CHAPTER XII

57. Keiji Nishitani, *Religion and Nothingness*, translated, with an Introduction by Jan Van Bragt, Nanzan Studies in Religion and Culture (Berkeley: University of California Press, 1982), p. 1.

58. *Ibid.*, pp. 1-2.

59. *Ibid.*

60. *Ibid.*

61. *Ibid.*, pp. 2-3.

62. *Ibid.*, p. 3.

63. *Ibid.*, pp. 3-4.

64. *Ibid.*, p. 4.

65. *Ibid.*, pp. 4-5.

66. The most important writing among many Shinran produced is called *Ken-Jōdo-Shinjitsu-Kyō-Gyō-Shō-Monrui*, which is often abbreviated to *Kyō-Gyō-Shin-Shō*. I refer to one of its English translaitons: *The True Teaching, Practice, and Realization of the Pure Land Way*, 4 vols., "Shin Buddhism Translation Series," Yoshifumi Ueda, general editor (Kyoto: Hongwanji International Center, 1983-1990), Vol. I, p. 63. Hereafter, this work will be cited as *TPRP*.

67. *Ibid.*, pp. 63-64.

68. *TPRP.*, Vol. IV, pp. 484-485.

69. *Ibid.*

70. *Ibid.*

71. *Ibid.*, pp. 507-508.

72. *Ibid.*, p. 508.

73. *Letters of Shinran: A Translation of Mattōshō,* "Shin Buddhism Translation Series," Yoshifumi Ueda, general editor (Kyoto: Hongwanji International Center, 1978), p. 87.

74. *Ibid.*

75. *TPRP.*, Vol. IV, p. 531.

76. *Ibid.*

77. Mircea Eliade, *Patterns in Comparative Religion*, translated by Rosemary Sheed (New York: New American Library, 1974), p. 30.

78. *Ibid.*, p. 29.

79. Mircea Eliade, "Methodological Remarks on the Study of Religious Symbolism" *The History of Religions: Essays in Methodology* (Chicago: University of Chicago Press, 1959), p. 101.

80. Mircea Eliade, *Patterns in Comparative Religion*, pp. 28-29.

81. Paul Tillich, *Systematic Theology*, 3 volumes (Chicago: University of Chicago Press, 1951-1965), Vol. I, p. 128.

82. *Ibid.*, p. 133.

83. Mircea Eliade, *Patterns in Comparative Religion*, p. 25.

84. Paul Tillich, *op. cit.*, p. 133.

85. *Ibid.* See also Wilfred Cantwell Smith, *Islam in Modern History* (Princeton: Princeton University Press, 1977), p. 13.

NOTES TO CHAPTER XIII

86. *Webster's Third International Dictionary of the English Language* (Springfield, Massachusetts: G. & C. Merriam Company, 1976).

87. *Gobunshō*, a collection of Rennyo's Letters, 1-15, *Shinshū Shogyō Zenshō* III (Kyoto: Oyagi Kobundo, 1964), p. 422.

88. D. T. Suzuki, *Shin Buddhism* (New York: Harper & Row, 1970), pp. 13-14.

89. *Ibid.*, p. 15.

90. Nagarjuna, "Chapter of Easy Practice," quoted in *The True Teaching, Practice and Realization of the Pure Land Way: A Translation of Shinran's Kyōgyōshinshō*, Yoshifumi Ueda, gen. ed., "Shin Buddhism Translation Series" (Kyoto: Hongwanji International Center, 1983), Vol. I, pp. 85-86.

91. Shusaku Endo, "A Trifle Question," in *Shinran and Shinshu* (Tokyo: Yomiuri Shimbunsha, 1985), pp. 46-47. The translation is mine.

92. *Letters of Shinran: A Translation of Mattōshō*, Yoshifumi Ueda, gen. ed., "Shin Buddhist Translation Series" (Kyoto: Hongwanji International Center, 1978), p. 83.

93. As quoted by D. T. Suzuki in his *Mysticism: Christian and Buddhist* (New York: Harper & Brothers, 1962), p. 115.

94. This poem has been passed down in oral tradition. The translation is mine.

95. This poem has been passed down in oral tradition. The translation is mine.

96. *Tannishō: A Primer -- a record of the words of Shinran set down in lamentation over departures from his teaching*, translated by Dennis Hirota (Kyoto: Ryukoku University, 1982), p. 23.

97. This poem has been passed down in oral tradition. The translation is mine.

NOTES TO CHAPTER XIV

98. *Nihon Junsatsuki*, a Japanese translation of Alejandro Valignano's *Sumario de las cosas de Japón* (1583) and *Adiciones del sumario de Japón* (1592), Editados por Josi Luis Alvarez-Taladriz, Tomo I, "Monumenta Nipponica Monographs," No. 9 (Tokyo: Sophia University, 1954), translated by Kiichi Matsuda (Tokyo: Heibonsha, 1973), p. 31. The translation from the Japanese is mine.

99. From the *Sūtra of the Bodhisattva Precepts* as quoted in the "Chapter on the Transformed Buddha and Land" in *The True Teaching, Practice, and Realization of the Pure Land Way: A Translation of Shinran's Kyōgyōshinshō*, "Shin Buddhism Translation Series," Yoshifumi Ueda, gen. ed. (Kyoto: Hongwanji International Center, 1990), Vol. IV, p. 587.

100. Translated by Masao Abe in his essay, "God, Emptiness, and the True Self," in *Buddha Eye: An Anthology of the Kyoto School* (New York: The Crossroad Publishing

Co., 1982), p. 63.

101. *The New English Bible* (Oxford: The Oxford University Press, 1970),

102. *Ibid.*

103. *Tannishō: A Primer*, translated by Dennis Hirota (Kyoto: Ryukoku University Translation Center, 1982), p. 43.

104. *Ibid.*, p. 22

105. *Ibid.*, 23.

106. *Ibid.*, 43.

107. *The True Teaching, Practice and Realization of the Pure Land Way: A Translation of Shinran's Kyōgyōshinshō*, "Shin Buddhism Translation Series," Yosifumi Ueda, gen. ed. (Kyoto: Hongwanji International Center, 1985), Vol. II, p. 249.

108. I have translated this from *Hajakenshōshō*, in *Shinshū Shogyō Zenshō*, Vol. III, p. 173.

109. *Mappōtōmyōki*, translated by John Ishihara and James Dobbins, in *Shōzōmatsu Wasan: Shinran's Hymns on the Last Age* (Kyoto: Ryukoku University Translation Center, 1978), p. 125.

110. *Okite* issued by Rennyo in *Shinshū Shiryō Shūsei* (Kyoto: Dobōsha, 1978), Vol. II, pp. 168-169.

111. Many expressions of this kind appear in *Gobunshō*, a collection of Rennyo's letters, *Shinshū Shōgyō Zensho*, (Kyoto: Oyagi Kobundo, 1954), Vol. III.

112. *Tannishō: A Primer*, p. 23.

113. *Ibid*, p.24.

114. *Letters of Shinran: A Translation of Shinran's Mattōshō*, "Shin Buddhism Translation Series," Yoshifumi Ueda, gen. ed. (Kyoto: Hongwanji International Center, 1978), pp. 26-27.

NOTES TO CHAPTER XV

115. See W. G. Aston, translator, *Nihongi: Chronicles of Japan from the Earliest Times to A. D. 697* (London: George Allen & Unwin Ltd., 1956 [reprint edition]), Part II, p. 101.

116. *Ibid.*, Part II, pp. 113, 118 *et. al.*

117. In the ancient matrilineal society, a man visited his lover at her home. The belief in a visiting deity is based on such a social structure in which women were in the service of local and/or ancestral deities and provided divine protection of their kin through their mediation. It was in 645 that the legal system of the society was made patrilineal on the Chinese model, but the social convention of the matrilineal tradition in naming children after the mother's surname, going to the wife's home for courtship and marriage, and so on, persisted for the following centuries. In the Okinawa islands farther south of Kyushu, we find even today female mediums in matrilineal succession monopolizing the service

to the divine in spite of the patrilineal social system. At the court, and later at the Grand Shrine of Ise, it has been the princess-priestess that has served Great Goddess Amaterasu, the ancestress of the imperial family. Originally, she enshrined Amaterasu and the local deity at her palace, but when the shrine was built in the mid-seventh century, it was managed by the two families assigned and sent by the imperial court. The princess-priestess visited the shrine on great festivals, three times a year, but later only once a year. Now, her presence there has become only nominal.

118. Aston, *Nihongi*, Part II, p. 154 (Suiko Tenno, 32nd year, 9th month).

119. See Kyoko Motomochi Nakamura, translator, *Miraculous Stories from the Japanese Buddhist Tradition: The Nihon ryōiki of the Monk Kyōkai,* translated and annotated with an introduction by Kyoko Motomochi Nakamura (Cambridge, Mass.: Harvard University Press, 1973), pp. 72-73 and 246-248.

120. For further details, see *ibid.*, pp. 140-142.

121. *Shozan Engi* (Histories of Sacred Mountains of Shugendo) in *Jisha Engi* (Histories of Temples and Shrines) (Tokyo: Nihon Shiso Taikei 20, Iwanami shoten, 1975), pp. 113-115, 131-134.

122. See H. Byron Earhart, *A Religious Study of the Mount Haguro Sect of Shugendō* (Tokyo: Sophia University, 1970, a Monumenta Nipponica Monograph), for a symbolical complex.

123. For Tendai Buddhism, see *Japanese Journal of Religious Studies*, Vol. 14, nos. 2-3, 1987 (a special number on Tendai Buddhism in Japan). See also *Sources of Japanese Tradition*, compiled by R. Tsunoda, W. T. de Bary, and D. Keene, (New York: Columbia University Press, 1967 [3rd edition of the work first published in 1958]), Vol. I, pp. 112-132.

124. See, for example, *Dainihon Koku Hoke-kyō Kenki* (Records of Wonders Related to the Hoke-kyō in Japan, edited by Chingen) in *Ōjō-den: Hokke-kenki* (Tokyo: Nihon Shisō Taikei 7, Iwanami shoten, 1974), pp. 166-168 (III. 87).

125. For Ryogen, see *Japanese Journal of Religious Studies*, Vol. 14, nos. 2-3, pp. 161-184.

126. For Genshin, see *Sources of Japanese Tradition*, Vol. I, pp. 188-197.

127. For Zouga, see *Dainihonkoku Hoke-kyō Kenki*, Vol. III, p. 82. As to Ryogen's involvement with power politics, see McMullin, "The Enryaku-ji and the Gion Shrine-Temple Complex in the Mid-Heian Period," *Japanese Journal of Religious Studies*, Vol. 14, nos. 2-3.

128. *Konjaku Monogatarishū* (Collection of Tales Present and Past), XV, 39, in the third volume of *Konjaku Monogatarishū* (Tokyo: Nihon Koten Bungaku Taikei 24, Iwanami shoten, 1961). For his sister, see *ibid.*, XII, 30 and *Dainihonkoku Hoke-kyō Kenki*, Vol. III, 100.

129. The number of members presented is based on the statistics provided by the Ministry of Culture. See *Shūkyō Nenkan* (Almanac of Religion), (Tokyo: Bunkachō, 1992).

130. See Kyoko (Motomochi) Nakamura, "Revelatory Experience in the Female Life Cycle: A Biographical Study of Women Religionists in Modern Japan," *Japanese Journal of Religious Studies*, Vol. 8, nos. 3-4, and "No Women's Liberation: The Heritage of a Woman Prophet in Modern Japan," in *Unspoken Worlds: Women's Religious Lives*, edited by Nancy Auer Falk and Rita M. Gross (Belmont, California: Wadsworth Publishing Company, 1989).

131. See Anne Page Brooks, "*Mizuko Kuyō* and Japanese Buddhism," *Japanese Journal of Religious Studies*, Vol. 8, nos. 3-4, 1981.

NOTES TO CHAPTER XVI

132. There are illustrations similar to the Oxherd pictures employing an elephant rather than an ox, suggesting South Asian provenance, but these may post date the ox versions. Also, analogies involving crossing a river in Indian Buddhist literature are sometimes cited as sources for the parable of the white path, but they lack the elaborateness of the Chinese narrative.

133. The *Nō* master Zenchiku devised a set of emblematic illustrations for different levels of accomplishment in the art, but it lacks narrative structure.

134. Ueda, Yoshifumi and Dennis Hirota, *Shinran: An Introduction to His Thought,* (Kyoto: Hongwanji International Center, 1989), pp. 291-293. See also Dennis Hirota *et al*, trans., *The Collected Works of Shinran* (Kyoto: Jodo Shinshu Hongwanji-ha, 1997), Vol. I, pp. 89-91.

135. "Tract on Steadily Holding to the Faith" (*Shūji-shō*), translated by Kensho Yokogawa (*The Eastern Buddhist*, vol. 7, nos. 3 & 4, 1939) in Daisetz Teitaro Suzuki, *Collected Writings on Shin Buddhism*, edited by The Eastern Buddhist Society (Kyoto: Shinshu Otaniha, 1973), p. 123.

136. *Tannishō: A Primer -- a record of the words of Shinran set down in lamentation over departures from his teaching,* translated by Dennis Hirota (Kyoto: Ryukoku University, 1982), p. 23.

NOTES TO CHAPTER XVII

137. Quoted from Dennis Hirota, "In Practice of the Way: *Susamegoto*, an Instruction Book in Linked Verse," *Chanoyu Quarterly*, 19 (1977), p. 25. Also see Hirota's *Wind in the Pines: Classic Writings of the Way of Tea as a Buddhist Path* (Fremont: Asian Humanities Press, 1995).

138. Yamanone Sojiki, *ibid.*

139. Kamo no Chomei, "Tales of Aspiration for Enlightenment (Hosshinshu)," as quoted

in my *Plain Words on the Pure Land Way: Sayings of the Wandering Monks of Medieval Japan* (Kyoto: Ryukoku University, 1989), p. xliv. For a discussion of the life and thought of one of the foremost examples of the wandering holy man, see my *No Abode: The Record of Ippen* (Honolulu: University of Hawaii Press, 1997).

140. As quoted in *ibid.*, pp. xliv-xlv.

141. As quoted in my article, "The Wabi Zen of Takeno Jo-o: The Letter on Wabi and Related Documents," *Chanoyu Quarterly*, 23 (1980), p. 10.

142. *Ibid*, p. 11.

143. Shintei, *Hitorigoto*, as quoted in "In Practice of the Way," *op. cit.*, p. 28.

NOTE TO APPENDIX I

144. A *sūtra* passage concerning women's transformation into men when they are born in the Pure Land (the 35th Vow named the "Vow of Transformation into Men" in *The Sūtra of the Buddha of Immeasurable Life*, i.e, *The Larger Sukhāvati-vyūha Sūtra*):

> The Thirty-fifth Vow of Amida: If when I attain Buddhahood, women in the innumerable and inconceivable Buddha lands of the ten quarters who, having heard my name, awaken joyful serene faith, raise the mind of enlightenment, and thus despise their female bodies, should again assume female forms, may I not attain the perfect enlightenment.

This Vow is based on the view of women at that time in India, which is reflected in Buddhist texts as "women having five hindrances and three bonds." The "five hindrances" are that women cannot become (1) Brahman, (2) Indra, (3) King of devils, (4) Cakravartin monarchs, or (5) Buddha. The "three bonds" are (1) when young, women must obey their parents, (2) when married, women must obey their husbands, and (3) when bereft of their husbands, women must obey their sons and daughters.

Such a view of women as this is today exposed to a severe criticism and attack by women's liberation movements. Some of us think, however, that the 35th Vow is intended to liberate women who were having a hard time in those social settings discriminating against women. The following wasan composed by Shinran, based on the 35th Vow, should also be appreciated in this way.

> So profound is Amida's great compassion
> That, manifesting inconceivable Buddha-wisdom,
> He established the Vow of transformation into men,
> Thereby vowing to enable women to attain Buddhahood.
> (*Jōdo Wasan* #60, in *Hymns of the Pure Land: A Translation of Shinran's Jōdo wasan*, "Shin Buddhism Translation Series" [Kyoto: Hongwanji International Center, 1991], p. 53.)